D1522389

Frontiers *of* Femininity

Space, Place, and Society
John Rennie Short, *Series Editor*

Selected titles from Space, Place, and Society

Alabaster Cities: Urban U.S. since 1950
  John Rennie Short

At Home: An Anthropology of Domestic Space
  Irene Cieraad, ed.

The Boundless Self: Communication in Physical and Virtual Spaces
  Paul C. Adams

From Abbotts to Zurich: New York State Placenames
  Ren Vasiliev

Inventing Black-on-Black Violence: Discourse, Space, and Representation
  David Wilson

Migrants to the Metropolis: The Rise of Immigrant Gateway Cities
  Marie Price and Lisa Benton-Short, eds.

Placing Autobiography in Geography
  Pamela Moss, ed.

Pleasure Zones: Bodies, Cities, Spaces
  David Bell et al.

Tel Aviv: Mythography of a City
  Maoz Azaryahu

Women, Religion, and Space: Global Perspectives on Gender and Faith
  Karen M. Morin and Jeanne Kay Guelke, eds.

FRONTIERS OF
Femininity

A New Historical Geography of the
Nineteenth-Century American West

KAREN M. MORIN

Syracuse University Press

Copyright © 2008 by Syracuse University Press
Syracuse, New York 13244-5160

All Rights Reserved

First Edition 2008
08 09 10 11 12 13   6 5 4 3 2 1

The paper used in this publication meets the minimum requirements of
American National Standard for Information Sciences—Permanence of
Paper for Printed Library Materials, ANSI Z39.48–1984.∞™

For a listing of books published and distributed by Syracuse University Press,
visit our Web site at SyracuseUniversityPress.syr.edu.

ISBN-13: 978-0-8156-3167-5   ISBN-10: 0-8156-3167-7

Library of Congress Cataloging-in-Publication Data

Morin, Karen M.
Frontiers of femininity : a new historical geography of the nineteenth-century
American West / Karen M. Morin. — 1st ed.
p. cm. — (Space, place, and society)
Includes bibliographical references and index.
ISBN 978-0-8156-3167-5 (cloth : alk. paper)
1. Feminists—United States—History—19th century.   2. Suffrage—United
States—History—19th century.   3. Women's studies—United States—History.
I. Title.
HQ1410.M67 2008
305.420978'09034—dc22
2008034675

Manufactured in the United States of America

Contents

Illustrations

KAREN M. MORIN is professor of geography at Bucknell University in Lewisburg, Pennsylvania. Her research focuses on relationships among nineteenth-century women's travel writing and British and American imperialisms, providing new angles for understanding questions of identity and gender in social geography. In addition to her interest in women's religious landscapes of North America, she is also working on a study of geographical thought in the United States during the nineteenth century. She has published more than forty research articles, book chapters, and commentaries and serves on several editorial boards. Her articles have appeared in the *Annals of the Association of American Geographers, Transactions of the Institute of British Geographers, Gender, Place and Culture,* and the *Journal of Historical Geography,* among others. She is coeditor of *Women, Religion, and Space: Global Perspectives on Gender and Faith,* also published by Syracuse University Press.

Acknowledgments

THE CORE IDEA FOR SEVERAL of these essays developed over a decade ago as a doctoral dissertation in geography at the University of Nebraska–Lincoln (1996) and subsequently spun out over the next few years into a number of distinct but related research projects on women, gender, travel, and the nineteenth-century American West. My intention for bringing them out in the present form is, hopefully, to reach a broad, interdisciplinary audience of scholars beyond those who read geography journals. While at Nebraska I was lucky to become the student of Jeanne Kay Guelke, who, during her short stay there in the early 1990s, was doing pioneering work in feminist historical geography of North America (e.g., Kay 1990, 1991). Jeanne was the best advisor one could hope for: a superb researcher, intellectually exciting and broad minded, with abundant generosity toward her students. Since those days we have worked together on many projects, and I continue to be dazzled by the connections she is able to make between seemingly disparate places, histories, and theories.

As a graduate student at UNL I also took classes from and worked as editorial assistant to Frances W. Kaye, English professor, former editor of the *Great Plains Quarterly*—and still, undoubtedly, the coolest person on that campus. I admired everything about Fran, including her decades-long protests against the death penalty in front of the governor's mansion in Lincoln, every Wednesday at noon, usually by herself. It was Fran's ability to articulate a keen sense of the places she knew—the American Great Plains, the Canadian Plains, and the American West more generally—that rubbed off on me and fueled my own desire to study these landscapes and places in depth. And it was David Wishart—a postcolonial critic ahead of

ix

his time—whose creative yet commonsense questions always forced me to think about American historical geography in a synthetic way. David had a subtle way of convincing me to not throw out the baby with the bathwater when comparing older versus newer theories and methodologies, advice that I never really appreciated at the time, but do now.

To these amazing mentors as well as to UNL and the Center for Great Plains Study for the support given by several grants and fellowships—thanks again.

Following my days at UNL I relied on the same small but dedicated cadre of colleagues to comment on my work. I cannot thank them enough for their collegiality, advocacy, and good will over many years—especially Jan Monk, Mona Domosh, Alison Blunt, Cheryl McEwan, and colleagues at the University of Waikato in Hamilton, New Zealand, who financially supported me and in whose company many of the ideas of this volume took shape: Dick Bedford, Robyn Longhurst, Lynda Johnston, Lawrence Berg, and the late Evelyn Stokes. The editors of the respective journals in which these essays first appeared, and all the anonymous referees who gave me such generous advice and helped me clarify my thoughts—thank you again. Thanks also to the late Denis Cosgrove, Ron Martin, Bonnie Poteet, Judith Kenny, Don Mitchell, Jenny Robinson, Gary Moulton, George Jenks, and Brian Page who are among the many others who read drafts of my work and provided inspiring direction to my thinking on these various projects. I also owe so much to Mary Selden Evans and her staff at Syracuse University Press for their continued support and guidance.

I was blessed with great colleagues at Bucknell University during the writing of these essays as well, and I especially look back and appreciate the good old days with the postcolonial theory group, the research and production assistance of Candice Hinckley and Deb Cook-Balducci, and the support from my friends in Coleman Hall, especially Kim DiRocco, and Paul Susman. The incomparable Annie Randall inspired the book's title. I also appreciate Bucknell's generous financial support, in the form of grants, course releases, and subvention fees, that allowed me to get these works into print, and provided me with the best undergraduate teaching assistants one could hope for. My deepest gratitude goes to Susan Holencik for her energy and efficiency in moving this project through the production phase.

I could write pages profusely thanking my great friends and big beautiful family, near and far, for their hospitality, fun, and engaging conversations during the writing of these essays—especially my eternally generous sister Ann Baker, Mark and Matt Mattern, and my father, the indomitable T. R. Morin, who is the only person as far as I know who read my entire dissertation who didn't have to. And as an academic who has always tried to balance a book on one hip with a child on the other, with both slipping off from time to time, I want to express my most profound gratefulness for Nina Theresa and Nicholas Hunter, centerpiece of my world, full of surprises, hugs, and tolerance for a little-bit weird mother. Finally to my sweetheart Dan Olivetti, Zen master of bending gender rules and of all things funny, thank you, I owe you just about everything.

I dedicate this work to the brilliant life that was my mother's, Margaret Ann Morin (1928–1998).

Versions of chapters 2 through 8 originally appeared in the following publications, and I gratefully acknowledge permission from the publishers to reprint the works here.

Chapter 2: "Trains Through the Plains: The Great Plains Landscape of Victorian Women Travelers," *Great Plains Quarterly* 18 (Summer 1998): 235–56.

Chapter 3: "Peak Practices: Englishwomen's 'Heroic' Adventures in the 19th Century American West," *Annals of the Association of American Geographers* 89, no. 3 (1999): 489–514.

Chapter 4: With Jeanne Kay Guelke, "Gender, Nature, Empire: Women Naturalists in 19th Century British Travel Literature," *Transactions of the Institute of British Geographers* 26, no. 3 (2001): 306–26.

Chapter 5: "Surveying Britain's Informal Empire: Rose Kingsley's 1872 Reconnaissance for the Mexican National Railway," *Historical Geography* 27 (1999): 5–26.

Chapter 6: "British Women Travellers and Constructions of Racial Difference Across the 19th Century American West," *Transactions of the Institute of British Geographers* 23, no. 3 (1998): 311–30.

Chapter 7: Reproduced with permission from Karen M. Morin, "Post-colonialism and Native American Geographies: The Letters of Rosalie La Flesche Farley, 1896–1899," *Cultural Geographies* 9, no. 2 (2002): 158–80. © Sage Publications, 2002, by permission of Sage Publications Ltd.

Chapter 8: "Mining Empire: Journalists in the American West, ca. 1870," *Postcolonial Geographies,* eds. Alison Blunt and Cheryl McEwan (New York: Continuum, Writing Past Colonialism Series, 2002), 152–68. Reprinted by kind permission of Continuum International Publishing.

Frontiers *of* Femininity

❧ 1 ❧

Introduction

The Frontiers of Femininity

This is no region for tourists or women.
—Isabella Bird, *A Lady's Life in the
Rocky Mountains* (1969, 54)

THE RENOWNED BRITISH EXPLORER Isabella Bird's infamous and incongruous statement that tourists and women did not belong in the Colorado mountains that she herself was climbing in 1873—as a tourist and as a woman—provides a good launching point for the essays collected in this volume. Bird's *A Lady's Life in the Rocky Mountains* (1879), still popular among tourists and women (and others) in bookstores around Estes Park, Colorado, reminds one of just how complicated a task it was for women such as Bird to capture and retain a reading audience. Bird, not atypically for women of her (bourgeois) social class and time, took pains to distance herself from anything resembling crass, commodified, mass tourism of the day, as well as the period's emergent "New Woman" image, though she implicitly embraced both in her life and work. Her class privilege allowed her to travel the world, become one of its foremost mountaineers and the first woman elected to London's Royal Geographical Society (in 1892), and publish nine travel books. She traveled and wrote widely on Japan, the Middle East, Tibet, and China; she is certainly among the best known and most studied of Victorian women travelers to North America, with two popular books on the subject. (She also wrote *An Englishwoman in America*, published

1

in 1856.)[1] Not incidentally, she was one of the first Euro-American women to wear pants in public.

Meanwhile, her books abound with a self-representation of the conventional, proper lady, feminine and domestic in all manner of behavior and values. This, of course, had as much to do with Bird's aligning herself as a superior British citizen as much as anything else, as she traveled through an American West in the late nineteenth century that was experiencing tumultuous mass immigration and was rife with an appalling resource, money, and land grab like no other. How "American" space, and along with it a range of nationalist, imperialist, and class discourses, influenced Bird's own self-expression as a woman, is the stuff out of which this book takes shape.

The essays collected here represent my attempt to understand how women's gender identities were produced "in place" in nineteenth-century North America. The essays critically examine the writings of women who traveled or lived in the American West and Mexico in the latter nineteenth century—mostly British women travelers and naturalists but also American journalists and a Native American tribal leader. My main intention is to explore how a set of discourses, about Victorian gender relations and imperial geographies (both American and British), combined to influence these women's writings as they moved through touristic and other spaces in North America. These included western parks, major cities, and train stations along the railroad's main transect as well as more remote locations off the tourists' itinerary, such as Native American reservations, rural farms and ranches, and the mountains of northern Mexico.

This collection draws from a number of primary source materials, from published travelogues and newspaper reports to unpublished archival sources such as letters and diaries. The women's writings reveal how experience of place is so important to the formation of women's self-identities

1. For biographical background on Isabella Bird, see Birkett (1989), Middleton (1965), Boorstin (1969), and Barr (1970). *A Lady's Life in the Rocky Mountains* was originally written as letters to her sister, then appeared serially as "Letters from the Rocky Mountains" in the genteel English weekly *Leisure Hour* in 1878, and flourished through eight editions by 1912 (Boorstin 1969, xviii–xix).

("subjectivities")—*as women* and also as members of particular races or ethnicities, classes, and nations. In turn, the women's subjective sense of themselves produced out of their encounters with places greatly influenced how those places were represented in their writing. I thus can problematize geographical context as fundamental to the formation of what has come to be known as gendered and colonialist discourses (originally after Said 1978), and hence to gender and colonial or imperial relationships themselves.

The essays question how competing discourses of conventional femininity and more transgressive forms of Victorian womanhood converged with discourses of colonialism and imperialism in women's writing. I take a broad view of how female liberation was imagined and lived for groups of women in the context of American expansionism, for example, in narratives of mountaineering and adventure, as noted in the case of Isabella Bird's (1879) narrative as well as those of lesser known writers such as Thérèse Longworth (1872), Rose Kingsley (1874), and Rose Pender (1888), examined in chapter 3. Bird captures the quintessential tension between a heroic description of the "conquest" of Colorado's Long's Peak—with language that might be interpreted as imperial mastery over place—with more feminine discourses of frailty, humility, and emotional attachment to place.

These essays can be situated thematically and theoretically within scholarly works about "the Englishwoman abroad" in the nineteenth century (Mills 1991; Blunt and Rose 1994; S. Morgan 1996; M. Morgan 2001). Studies of nineteenth-century women's travel and writing have found clear and still growing niches in geography, history, literary criticism, and cultural and postcolonial studies. Across disciplines, much of this literature has focused on elite women's complicity with, but also resistance to, European colonialism and imperialism; on intersections between nineteenth-century western feminism and colonialism; and on representations or experiences of colonized women (Chaudhuri and Strobel 1992; Sharpe 1993; Burton 1994; Raju, Kumar, and Corbridge 2006). I take up all of these themes here within the context of nineteenth-century American continental expansionism in its western regions.

The rhetorics of women's domesticity and conventional femininity have been tied to British imperial projects by scholars across disciplines and geographical arenas (Davin 1978; Callaway 1987; Foster 1990; Strobel 1991; Ware 1992; Burton 1994; McClintock 1995; S. Morgan 1996). Part of my project here is to examine British women's expressions of hegemonic femininity and enactments of domestic relations during their journeys to the American West, framing them in terms of class management, nation, and empire. Masculinist political, corporate, educational, and religious institutions produced a hegemonic version of upper- and middle-class womanhood in the late Victorian period that rested on an ideology of women as gifted with superior moral character. The idealization of motherhood in particular was tantamount to the social identity women presumably derived from their families and homes. In such hegemonic constructions of gender difference, bourgeois women were not only to be moral and innocent, but bound by duty and self-sacrifice to their families, and by extension, to society and nation. Ware (1992) and Davin (1978) have shown how the idealization of motherhood in particular came into the service of empire. McClintock (1995) demonstrates the power of the Victorian middle-class home and its domestic commodities in connecting the "cult of domesticity" to imperial race relations. Others have shown how women's domestic relations served to establish the class structure fundamental to British (inter) national identity and its "ideological clusters." Langland (1995), for instance, argues that bourgeois women performed extensive economic and political roles as household managers and employers of servants and thus were instrumental in class management and in erecting class barriers.

Victorian gender relations experienced through the power relations of colonialism and imperialism worked to produce many "subject positions" in women's writing about North America. It was a place with very different historical exigencies than the British colonial contexts under which most theorizations of the Englishwoman abroad have been developed. Thus I am testing how such theories might themselves "travel" to an American context. Edward Said (1993), in his essay, "Traveling Theory," developed a geographical model of how ideas or theories travel from place to place, and what happens to them when they do. He argued that because theories develop within particular sociohistorical contexts, they lose their oppositional weight when moved and "domesticated" into other contexts. He later revised this position, conceding that possibilities exist for theories to be effectively reconstituted in new political situations (see Brennan 2000). The phenomenal force of Said's theory of Orientalism and the "traveling" it has done throughout colonial and postcolonial thought allows me to take this later view as a starting premise in the essays that follow.

In these essays I address some concerns arising out of other works that have examined women's travel writing and experiences in the nineteenth-century American West but have not theorized them apart from the writings of other visitors and settlers. Martha M. Allen, in her *Traveling West: 19th Century Women on the Overland Routes* (1987), for example, undertook the monumental task of analyzing 143 book-length accounts of travel by women in the American West in the later nineteenth century. Though theorizing what would now be considered an essentialist, generic "female identity" and response to the region that did not take into consideration the many layers of differences among women, Allen nonetheless provided scholars like me with a provocative starting point for further analysis. Likewise, Brigitte Georgi-Findlay's *The Frontiers of Women's Writing: Women's Narratives and the Rhetoric of Westward Expansion* (1996), though addressing the intersections between imperialism and gendered subjectivity that bound white women together (particularly as agents of exploitation of Native peoples), did not discuss how these identities and narratives were dynamically produced "in place." Shirley Foster's *Across New Worlds: Nineteenth-Century Women Travellers and Their Writings* (1990) discusses Englishwomen's writing about America, but her focus is primarily the East in the first half of the 1800s. And finally, Krista Comer's *Landscapes of the New West: Gender and Geography in Contemporary Women's Writing* (1999), another example, identifies a new regional paradigm of women's fictional writing about the West. With much to recommend itself otherwise, the book does not critically unpack the complex society-space interactions that women experience, but instead relies on a territorial notion of geography for analysis (Morin 2001). Though I will have undoubtedly opened new gaps of my own, I hope I have closed some of these.

The title to chapter 3, "Trains Through the Plains," refers to travel through the middle part of the transcontinental (New York to San Francisco) railroad journey that many travelers and tourists took in the later nineteenth century. Though the places studied in the book extend well beyond the Great Plains portion of North America, the Great Plains are a particularly useful starting point for considering ways in which women's writing was influenced by both the material circumstances of travel—literally the spaces available to them as women—as well as cultural ideologies about womanhood and femininity. These include discourses about the proper upper-class lady; emerging first-wave feminism; Victorian reform rhetoric; a type of environmentalism that articulated well with women's garden aesthetic; and women's individual and national relationships to capitalist advancement in America. Study of a variety of domestic, wilderness, and urban landscapes encountered on women's journeys reveals both "women's spaces" and "women's knowledge" that developed about them.

British women travelers on board the westward moving trains often wrote a great deal about the interior train compartments themselves, for example, articulating through their levels of comfort or discomfort their upper-class social positioning and superior nationality (see chapter 2). Women's views on the situation of Native American land dispossession, to take another example, were considerably influenced by the site of their encounters with local Native peoples—from a distance on board a swiftly moving train local Natives became ugly or beautiful aesthetic objects, yet those encountered "intimately" (face-to-face) at the many train stations along the railroad route oftentimes became subjects of the women's philanthropic reform doctrine, to be saved from the unscrupulous, greedy Americans (see chapter 6).

Said (1978), Pratt (1992), Hulme (1986), and scores of other colonial and postcolonial theorists have demonstrated links between Europe's political-economic-administrative goals for its colonies and their manifestations in cultural practices, such as in the writing of travel books. These scholars have identified ways that explorers and travelers served an important function in validating and justifying British control in the colonies, citing evidence of imperialist language that posits British ethnic and racial superiority and the vast quantities of raw materials available for extraction. To them, the hallmarks of imperial language were expressions of nationalism, ethnocentrism, and expansionism. MacKenzie (1984) further identifies late nineteenth-century British imperialism as an "ideological cluster" comprising renewed militarism, devotion to royalty, identification and worship of national heroes, and racial views consistent with social Darwinism (as cited in Ware 1992, 119; see also G. Jones 1980).

Feminists concerned with colonial discourses have been in the forefront of highlighting the extent to which nineteenth-century British imperialism took many diverse ideological and discursive forms, emphasizing the tensions between discourses of white, Christian, bourgeois superiority and expansionism in the colonies with those surrounding women's gendered subjectivity (e.g., Callaway 1987; Strobel 1991; Chaudhuri and Strobel 1992). By examining the texts of women travelers, administrators' wives, missionaries, reformers, nurses, and writers, these and other scholars have investigated ways that women were both "inside" and "outside" British and European imperial projects—inside them by virtue of their race, class, or national identities but sidelined by their gender. The social and spatial outcomes for this multipositionality took many forms. Works often cited in geography (such as Mills 1991, 1996; Blunt and Rose 1994) emphasize tensions between imperialism and a particular form of conventional, bourgeois, Victorian femininity, which played out in many women's writings as an uneasy ambivalence toward imperialism and its bald expansionistic and nationalistic policies. Geographers sensitive to issues of spatiality have also shown how British women's whiteness aligned them with the ruling power and thus reconfigured their spatial frameworks in the colonies (see, e.g., Blunt 1994; Blunt and Rose 1994; McEwan 1996).

Another important aspect of my project is a critique of the seemingly unilateral power and control that "the European subject," via metropolitan modes of thought, is able to exert over representations of colonized people and places. A postcolonial perspective demands a deconstructing of the writer and metropolitan ideology and is sensitive to varied and multiple representations of the same people and places. A postcolonial perspective also demands, though, a "decentering" of the writer, such as by focusing on how subjugated peoples may be positive actors in the formation of what come to be dominant understandings about them, as mediated through popular texts. (That is, how what the trave*ler* writes is influenced by what the trave*lee* does.) Chapter 6 takes up this task explicitly, but all the chapters in one form or another adopt perspectives from colonial and postcolonial discourse theory, again first outlined by Edward Said (1978, 1983, 1993), influenced himself by Michel Foucault (1970, 1972), and later refined by other theorists such as Gayatri Spivak (1988), Sara Mills (1991), and Mary Louise Pratt (1992).

To complement the inclusion of writings by women from the metropole I also study the writings of a prominent Native Omaha woman, Rosalie La Flesche Farley (chapter 7). There remains a pressing need to continue "writing women in"—especially women who represent minority cultures and ethnicities—to historical geographies of North America. To do so requires reaching beyond public or published documentary sources to the women's private sphere of letters and diaries, the significant genre of literate women's self-expression in the nineteenth century. The chapter on La Flesche Farley links with other chapters on women's gendered subjectivity and racial difference but also departs from them, by explicitly engaging the processes of "internal colonialism" in the American West from the perspective of the colonized (Singh and Schmidt 2000; Rowe 2000; R. C. King 2000). La Flesche's letters locate her gendered subjectivity within a set of competing economies, patriarchies, and cultures—an individual political contest that influenced those at a much larger social scale.

Feminist postcolonial scholarship (e.g., Ballantyne and Burton 2005, to take one recent example) has thus far paid little attention to nineteenth-century American women who traveled in and wrote about the United States and its empire-building practices. Such closure would seem to be an outgrowth of more general trends in American studies that have, until recently, posited an "American exceptionalism" to histories of colonialism and imperialism (Kaplan and Pease 1993; Pease and Wiegman 2002). Chapter 8, on early newspaper writing by American women Miriam Leslie and Sara Lippincott, allows for cross-cultural comparison with their British counterparts. These women focused much attention on capitalist expansion in the West, such as on emerging industrial mining, displaying contradictory and paradoxical attitudes toward the colonial practices taking place within the United States; that is, the consolidation and incorporation of different territories, peoples, languages, and currencies into the American nation. This chapter, as well as that about the American capitalist vanguard and the British aristocrat Rose Kingsley (1874) involved in the development of the Mexican Railroad (chapter 5), helps develop a spatialized conception of the ways in which women's writing engaged the narrative rhetorics of capitalist development in highly gendered, classed, and racialized ways, within quite different contact zones.

All of the chapters implicitly or explicitly assert a relationship between gendered subjectivity, colonial and imperial relations, and gendered knowledge itself. Rhetorical venues and genres available to women, women's ability to exercise narratorial authority, the social and spatial locations of differently positioned actors, and of course the erasure of or marginalization of certain knowledges are all important considerations in the construction of American history and historical geography. In chapter 4 I and my co-author Jeanne Kay Guelke address these issues by questioning the potentiality of a women's "naturalist knowledge" and its relationships to nineteenth-century scientific traditions and imperialism.

Geographers have made convincing arguments about the important roles that women travelers and explorers played in the history of geography as an academic discipline. Gillian Rose (1995, 414) eloquently critiqued the "Great Man" tradition of geographical inquiry more than a decade ago, arguing that *The Geographical Tradition* by David N. Livingstone (1992) offered a

> paternal tradition [that] can be used as a kind of legitimation process,
> in which would-be great men cite men already-established-as-great
> in order to assert their own maturity: what might be described as the
> "dutiful son" model of academic masculinity.

Other feminist geographers have likewise noted the paternalism, sexism, and masculinism inherent in histories and historiographies of geography—the gendering of geographers, of the knowledge and science they created, and of the social milieus within which they worked. Mona Domosh's (1991a) incisive feminist historiography of geography, for example, exposed the sexism inherent in David Stoddart's acclaimed 1986 history of geography, *On Geography and Its History*. Stoddart, for his part, offered a "dutiful son" maneuver when he explained that he did not include any women or women's experiences in his book because they had "nothing to do with" his history of geography and that "there is therefore no reason to mention them" (1991, 484). "Isn't that the point?" Domosh retorted (1991b). Stoddard's explanation elided the fact that histories or historiographies such as his *produce* the realm or limits of geography as much as they reflect some preexisting condition of it as a coherent, mutually agreed upon body of knowledge.

Work such as Domosh's has served a much wider purpose in grappling with geography's paternal lines of descent, which has created a "masculinist" tradition of geographical knowledge (Rose 1993, 1995). Masculinism here refers to claims that knowledge is exhaustive, objective, and universally applicable; has been gathered and developed through the "manly virtues" such as competition for firsts (being the first to find a route or draw a map, going the farthest or longest or highest, or collecting the most); or is devoted to the development and exploitation of people and resources.[2] Both men and women can be and are, of course, complicit with creating masculinist knowledge, and in turn, supporting and enabling the masculinism embedded in American development and expansionism.

This issue of geography's disciplinary knowledge, and its accompanying language and values, is an important one. Who creates knowledge, how do they do so, and for what ends is it used? Questions of epistemological orientations, narrowly defined subjects of study, available evidence, and research methodologies remain at the forefront of producing more critical and polyvocal historical geographies. Meanwhile, though, we need also to think very carefully about *how* we recover women or other silenced voices in historical geography, and for what ends. These are big questions that essays in this volume only begin to address. With them in mind though, I want to turn briefly in the next section to my concerns about feminist

---

2. Though not addressed in this volume, certainly geographical knowledge produced for wartime purposes would be another masculinist tradition in geography. As Ambrose Bierce once famously remarked, "War is God's way of teaching Americans geography."

historical geography of North America, to underscore my approach and goals for bringing these essays together.

Travels with Feminist Historical Geography

When I began my doctoral study in the early 1990s, an explosion of new, multiculturally sensitive books on "western women" had been appearing for a decade or more (e.g., Armitage and Jameson 1987).[3] As a geography student I detected early on a similar way that western women's historians and feminist geographers (though there were far fewer of the latter) tended to write about women's experiences and emplacement in the West, compared to that of other historians and scholars. As I would put it today, the distinction was that to feminist historians and geographers, landscape "acted" on one's sense of self and one's experiences—and I would cite Vera Norwood's and Janice Monk's *The Desert Is No Lady* (1987) as one of the best, early examples of this approach; however, in more traditional historical studies, landscape was often depicted as an inert stage or platform upon which one acted or one's experiences unfolded. This is a gross overgeneralization but an important distinction to make in how scholars might think about the power of place in shaping one's identity.

At the same time, though, social and environmental historians were leading geographers in offering compelling, sophisticated analyses of the myriad social, cultural, and environmental issues of nineteenth-century North America (e.g., Worster 1985). Although my interests fit conceptually best within the subdiscipline of historical geography, its project still into the 1990s seemed antiquarian by comparison—empirical studies of exploration, descriptions of migration trends, settlement patterns and sequence, types of survey systems, staple export production, and emerging urban and economic integration. Historical geography seemed to represent one of the last bastions of an empirical geography that was complicit with masculinist language and values. Annette Kolodny (1984) would have had a field day with all of the thrusting and penetrating of new lands by the bold men described in historical geography volumes

---

3. This section's title, and some of the ideas presented here, first appeared in Domosh and Morin (2003). I thank Mona for permission to reuse them here.

at the time (such as by J. Allen 1997). (Kolodny's often-cited work had demonstrated that men gendered the American landscape as passively feminine and awaiting transformation and domination, whereas women writers imagined it as place of idealized domesticity and other female archetypes.)

Lack of self-reflective and critical analyses of American imperialism had simply been neglected in the subfield, unlike history but also unlike historical geographies from other places such as Great Britain, which had a long critical engagement with British colonialism and imperialism.

In addition, Anglophone historical geography for the most part lacked critical attention to women and gender. Women entered the picture in American historical geography almost exclusively in their roles in sex and reproduction, and their activities were typically subsumed under men's. Jeanne Kay Guelke persuasively argued that by excluding women's spheres of influence and ignoring the workings of gender difference in society and space, inaccurate understandings of the past were being propagated (Kay 1990, 1991). Such arguments propelled me to combine my interests in history and geography in the study of women's travel, landscape interpretation, and the historiography of the discipline of geography. I suppose one might thus call me a "dutiful daughter" (cf. Rose 1995) in extending this type of research in my own career.

This collection of essays is, then, as much as anything else, a statement on historical geography—what it ought to be concerned with and how it ought to be practiced. If that sounds a bit audacious, it should not, as feminist theories and methods have been widely adopted in many other subdisciplines within human geography, most notably urban, political, and cultural geography. Here I want to make a compelling case for the need to incorporate feminist and gender theorizing and approaches in American historical geography and thus resist reproducing a historical geography that remains largely masculinist and empiricist.

It remains the case that major works in historical geography of North America too often lack a critical, social-theory type of orientation. D. W. Meinig's highly praised four-volume "synthesis" of American historical geography, *The Shaping of America* (1986–2004), provides just one of hundreds of examples. (See Hurt's 2006 study of those considered the most important American historical geographers for additional examples.) Much research in historical geography is highly empiricist, with too little attention to the ways in which empirical findings are always rooted in specific social and political perspectives. While I (still) find historical geography in urgent need of including women and feminist theorizing in particular (Morin and Berg 1999), the essays that follow illustrate at a broad level the usefulness of a clear theoretical commitment applied to deep empirical case studies.

And if historical geography is often unmoored theoretically, feminist theorizing is just as often empirically thin and often makes little analytical use of the past or a developing present. The essays collected here are marked by extensive use of historical archival sources, well grounded and contextualized within historical places and developments. Meanwhile, they engage feminist geographical theories about social spaces, the operation of power relations, and the construction of gender. Such an approach is uncommon in a feminist geography that tends to focus more on contemporary topics and qualitative research methods and interviews, focus groups, and ethnography as primary sources of evidence (Limb and Dwyer 2001). Perhaps because of the long-standing commitment to participatory research or research "from the bottom up," gathering ethnographic evidence appears to many feminist geographers as the most compelling manner in which a researcher might deeply engage with the materiality of space and place. Obviously, ethnographic research is not possible on long-deceased historical subjects. This raises the thorny issue of *who* historical geography research is *for*. In other words, the apparent lack of specific subjects to emancipate might lead some to wrongly assume that historical geography is apolitical or lacking in political weight.

The archival focus of most historical geography presents a challenge to feminist geographers. The politics of archives are such that what remains as evidence is often written and preserved by white, literate, power-wielding men, and the issue of how one might read the silences or hidden spaces in the archives is an important though complicated one. It has long been acknowledged that scholars must search out nontraditional sources—such as diaries, letters, and journals—to recover women's historical geographies, but such sources are not always readily available.

Moreover, concepts of history itself, and of historical geography, are shaped not only by what is in the archive but by how what is there is read, a topic discussed in some depth in chapter 7. Many feminist geographers have addressed the question of who has the power to make, record, and interpret history (e.g., Rose 1995), and others continue the important work of discovering appropriate strategies for approaching the archives and reading the silences embedded in them (e.g., Barnett 1998). Much has been accomplished in recent years in producing historical geographies of the United States and Canada that are not gender blind and that include women's spheres of influence (e.g., Schuurman 1998). Yet uncovering historical information about women cannot in itself say anything about the relative importance placed on them, their work, or their activities (after Scott 1988a). For that we need to understand the origins of gender differences—how gender difference is produced in place historically and the ways that gender differences worked through other economic, political, cultural, and sexual differences in the creation of past geographies.

Moving analysis away from the gendered subjects themselves and onto the historical conditions in which those subjects have come to be constituted as such has certainly broadened the ways in which archival material can be used by historical geographers. It has also aided in questioning the extent to which feminist geographers can rely exclusively on ethnographic data in their studies. Nonetheless, methodological problems remain. Those feminist geographers who have incorporated historical perspectives into their work have almost always used them as backdrops to their analyses of contemporary gendered identities, rarely as constitutive of those identities, thus "fixing" their subjects' identities in time and place. Using historical analysis to understand the social, political, and economic systems in which identity and difference are constructed, therefore, would contribute to a politics of change. This would enable a questioning of how constellations of power and knowledge are quite literally inscribed in space and place and thus advance discussions about how gender and other social roles and relations are formed, sustained, challenged, and changed.

These essays in many ways follow a British feminist historical geography tradition that has been concerned with the nature of historical narratives themselves, their rhetoric and structure, and women's relative participation in empire building through their writing. Scholars have moved away from simply adding women to histories of travel and exploration (e.g., Birkett 1989) toward theorizing women's imperialist motives in their travels abroad, questioning authorial "intention" and problematizing the ways that women negotiated the complex material and discursive webs of power in the colonies. The goal of much such work has been to expose the part that women—wives of military men and colonial administrators, missionaries, travel writers, tourists, nurses and others—played in colonialism and imperialism, supporting or critiquing "empire" and patriarchy, or to question how inclusion of women travelers might reconfigure a historiography of disciplinary knowledge (e.g., Blunt and Rose 1994; Mills 1996; McEwan 1996). The "fragmented" nature of women's subjectivities across space has become an important problematic in such work, as scholars study the tensions women experienced being part of colonial and imperial social relations but also caught within the often conflicting parameters and discourses of Victorian womanhood.

Contents of the Volume

All of the essays in this volume were previously published, appearing in geography journals or books over a four-year period, from 1998 to 2002. The texts are reproduced here in only slightly revised form, followed by a new afterword that provides some reflections on what we might learn from and about the people and places discussed in the volume. What follows here are additional details on each of the chapters.

Chapter 2 examines how a group of fourteen British women travel writers responded to the central prairies and plains between Chicago and Denver during their late nineteenth-century travels. Some responded emotionally, others aesthetically, others focusing empirically on natural history, and still others with an eye to future economic development of the region, particularly in farming and ranching. The chapter locates some of the social and cultural influences that combined to shape the women's varying responses to the rural grasslands. Train transportation itself deserves attention, in that responses to the landscape rested to some degree on the type of engagement with the land—whether firsthand and intimate or detached, from the train. Romantic literary conventions combined in the narratives as well, producing particular aesthetic responses to the landscape. And the women's social positioning, as professional or upper-class women who had to some degree escaped the confines of Victorian domesticity through travel, was also relevant to the ways in which the vast, often uninterrupted horizons of the prairies and plains were portrayed in the women's travelogues.

Many Englishwomen explored the mountainous regions of the American West in the 1870s, 1880s, and 1890s, hiking and taking excursions into popular tourist destinations such as the Rocky Mountains and Yosemite Valley. Chapter 3 examines the writings of seven women who toured these regions and published accounts of their journeys. These travelers produced a complex array of gendered subjectivities in their writings. They represented themselves as actively "conquering" mountain peaks as well as passively waiting for the men to do it; as fearing danger and fatigue but also ridiculing the incompetency of local male guides; and as "resisting" adventure yet expressing female empowerment and abandonment in it. The chapter examines feminine codes of behavior, first-wave feminism, and convergence of these within nineteenth-century British imperialism and narratives of adventure to show how conventional as well as more transgressive discourses of Victorian womanhood worked with imperialist, nationalist, and class discourses. The chapter explores what women wrote about both the indoor spaces of mountainous landscapes and their outdoor mountaineering adventures. In many ways, the women reinscribed themselves as feminine domestic subjects in wilderness environments, yet they also explored and contested the powerful inscriptions of conventional Victorian womanhood.

Among the many British women abroad in the late nineteenth century were a number of travelers who toured the American West with a naturalist's pen and sketchbook. California, with its giant sequoias and redwoods, scenic Yosemite Valley and Sierra Nevada, and the Mediterranean flora of the southern coasts, especially attracted travelers with a naturalist orientation. Chapter 4 examines the botanical and naturalist writings and art of two well-known world travelers—Constance Gordon Cumming and Marianne North—and another less-well-known British aristocrat, Theodora Guest, sister of the Duke of Westminster. The chapter examines relationships among these elite women's association with the Romantic aesthetic and naturalist traditions, natural sciences, class-based associations between women and flowers, and emergent environmentalism. The works of these women indicate the process by which natural history rhetorics and styles became embedded within gender, class, and imperial relations and how the division of natural history into professional and amateur domains relegated women to the margins.

Chapter 5 focuses on Rose Kingsley, a member of England's prominent clerical and literary Kingsley family, who traveled to Mexico in 1872 as part of a reconnaissance team for the Mexican National Railway, headed by the American railroad promoter William J. Palmer. Kingsley detailed her participation in this reconnaissance trip in her travelogue, *South by West or Winter in the Rocky Mountains and Spring in Mexico* (1874). The lasting impact of such reconnaissance trips should be made visible. Six hundred forty kilometers of Mexican railroad had been completed from 1862 to 1876, consisting almost exclusively of the British-owned Mexican Railway between Mexico City and Veracruz. This chapter examines Rose Kingsley's account of her participation in the development of the railway and Britain's "informal" empire in Mexico, drawing out the classed, gendered, and racialized structure of capitalist development abroad and its implications for women's travel and travel writing. Kingsley engaged the narrative rhetorics of capitalist development in Mexico by inscribing herself in the text as both a bourgeois rational capitalist and a genteel, English lady. This chapter adds an important dimension to the volume in that Mexico has been virtually ignored in studies of British travel writing and imperialism.

At a time coinciding historically with the height of the British Empire, immigrants' rush to occupy American West lands, and the wholesale removal of Native Americans onto reservations, encounters between Native peoples and British women travelers became emblematic of a whole range of sociospatial relationships of domination, subordination, and resistance. Chapter 6 examines representations of western Native Americans in the travelogues of ten British women travelers to the late nineteenth-century American West, produced primarily during encounters at sites along the western rail lines. The travelers described Native peoples as aesthetic objects and "vanishing Americans," but they also asserted a great deal of reform rhetoric sympathetic to the situation of those dispossessed of their lands. How the women interpreted race and gender differences can be tied to ideologies embedded in British colonial discourses, but also to the social relations inherent in the multiple contact zones within which their encounters with Native peoples took place, such as on board the trains and at train stations in white settlements. This chapter takes a postcolonial perspective in suggesting ways that Native peoples influence what gets written in travel texts.

Chapter 7 focuses on the writings of Rosalie La Flesche Farley, daughter of the last chief of the Omaha tribe of eastern present-day Nebraska, known contentiously as the classic "assimilationists" upon whose experiences of allotted reservation land the 1887 Dawes Act was modeled. Rosalie was the Omaha bookkeeper and business manager during the tumultuous period of land alienation and pasturage leasing and was often accused of cheating her tribe. She moved in numerous Omaha and Anglo-American social contexts, on and off the reservation. This chapter attempts to make sense of how Rosalie negotiated the many social spaces and subjectivities through which she maneuvered within the larger context of American colonization of the Great Plains. I draw attention to the letters that Rosalie wrote to her brother Frank during the years 1896–1899 when he worked for the Bureau of Indian Affairs in Washington, D.C. The letters speak of her efforts to prevail upon her family, other Omaha, encroaching white squatters, local businessmen, and numerous government officials in the allotting, selling, and leasing of Omaha land. These letters provide a unique opportunity to hear the voice of one influential Indian woman who was caught amid a range of competing cultures, economies, and patriarchies. Rosalie occupied numerous conflicting, obviously distraught, but ultimately personally advantageous spaces of "Indianness" in late nineteenth-century America.

Chapter 8 examines the published volumes of two widely read, influential American magazine and newspaper correspondents, Miriam Leslie and Sara Lippincott (a.k.a. Grace Greenwood). These women took well-publicized transcontinental tours of the United States in the 1870s. The chapter concentrates primarily on what these journalists wrote about

American national consolidation via the development of large-scale industrial mining in the American West, such as at Nevada's Comstock Lode.
Western mining was then entering a new phase of industrial-scale, technologically advanced operations that relied on both large capital investments and waged laborers. This chapter asserts that the women deployed
reform rhetoric in the cause of exploited mine workers, rhetoric that complicates a straightforward reading of their imperial politics. Development
of industrial mining depended on the hierarchies produced out of ethnic,
class, and gender differences. The "internal colonization" processes and
practices that these women's texts supported were integral to American
continental expansion. Lippincott's and Leslie's writings provide useful
sites for exploring the intersections between the women's gendered subjectivity and imperial development in the American West and also demonstrate sites of both opposition to, and support of, that development.

Chapter 9, the afterword, offers ruminations on what we might learn
from the study of these gendered geographies, particularly what they might
mean for our understanding of historical geography of North America.
What "imprints" did these women make on the people and places they
visited, and in turn, how can those imprints be incorporated into our historical geographical studies? Such ruminations are contextualized within
more recent studies of women, travel, gender, and nineteenth-century
North America.

2

Trains Through the Plains

The Great Plains Landscape of Victorian Women Travelers

> Arriving in San Francisco by the Overland Route impresses us as a coming back to the world again after a lapse into the wilderness. For, in leaving the wonderful Phoenix City of Chicago for the West, it seemed that we left the world behind: in Omaha, our next stage, we felt as if we had got to the outside fringe of civilization and cultivation, and wondered vaguely what could be beyond? Into what wild exile were we about to plunge?
>
> —Iza Duffus Hardy, *Between Two Oceans* (1884, 136)

THE YOUNG BRITISH NOVELIST Iza Hardy, during her travels to America in 1881–1883, anticipated the American West as terra incognita, a place completely beyond civilization. Like many other British tourists to America in the late nineteenth century, Hardy traveled extensively throughout the East Coast and South and took a transcontinental journey to the Pacific Coast by train. Out of her American travels Hardy produced *Between Two Oceans: Or, Sketches of American Travel* (1884) and a book about Florida. Hardy's coverage of the western portion of her American journey followed the transect of the railroad, with chapters of her book titled accordingly.[1]

---

1. Travelers discussed in this study, like Hardy, typically departed on the western portions of their journeys at Chicago and followed a transect across the West though Kansas City, Omaha, the central grasslands, Denver, the Rocky Mountains, Salt Lake City, and the

And like many other books in the genre, her travelogue includes extensive coverage of scenic attractions such as the Rocky Mountains and western cities such as Denver, Salt Lake City, and Sacramento, but little discussion of the central prairies and plains between Chicago and Denver. The minor attention Hardy did pay to the central grasslands reflects disappointment and boredom with the scenery. She wrote of the oppression she experienced during her "four long days and nights of speeding across the seemingly limitless desolation of the prairies" (1884, 136–37) on her way west, during which time she apparently never left the train.

In this chapter I examine how a group of fourteen well-to-do British women travel writers like Iza Hardy responded to the central prairies and plains during their tours of America in the late nineteenth century. These women's travel texts, largely as yet unstudied,[2] were among the many wealthier British citizens who took grand tours of North America by train just after the first transcontinental railway line from the Atlantic to the Pacific Coast was completed in 1869. During the last three decades

Sierra Nevadas, finally reaching the Pacific at San Francisco. The travelogues typically follow the transect the railroad followed, with chapters dated and titled chronologically and geographically east to west. A northerly or southerly leg was typically added to the travelers' journeys either going west or returning east. Lady Theodora Guest (1895), for instance, rode the Northern Pacific Railroad onto Vancouver and then crossed through Montana and Yellowstone Park and the northern Plains states before returning east.

2. The names and social titles I use here are those that appear on the covers and title pages of the books themselves. Although this produces inconsistency in naming conventions, these are the names and titles under which the women themselves apparently wished to be known publicly. Brief biographical sketches are available on most of these authors in J. Robinson (1990), Athearn (1962), and Rapson (1971) as well as from the travelogues themselves. With the obvious exceptions of Isabella Bird and Emily Faithful, most of these authors have not yet, to my knowledge, been studied in any depth. Of these books, only Isabella Bird's *A Lady's Life in the Rocky Mountains* has received extensive scholarly attention in the English-speaking world during the past hundred years. At least three of the volumes I discuss have been reissued for today's audiences: Bird's *A Lady's Life* by the University of Oklahoma Press in 1969; Rose Pender's *A Lady's Experiences in the Wild West* in 1883 by the University of Nebraska Press in 1978; and Thérèse Longworth's *Teresina in America* by Arno Press in 1974.

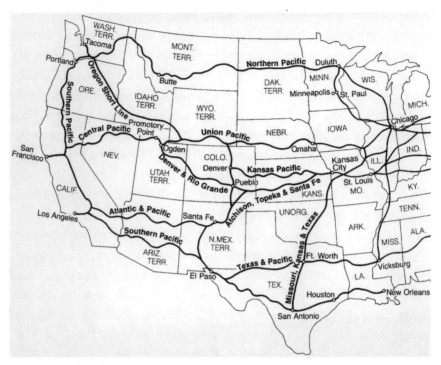

1. Early Pacific railroad lines, 1887. From *The National Experience: A History of the United States.* 8th edition by BLUM. 1993. Reprinted with permission of Wadsworth, a division of Thomson Learning: www.thomsonrights.com.

of the nineteenth century, travelers of all types were for the first time provided with a relatively fast, comfortable means of transportation coast to coast. Traveling at the rate of twenty miles per hour and stopping at 250 stations along the way, the portion of the trip from Chicago to San Francisco (where most were headed), if direct, would have taken six days (Athearn 1962, 17).

The women whose books I examine here were of wealthy aristocratic or professional-class society in England and Scotland, and all were published authors, however dissimilar their professional and personal motivations for travel. Some were travelers and travel writers by profession (e.g., Bird 1969 and Longworth 1974); others were known for other types of writing such as poetry, essays, and other works of nonfiction (e.g., R.

Kingsley 1874 and Pfeiffer 1885[3]); and still others presented themselves as wives traveling with their husbands or brothers on business or for pleasure (e.g., Guest 1895; Pender 1978; Howard 1897).

Many of the women rode in the Pullman cars of the Union Pacific railroad, sleeping cars designed specifically for long distance travel. As most of the women traveled by train straight through the region, they had little direct engagement with the land they were describing. However, a small number of them spent more time on the prairies and experienced the environment more intimately (cf. Sidonie Smith 2001). Lady Rose Pender, for instance, traveling with her husband, the Baronet Sir James Pender (director of a telegraph company), spent the spring and summer of 1881 inspecting the telegraph cable business as well as their personal investments in the cattle industry in America. Pender camped out in Wyoming and Nebraska and framed her 1888 narrative around the "search for a roundup." Another traveler, Thérèse Longworth, the Viscountess of Avonmore, during her 20,000-mile tour of North America in 1872–1873, reported that she stopped at nearly every town, settlement, and fort in the West (including Fort Laramie) during her seven-week stay there (Longworth 1974, 2: 8).[4]

These women expressed a wide range of motivations for travel. Many wrote of traveling west simply for pleasure's sake or to view the region's scenic attractions. Lady Mary Duffus Hardy, Iza's mother, a novelist popular with American audiences, took a trip similar to her daughter's in 1880–1881, identifying the Golden Gate as her "mecca" (1882, 133).[5] Twenty-three-year-old Mrs. Vincent, on a world tour with her husband

3. Emily (Davis) Pfeiffer, listed in the *Dictionary of National Biography* as a "poetess" (Athearn 1962, 198), discusses her travels throughout the Mediterranean region and America in her book *Flying Leaves from East and West* (1885).

4. Longworth published the extensive two-volume set *Teresina in America* (1974) and wrote three other travel books (Rapson 1971, 240; Athearn 1962, 195).

5. Rapson (1971, 233) reports that Iza followed her mother to America, though a comparison of the two women's texts raises the possibility that they traveled together. Parts of their texts are nearly identical, such as their descriptions of San Francisco's Chinatown (compare L. Hardy 1882, 137–89, and I. Hardy 1884, 138–87).

in 1884–1885, wrote that she too hurried across the continent, "fear-ful lest time should fail us at last for the Yosemite Valley" (1885, 1: 102). Lady Howard reported "having a little time to spare" for a pleasure trip throughout North America with her brother in the autumn of 1894 (1897, 1).[6] Rose Kingsley (1874), eldest daughter of the prominent English literary and clerical figure Charles Kingsley (and cousin to the more famous world traveler Mary Kingsley), described crossing the Atlantic as a Church of England representative to an 1871 convention in Baltimore. She later trav-eled west to visit her brother who was living in Colorado Springs.[7]

Other women wrote of expressly intending to collect material for books. Emily Faithful, a leading English suffragist, writer, philanthro-pist, and businesswoman, wrote *Three Visits to America* (1884), which first appeared as a compilation of articles published in English and American magazines and newspapers.[8] Her stated purpose for travel was "to write about the changed position of women in the nineteenth century . . . how America is trying to solve the problem" (1884, vi).

Although these and other women travelers expressed rather diverse goals for traveling, their books nevertheless closely follow the late nine-teenth-century travelogue genre and are in fact quite similar not only in structure and format but to some extent in content as well.[9] And though

6. The Baroness Winefred Howard of Glossop traveled extensively in continental Europe, the Middle East, India, and Burma. She set out on a pleasure trip with her brother in the autumn of 1894 (J. Robinson 1990, 115), at age thirty-three, and spent four months traveling throughout the United States, Canada, and Mexico. In 1897, she published *Jour-nal of a Tour in the United States, Canada, and Mexico*.

7. Rose Kingsley, unmarried and twenty-six years old, accompanied the dean of Ches-ter to the Baltimore convention. Afterward, she rode the transcontinental railway across the United States to Colorado Springs to visit her brother Maurice, who was working as a secretary for the Denver and Rio Grande Railway Company. She spent four months with him there and later traveled on to Mexico as part of a reconnaissance team for the Denver and Rio Grande (see chapter 5).

8. For biographical background on Faithful, see Frawley (1994).

9. After Pratt (1992, 171), I distinguish the eighteenth- and nineteenth-century bour-geois era travelogue as an "autobiographical narrative." In this form, the writer herself is the narrative's protagonist; the texts combine events surrounding the protagonist with observational detail. The travelogues in this study are remarkably similar in form and

attention paid to the central prairies and plains sometimes occupies only several pages of a 200- or 300-page book, these travel writers responded to that landscape in a wide range of ways. Some responded emotionally, whether bored by the uninterrupted horizon or enraptured by the wide open spaces. Others expressed admiration for certain aspects of the landscape, such as the glorious color and light displays in sunrises and sunsets, or they found fascination in monotony or barrenness—both views consistent with nineteenth-century romantic conventions for the beautiful and the sublime. Other travelers responded more empirically to the landscape, writing about buffalo and prairie dogs and the natural history of the area. Still others focused more attention on what the grasslands held for the future economic development of the region, particularly in farming and ranching. Often the same individual responded in multiple ways to the landscape.

My purpose in examining these seldom-explored travel accounts is to locate some of the social and cultural influences that combined to shape the women's responses to the rural grasslands. Train transportation itself deserves attention, in that responses to the landscape rested to some degree on the type of engagement with the land—whether firsthand and intimate or detached, from the train. Romantic literary conventions of the time seem to especially combine in the narratives as well, producing particular aesthetic responses to the landscape. And the women's social positioning, as professional- or upper-class women who had to some degree "escaped" the confines of Victorian domesticity through travel, also seems relevant to the ways that they portrayed the vast, often uninterrupted horizons of the prairies and plains.

---

itinerary. Most are introduced with elaborate frontispieces and characteristic lengthy and detailed tables of contents. They then proceed with descriptions of departures from British ports such as Liverpool or from the author's entry into New York Harbor. They then continue chronologically and geographically (typically east to west) as the journey progresses. The subject matter of the narratives primarily reflects the route and destinations of railroad travel circa 1880. Generally, and as will be developed throughout this and subsequent chapters, all of the women wrote about American society and culture, scenic attractions, and hotel and train accommodations. Beyond that they concentrated on a diverse range of American physical and cultural landscapes.

Although my main focus is on the outdoor, rural landscapes of the central grasslands, I begin my discussion with the interior spaces of the trains themselves, to which the women's attention was frequently drawn on their journeys westward.[10] For my main purposes, though, I focus on the outdoor and rural prairies in western Iowa and Missouri and the plains of Kansas, Nebraska, and eastern Colorado and Wyoming—to form a homogeneous "grassland" zone, what the women themselves almost exclusively referred to as prairie. These central grasslands were primarily defined for these writers as the geographic transect that the railroad followed between Chicago and Denver (though not incidentally, the writers often failed to note exactly which prairie landscape they were describing along that transect). The prairies and plains experienced different periods of settlement. A prairie is generally characterized by tall grasses intermixed with forested and hilly zones, with richer soil and more plentiful rainfall, and the plains tend to be more level, treeless, semiarid, with short grasses. However, these differences went largely unnoticed by the travelers. The rural landscape on both sides of the Missouri River in the late nineteenth century appeared largely as an uncultivated and unaltered grassland: vast, unbounded, lacking in scale, and open to the sky. These are the kinds of features the travel writer noticed.

Trains, Plains, and Tourism

Historian Robert Athearn argues that during the late nineteenth century, after transportation and accommodations became available, "no place on the earth's surface seemed to offer more all around attractions to the British than the American West." They came to invest their money in mining enterprises in the mountains or in agricultural or ranching ventures on the high plains; they came for the "bracing climate which attracted both the healthy and the ailing"; they came for hunting or fishing expeditions; and some came simply out of curiosity (Athearn 1962, 116–18). Many British who had settled in the Rockies provided focal points for some travelers'

---

10. I have omitted from the present chapter other important features of the prairies and plains landscape discussed by the travelers (e.g., Native American reservations) because they appear in subsequent chapters.

journeys (Rose Kingsley's, for instance). Whether the Rockies were a destination or an important stop on a longer journey en route to the Pacific, they must have served as a looming backdrop for women traversing the prairies and plains and modified their impressions of them accordingly. McFarling (1955, vii) asserts that travelers whose destinations were points west looked upon the plains as a barrier to get across as quickly as possible. While she was traveling between Omaha and Cheyenne and yearning for her San Francisco "mecca," Lady Hardy found little worthwhile in the prairie landscape: "We look out upon the vast prairie-lands, which roll before and around us like a gray-green, motionless sea. The prospect is wild and dreary. . . . The scene grows monotonous; nay, wearisome . . . the novelty of it has worn off" (1882, 93). Her return trip from California was more wearisome still:

> We rest one more night in Denver, and start early next morning for St. Louis, via Kansas City. We soon feel as though we have left all the beauty and brightness of the world behind; for anything more dreary than the road thither cannot well be imagined. The whole day long, from morning till night, we look out upon the dull, uninteresting prairie land; the icy peaks, snow-clad mountains, and verdant valley have all disappeared, as though the magic plains had collapsed with all their wonders. (1882, 278)

The central grasslands appear in these passages as a time-consuming, displeasurable obstacle en route to other, more interesting destinations. Her response to the same landscape on her return from California also suggests how important the stage of journey is in landscape perception, in that the return journey is inevitably more monotonous.

Unlike their experiences hiking and taking stagecoach excursions into the Rocky Mountains and other well-advertised tourist destinations, these travelers had very little direct and intimate engagement with the central prairies and plains. Thus, most of their observations of the area were "detached" and primarily visual, made in the context of the relative comfort (or discomfort) of the railroad car. Emily Faithful mentioned that she "left Chicago on Saturday morning, and traveled for two nights and a day without leaving the cars, chiefly over barren prairies extending for hundreds of miles" (1884, 127). From the inside of a swiftly moving train car, Faithful described the landscape as "barren prairies," even though she must have passed some agricultural country. Statements such as hers and Lady Hardy's suggest that the type of engagement with the land influenced particular responses to it.

Spending a good deal of time on trains, the women often wrote and reflected on their journeys within the confines of the closed, intimate, interior "home-like" spaces of train compartments. Many scholars have noted that the experience of this interior space can affect travelers' writings about the exterior landscapes passing by. Mark Twain asserted that "nothing helps scenery like ham and eggs" (quoted in Farrar-Hyde 1990, 115). Foster argues that the enjoyment of a journey rested both on how well the traveler liked her or his traveling companions and on the traveler's health (1990, 76). Martha M. Allen (1987, 14) and Jeffrey (1988, 70) suggest as well that the means of transportation determined to a large extent how people responded to western American landscapes. First-class train travelers were ensured of a relatively comfortable, carefree, experience. Train travel also provided a distinctly visual experience of a landscape in which the visitor could enjoy an ever-changing view.

Certainly the relative speed of train travel distinguished travelers' responses to passing landscapes as well and perhaps even drew attention away from the exterior landscapes passing by. Wolfgang Schivelbusch argues that nineteenth-century rail travel refigured time, space, and geographical imagination (1978, 41–76). Among other points, Schivelbusch asserts that the speed of railroad travel annihilated the familiar time-space continuum of other forms of transport such as coach travel, such that the experience of an area's geography was reduced to destinations or stopping places. "The railroad knows only points of departure and destination." The outcome, to Schivelbusch, was an erasure of the space traversed between, and a disconnection between the traveler and traveled space (1978, 44). From a covered wagon, the "grain" of the country could be seen, but from a fast-moving train such microscale details might become aggregated into larger and perhaps more repetitious scenes. And at an aggregated grand scale, one exterior view of the vast horizons of places like the North American Great Plains may have seemed like any other, in which case the

2. Pullman car. Reproduced with permission of the Pennsylvania Historical and Museum Commission and the Railroad Museum of Pennsylvania.

traveler's attention could easily turn to the immediate surroundings of the train compartments.

Lady Hardy commented that the "blinding sunlight" of the prairies caused her to withdraw from the scene and "glance round upon the cheerful prospect within" (1882, 94). She reported that fellow passengers were occupied with a variety of activities, including indulging in reminiscences, playing or watching whist or poker, sitting idly, or making lace. Iza Hardy wrote of the "cozy little social circle" within the trains that helped alleviate her boredom amid the "seemingly limitless desolation of the prairies" (1884, 136–37).

Train travel presents some interesting questions about the construction of gender in women travelers' texts. Sara Mills argues that women's writing often focused on appropriately feminine topics, such as domestic affairs, duty to family or community, the protagonist's own thoughts and feelings, interpersonal relationships, and proper, English upper-class manners (1990, 128–32; 1991, 94–106). And in fact the quality of railroad accommodations, hotels, and food figured centrally in the writings of travelers through the American prairies and plains, a response that is consistent with a feminine voice that derives its authority through association with interior domestic spaces. These travelers wrote at length about the extent to which the railroad accommodations fit their expectations and needs. Some were complementary. Lady Hardy enthused over the food on her train:

> It was an *embarras de richesses*. There were so many good things that we held a consultation as to what would form the most desirable meal. We decided on mulligatawny soup, broiled oysters, lamb cutlets, and peas. . . . Towards six o'clock every table was spread with dainty linen, and the dinner was exquisitely served . . . The simplest dish, as well as the most elaborate, was cooked to perfection. (1882, 80–82)

But complaints about the deficiencies of train travel were more common. Complaints about the lack of privacy on the trains, inadequate toilet facilities, stuffiness, and unpalatable food and the manner in which it was served were commonly noted. These tropes may be understood as expressions of both genteel class superiority and British chauvinism. The well-traveled E. Catherine Bates, who spent a year crossing North America in the late 1880s, was horrified at the way food was served: she wrote that one has to "degrade [one]self to the level of a pig by eating every course of a meal off one platter" (1887, 2: 6). Emily Pfeiffer complained that in America "the fact that you are in a democratic country is pressed upon you from every side; no exclusiveness is here possible" (1885, 119). Thérèse Longworth similarly objected to the lack of privacy on trains, protesting that there was no place to change or store her clothing (1974, 2: 5–6). Many of the travelers resented going to bed earlier than preferred and complained of the heat and closeness of the train cars. Mrs. E. H. Carbutt alleged that the sleeping arrangements were "very much like being in one's coffin" (1979, 24), and Lady Howard declared, "How one longs for an English first-class compartment, or even second or third! . . . no words can describe the discomfort and suffocating *désagréments* of the 'sleepers'" (1897, 8). Marianne North, the celebrated world traveler and painter who crossed North America twice in her career (in 1875 and 1881), concurred: "If I opened the scrap of window next to my face, I was blown away and smothered with dust; if I shut it, I was stifled (1892, 1: 200–201).

Although Athearn points out that men also wrote of western train and hotel accommodations, women were more critical of them (1962, 18), suggesting that such a "discourse of complaint" was not equally available to men and women travel writers. In addition to their focus on domestic scenes and personal feelings and relationships, Mills argues that further components of Victorian women's travel writing were expressions of weakness, passivity, the need for help, as well as complaints about how emotionally difficult travel had become. All of these were, Mills persuasively argues, the outcome of Victorian women's inability to participate fully as adventurers in a foreign land simply because they were women (1991, 78).[11] Moreover, British women's complaints about accommodations also may be understood as a means of solidifying their gendered class positions, as a sort of "princess and the pea" narrative device. From this perspective, narratives about the grasslands that were turned inward, toward the social settings of train compartments themselves, provided travelers opportunities to disclose proper English manners reserved for the genteel classes (counterdistinguished from American crassness) as well as the delicacy and refinement reserved for ladies. Thus, these narrative devices served to consolidate both their superior class position and superior nationality, even if at other points in their texts the women were critical of dominant constructions of Victorian femininity at home.

Views from the Train: Monotonous and "Empty"

When the women's attention turned outward, onto the grand-scale vast horizons of the central American grasslands, one exterior view often

11. Nevertheless, both men's and women's emphasis on the difficulties of travel served as a means of "improving" their achievement, although this seems more relevant within the context of mountaineering or other explorations into remote districts than within such "domestic" train scenes.

appeared as any other. Many of the travelers who described the prairies and plains from within their train compartments found the terrain hopelessly dreary, desolate, visually tedious, and psychologically overwhelming. Many pointed to the absence of variety in nature, of streams, rocks, trees, as well as to the absence of human features. Negative terms such as "dull," "monotonous," "dreary," "desolate," and "barren" were common. The aristocratic Theodora Guest wrote of the plains just east (and within sight of) the Rocky Mountains: "When we woke thus early it was to gaze on a most bare, hopeless, flat, treeless prairie, stretching as far as the eye could reach, in shades of yellow, grey and dull brown" (1895, 58). Mrs. Vincent described the prairies as "the blankness of desolation" (1885, 1: 72). Catherine Bates saw "not a building, not a hill to break the terrible monotony" (1887, 2: 17). Emily Faithful referred to the grasslands as "barren prairies" (1884, 127), and Rose Kingsley called the prairie a place of "utter desolation and monotony" (1874, 40).

Mrs. Vincent "look[ed] for some sign of life, some tree or green plant" (1885, 1: 72). Her suggestion that nature should be green is significant. The seeming uniformity of plant life and the absence of the trees and shrubs found in eastern woodlands, the season of the year in which most journeys took place—late summer or autumn when much of the vegetation may have turned brown and seemed unattractive—and the fact that riding in a train was not conducive to picking out individual flowers or plants, all suggested to the traveler that nature itself was absent from the surroundings. Vincent elaborated on the point by referring to nature there as "grim and stingy" (1885, 1: 72).

Martha Allen asserts that women (travelers as well as immigrants on the overland routes) "showed a surprising lack of interest in flora and fauna" of the region and that "to a certain extent this apparent oversight is a reflection of the nineteenth-century understanding of the plains rather than a lack of curiosity or keen eyesight" (1987, 14). But it is not surprising that travelers detached from the landscape, moving swiftly through it by train, were unable to distinguish species of grass or herbs. Asserting monotonous uniformity of the region, particularly its plant life, can be directly related to mode of transportation and lack of direct engagement with the land. Most of these travelers were located not in the landscape but apart from it; their separateness from it must be considered in contrast to their claims to "know" the region without actually having stepped foot in it. Even most writers who noticed the difference between uncultivated grass and cultivated fields (typically east of the Missouri River) found the agricultural land monotonous and lacking in variation (Pfeiffer 1885, 116; Guest 1895, 57; but see note 11).

Nature's Aesthetic Relief

Though much of the prairie landscape appeared repetitious and even empty to British travelers, one of the few distinguishable features they often noted about the region were the (sometimes) plentiful prairie flowers and sagebrush, another component of a properly feminized discourse about a place. Women travelers' attention to flowers in these texts appears to be consistent with that of women settlers, as Annette Kolodny argues; women went about planting gardens and flowers to claim the frontier and as a way to produce a kind of sanctuary for domesticity (1984, xxii–xiii, 6–8; also see Norwood 1993 on women's garden aesthetic; and chapter 4).

The travelers placed great significance on flowers during their journeys, described them at length (often providing the botanical names for the different species), and collected them at train stations along the western routes. Mrs. Carbutt, who otherwise found little to appreciate about the northern prairies, found the wild sunflowers one of the only redeeming qualities of the landscape. She also praised the sagebrush covering the northern prairies for its aesthetic appeal and pungent smell: it was "a pale, silvery, olive-coloured plant with a delicious smell. I have some now sewn in muslin" (1889, 38).

Season of travel, of course, greatly influenced how the traveler experienced a flowered landscape. A typical cross-country tour began with an Atlantic steamship crossing in summer and arrival in the West by railroad in early autumn. By that time, the region's plentiful wildflowers had dried and turned brown and, to many observers, unattractive. Some women, especially those on longer or multiple trips to America, though, traveled through the interior country in the winter (e.g., Longworth) or in spring (e.g., Pender) and thus encountered an altogether different landscape. Rose Pender described the springtime Platte River valley as flourishing with plenty of cotton trees, and a river was winding its way through the valley. Such lovely prairie flowers, and all as green as only the early spring can produce. We halted by the river and made tea, and I rambled some distance along its banks, enjoying the delicious air after the rain, and gathering a lovely bouquet of quite unknown (to me) wild flowers. (1978, 94)

The women collected wildflowers at rural train depots and decorated their train and hotel rooms with them, notwithstanding defensively ranking them among "common weeds" or "rubbish" (R. Kingsley 1874, 40). Marianne North, the one traveler with a professional interest in flowers and plants (see chapter 4), observed all along the prairie country "hundreds of miles of sunflowers . . . we stopped long enough at the stations to pick a few flowers; and the train always started again slowly, so that any stragglers could catch it up (1892, 1: 200–1). After crossing the Rocky Mountains eastward, North wrote of coming down "on the vast and uninteresting plains . . . *Lupins, vetches,* and *oenotheras* were the only flowers I saw on that great green plain" (1892, 2: 203). Lady Guest, too, collected flowers throughout her American journey and dried them using her own press (1895, 61).

One job of the travel writer was to note those features of a place most unique and different from the home country. Descriptions of strange animals such as prairie dogs and especially buffalo worked well for British travel writers in this regard. With little else of the apparently empty landscape to draw their attention, women travelers textually "completed" the prairie scenery through discussion of notably western—and exotic—forms of wildlife (Farrar-Hyde 1990, 110), which aligned well with other aspects of romantic discourse discussed momentarily. Marianne North, for example, declared that a prairie dog city interested her more than Chicago did (1892, 1: 200). Many descriptions of prairie dogs combined observational detail with analysis of the animals' social characteristics (Vincent 1885, 1: 73; Bridges 1883, 410).

Rose Kingsley filled two pages describing a prairie dog scene west of Salina, Kansas, and included in her book a detailed pencil sketch of them. She concluded by declaring that they "are the quaintest little animals; and make charming pets, as they are very easily tamed" (1874, 36). Although this view toward domesticating prairie dogs seems congruent with a feminine desire to contain wild animals within the limits of domesticity, the narratives adopted more moral and ethical dimensions when the subject turned to buffalo.

Buffalo provided a welcome diversion to the largely uninterrupted prairie landscape, and many of the women who wrote of them expressed concern with how fast they were dying out.[12] Sometime after departing from Columbus, Nebraska, Thérèse Longworth assessed their situation:

> These plains, which extend for about five hundred miles, are the great buffalo runs . . . the buffaloes literally cover the plain, and can be shot from the platform and windows—a sort of cockney sport, but one which the American hunter seems to delight in. Sometimes the plains are blackened over with these animals, and shooting at them is like firing into a mountain. (1974, 2: 18–19)

Earlier in the passage Longworth provides buffalo with anthropomorphic intelligence and dignity, in contrast to the "cockney" (dull, stupid, low-class) American sportsmen who shot them. As Longworth continued describing ignorant American buffalo-hunting, she added that Americans "can never understand the English idea that danger enhances the pleasure of the sport" and so preferred instead to shoot buffalo from a position of safety and weakness (1974, 2: 20–21). Rose Kingsley, who observed a herd of thousands, was likewise appalled at the random shootings of buffalo from the trains: "A most cruel and foolish fashion prevails on these trains, of shooting the poor animals from the cars as they go along, for the mere pleasure of killing" (1874, 38–39, 42). Like Longworth, Kingsley located

---

12. White (1991, 216–20) reports that bison herds on the American plains probably peaked at about twenty-five million, with about six to seven million in the southern herds in the mid–nineteenth century, and three million as late as the 1870s. However, by 1875 the southern herd was virtually gone, due primarily to the industrial-style hunting of professional hide hunters who moved into the area. White reports that the most skilled hunters took 2,500 to 3,000 buffalo in a single year in the 1870s, inefficiently wasting most of their kill. "The slaughter was so thorough and quick that not even the hunters could believe what they had done" (1991, 219). By 1883 the northern herds had vanished as well.

herself in opposition to the random massacre of buffalo by thoughtless (male) railroad passengers, adopting a voice of compassion and feminine sympathy as well as providing a comparison of the English upper-class manner of hunting to that of the rough and uncouth American. (Never mind that buffalo were potentially far more dangerous than rabbits and foxes on an English hunt.[13]) These writers asserted their ethnocentric pride in proper hunting techniques, meanwhile ignoring altogether subsistence-based buffalo hunting among Native peoples. In that sense they did not seem to object to the killing of buffalo per se, as much as to the manner by which it was done.

Literary and Romantic Horizons

It is important to recognize the potentially vast range of commercial and literary influences on landscape interpretation in Victorian travel writing. Tourist guidebooks on America, such as *Crofutt's Trans-Continental Tourist's Guide* (1872), were one such commercial influence (Farrar-Hyde 1990, 120–21). Widely available to British travelers, they provided practical and useful information about the transcontinental journey.

The main source of tourist information about western America, however, was provided by the major railroad companies. Advertisements praising the virtues and qualities of scenery and recommending preferred travel routes and points of interest were found in British newspapers and journals beginning in the 1840s and 1850s. Such promotional material was also available through the railroad land offices and private land companies (some with offices in Britain), at depots across the West, as well as on board the trains (Davis 1975, 182; Farrar-Hyde 1990, 96–146). These probably had less than the desired effects for the railroad companies, however, as travelers frequently expressed contempt for how unsatisfactorily their western experience measured up to that promised (e.g., Pfeiffer 1885, 116).

Not surprisingly, residents and nonresidents of an area embody distinctly different types of landscape observers. A tourist or traveler, disengaged from qualities of land such as economic productivity, can "enjoy"

---

13. My thanks to Fran Kaye for clarifying these distinctions.

3. Cover to *Crofutt's Trans-Continental Tourist's Guide,* 2d ed. (1871). Reproduced courtesy of the Bancroft Library.

a landscape and therefore might respond mainly to its aesthetic qualities (Norwood and Monk 1987, 4). The influence of the romantic movement on Victorian travel writing seems especially relevant to descriptions of the aesthetic qualities of the central American grasslands. Romanticism, originating as an artistic and intellectual movement in the late eighteenth century, stressed the importance of emotions and sentiment, imagination, self-improvement, and anticlassical artistry (Perry 1984, 207–59). Romantic writers were concerned with the impact of scenery on their senses; they observed and recorded their subjective reactions to beautiful and sublime landscapes in a way contrary to the transparent, uninvolved scientific observer. Romanticism stressed the individual, and in terms of landscape, how a landscape made one feel. Thus, while feminist scholars of Victorian women's travel literature have treated personal and introspective expressions of feeling as somehow feminine and related to women's domestic orientation, evidence also suggests that these expressions correspond to romantic literary conventions.

But the grasslands lacked all the features normally valued by Victorians in a landscape: they lacked the sublimity of the mountain or desert and were not picturesque like England and New England. As Thacker points out, the grasslands were (and are) "unlike any landscape conventionally thought pleasing. Rather than the variety and contrast of the picturesque, or the majesty of the sublime, the prairie seemed to embody a view vast and endless" (1989, 2). Farrar-Hyde argues that the "raw natural power" of American landscapes was potentially alienating to European observers in search of the beautiful or sublime in more familiar picturesque scenes. She explains that, primarily due to the influential eighteenth-century treatise of Edmund Burke, romanticism popularized another aesthetic category to exist alongside the picturesque. This category seemed perfectly designed for the American wilderness: an object or scene could be described as sublime if it produced fear, awe, or excitement, or if it evoked great size, power, or solitude. According to Farrar-Hyde, "wild, barren, harsh, jagged, and strange landscapes suddenly had aesthetic value" (1990, 17–18).

Likening the prairies and plains to the sea or ocean was a common literary device in the travelers' texts. As Martha Allen suggests, the sea metaphor was the only other physical form in the travelers' experiences with which they could draw a logical analogy (1987, 7)—it was as vast, trackless, and treeless. Rose Kingsley likened the plains to "long stretches of brown, rolling away wave upon wave, like some great ocean turned into land in the midst of a heavy ground swell after a storm" (1874, 35). Lady Howard wrote that "everywhere was a sea of green" and that "half of the passengers felt sea-sick" from the rocking motion of the train (1897, 28). Thérèse Longworth wrote of her experience as one of "rolling through these boundless plains of swaying grass, that now seemed to move in ripples, now in great undulating waves of the ocean"; she went so far as to describe smelling a "saltwater breeze" (1974, 2: 18). Longworth drew the analogy out in an image of a December winter scene as well: "The long prairie grass waving for miles around was topped with snow, like crested foam on the ocean" (1974, 2: 10–11).

Consistent with later nineteenth-century romantic conventions for the beautiful and the sublime, all the travelers turned at some point to what they considered the aesthetically pleasing aspects of the western grass-lands. They noted the special qualities in the colors, light, and shadows of the sun, particularly in sunsets and sunrises, in violent thunderstorms and other inclement weather, in extraordinary starlit nights, and in the sheer vastness of the wide open spaces. Those who experienced violent thunder-storms (from within the safety of a railroad car) found value in inclement weather, considering it grand, awesome, and sublime. On her approach to Omaha, Nebraska, Lady Hardy observed that the "wind howled like a shrieking demon, and came creeping in at every crevice, till we shivered in its icy grasp. Dreary without and dreary within!" (1882, 83). And Rose Pender, who traveled in the springtime by stagecoach from prairie ranch house to ranch house in Wyoming, described at length the many thun-derstorms she experienced; they were lovely, wonderful, and truly grand (1978, 88, 69; also 94). Locating herself out in the prairie, her descriptions of storms reflected her intimate, firsthand encounters with them.

Pleasing aspects of sunrises and sunsets also figured prominently in the texts (e.g., Guest 1895, 176). The poet Emily Pfeiffer declared that a Missouri sunset

> had indeed been surpassingly lovely . . . with its indescribable clearness, it stood as of heaven opened, and its delicate variation of tints; and no less exquisite was the starlit night. . . . The sunrise the following morn-ing was a glorious succession of changes, dark, upright-standing clouds, like battalions of fighting men, catching the red illumination on their fronts as they moved forward over the crystal clearness to melt into the roseate blaze. (1885, 117)

These travel writers adopted a range of rhetorical strategies to justify describing a landscape that otherwise held little interest, and this was most easily accomplished by describing the prairies as "fascinating" in all their monotony. Most of the writers who portrayed prairie scenery as boring also found romantic fascination in it. Mrs. Vincent described "the majesty of loneliness . . . Monotonous as they are, there is the greatest fascination about the prairies" (1885, 1: 73). She continued: "Those beautiful rolling plains—millions of acres, covered with the short, yellow buffalo grass— extend to the horizon in undulating lines, a wide, uninhabited, lifeless, uplifted solitude" (1885, 1: 72–73). Lady Howard described the region as "boundless plains of rolling grass—a sea of waving golden verdure, wild, solitary, and beautiful" (1897, 28).

The narrative tradition of romanticism undoubtedly provided British women travelers a language to describe the unfamiliar, grand-scale landscape of the North American grasslands. One might speculate that these tropes of romanticism enabled the writers to further articulate their class associations. From a sociological viewpoint, it could be argued that these writers employed certain romantic conventions in order to associate themselves with the British intellectual and literary elite. Furthermore, it might plausibly be argued that romanticism gave these writers a language to express the transformative effect of nature on their personal growth, as women. Given romanticism's stress on emotional responses and human perfectibility, the writers may have invoked a romantic style to signify the extent to which the "natural" environment of the prairie freed them from the constraints of their domestic lives in cities (even if contact with nature also produced an ennobling effect on men). Though romanticism stressed the "cult of the individual," this individualism stood in marked contrast to the feminine discourse of family ties and self-effacement. Many of these women did not travel until middle age, when their familial duties were complete, and thus their prior exposure to nature (outside of England's well-articulated landscape aesthetic focused on picturesque heaths, and so forth) may have been quite limited. In this sense direct exposure to the rugged, wild, outdoor landscapes of the prairies became the arena within which they expressed personal transformation, newfound pride, and self-satisfaction.

Lady Rose Pender's text provides a case in point. Pender, in describing prairie storms, stressed the many markers of romantic language to which Farrar-Hyde refers (1990, 17–18). Pender's courage stands out in the face of a terrifying storm, as do her explicit references to the awe-inspiring and grand-scale qualities of the scene. The individual that emerges is a more liberated figure, taking pride in withstanding dangerous natural hazards. Travelers such as Pender who experienced direct engagement with the land noticed details about it that were difficult, if not impossible, to recognize from the train. Whereas most travelers described the region as uniformly "flat," "monotonous," and "dull," Pender noticed variation across the terrain:

> I must try and give some idea of the Neobrara [sic] Ranche and the coun-try round it. Not a bit flat, much resembling Scotch lowland scenery, a broad green valley, through which a bright little trout stream wound its way, and along its banks we put up ducks, herons, and other water fowl. The hills rose in high undulations for ever and ever,—a country where one would get lost easily in an hour when once out of sight of the ranche and its enclosures. (1978, 72)

Not only did Pender notice variation in the physical landscape as she camped out in Wyoming and Nebraska, but her text provides a good example of the romantic mode in its fullest expression as she pondered the wide open spaces she actually stood in. Pender wrote of a sense of exhila-ration, freedom from constraint, and well-being she experienced in what she considered her unrestricted life in the Niobrara country of northwest-ern Nebraska: "I hunted for wild flowers, helped Bury to milk the cows, and washed all the clothes . . . in short, led the simplest and wildest lives, in the purest and most delicious air I ever breathed" (1888, 74). While vis-iting cattle ranches in Nebraska, she further contended that

> Never in my life had I enjoyed anything half so much as our wild rough life. . . . The delicious pure air, the scenery, the strange sights and experi-ences, the sense of utter freedom and independence, and above all, the immunity from any ailment whatever—a feeling of such well-being that to rise in the morning was a delight and to live and breathe a positive luxury—made our few weeks' drive over the prairies a happy time for me to look back upon for all my life. (1888, 123)

Pender also participated in "masculine" activities such as a cattle roundup (see below) and portrayed herself as strengthened by them. She quoted a ranchman who asserted that "if all English women were as strong as I was they must be a fine race, as I seemed to be a real 'Rustler.' This, I believe, is a term of approval" (1978, 117). In all of these excerpts, Pender expressed something demonstrably new and different—and empowering—about her experiences, and employed romantic language to articulate this newfound sense of self on the prairies.

Pioneers of Progress

Most travelers in this study rode the trains straight through the grasslands without stopping, and as already noted, described the region primarily as empty, devoid of interesting characteristics that the mountains in particular held and an obstacle to be crossed as quickly as possible. Whereas the mountains represented presence, the plains represented absence (R. Kingsley 1874, 44). In relational terms, the mountains were invested of meaning, the plains divested.

The plains were, moreover, consistently described in negative terms, terms that indicated the landscape lacked attributes found in other places: the region was constructed as treeless (lacking in trees and shrubs), flat (lacking in topographical variation), and monotonous and dull (lacking in interesting vegetation, geology, human features, picturesqueness). Some claims were exaggerated to stress a point, such as Kingsley's assertion that the plains ran east from the mountains to Kansas "without a single tree, for 400 miles" (1874, 60). Thus these writers primarily constructed the plains as essentially underdeveloped, as unfinished in comparison to other landscapes, and ultimately as lacking meaning, with nature itself absent from the surroundings as well (Vincent 1885, 1: 72–73, discussed above). This type of discourse implies that the region is in need of some sort of completion, either aesthetically or through human development in the form of civilization, industrialization, or especially agriculture.

Aesthetically the landscape might be completed by imagining a different landscape altogether in its place. To that end Rose Kingsley, traveling through the Kansas prairies, enjoined a beautiful landscape "mirage" of lush lakes and rivers to complete an otherwise unsatisfactory view (1874, 40). To Mrs. Vincent, the only way to aesthetically complete the landscape was to look past it, toward the mountains (1885, 1: 76). Pratt

(1992, 137–41) argues that constructions of landscapes as essentially lacking in meaning was characteristic of imperialist travel writing of the eighteenth century, wherein places such as South America were "reinvented" by explorers such as Alexander von Humboldt as needing European completion. Pratt argues that writers in this type of discourse are "oblivious to the limitations on their own perceptual capacities" to see the landscape out of scarcity, rather than density, of meaning (1992, 217–19). That is, if meaning is lacking in the landscape, it is the landscape's "fault," not the viewer's inability to see and interpret it. Gregory makes a similar point in his work on the travel writings of Florence Nightingale in nineteenth-century Egypt. Nightingale, unable to adequately describe the Egyptian landscape, turned her frustration into a focus on the inadequacy of her object; Egypt for her becomes hell itself, an inversion of the "ordered and Christian world of Europe" (Gregory 1995, 29–57). Such analyses are instructive; if a landscape is primarily represented in terms of deficiencies, in terms of aesthetic disappointments, the writer implicitly suggests that the hand of social or material intervention is required to bring it to fruition.

Several British women travel writers turned their attention to the future capitalistic development of the grasslands, and especially the potential for productive farming and ranching, as a means of textually completing the landscape for their home audiences. Discourses surrounding the nineteenth-century development of the plains region, as well as the American West more generally, have been well documented—the aesthetic as well as political-economic transformation of the West from the points of view of American settlers as well as industrialists, scientists, railroad developers, and media correspondents. Key works have focused on the mixed and paradoxical images of the West, particularly of the central prairies and plains as both "garden" and "desert" throughout the century (H. Smith 1950; Nash 1967; Marx 1964). From a textual perspective, these rhetorical strategies invoked the transformative powers of settlers and farming techniques that in effect completed an otherwise incomplete and immature western land. As such, these strategies are part of an (American) imperialist version of the world, especially as they are contingent upon the removal of the region's indigenous populations.

Athearn maintains that much of the attention of the "enterprising" Britisher in the later Victorian years was focused on the numerous investment opportunities in western mining, cattle ranching, and agriculture (1962, 122–24). Such economic interests produced particular kinds of discourse about the proper development of the region in the travelogues of writers personally invested. Again, Rose Pender's travelogue provides a good example of the way in which personal investment interests produced a kind of business discourse concerned with capitalist improvement of the land. The climax of Pender's narrative is her participation in a spring cattle roundup:

> In plain English, a Round-up is a search or hunt in the spring for all the cattle in the locality. Several owners join together. An outfit, which consists of waggons drawn by mules, a large herd of horses, and as many men from each owner as is necessary, is assembled, under the command of a headman or foreman. The country is systematically scoured for miles, sometimes for hundreds of miles. All the cattle collected are driven to some settled locality, when the calves are branded, and beeves destined for market are driven off, a rough estimate of profit or loss is made out, and when this part of the business is finished the Roundup terminates, and the men depart to their ranches. (1978, 3)

Within the context of the roundup, Pender's attention occasionally turned to the relative development of the cattle industry and availability or quality of pastureland for grazing. Somewhere in the vicinity of Fort Laramie Pender reported that "[we] drove for a long way . . . till we reached the enclosure of Players' Ranche, our destination for the night. 50,000 acres are enclosed with a ring fence, and as this was a new purchase of our manager's, we were anxious to inspect a part of it" (1978, 69). On approach of her own ranch she observed that

> such rich pasture land it all was, and near the stream was the hay land. Mr. R—— calculated that they would make some hundreds of tons that season. It simply requires cutting, the sun dries it thoroughly in two days, and then it is stacked as it stands. (1978, 72)

Significantly, though, such a business discourse was overlaid by Pender's romanticism and feminism, as she experienced "the most charming spot in the world" for the first time. The thrill of camping out during the roundup itself, her "first actual experience of roughing it," foregrounded her narrative (above). Here Pender captured the scene as one of romantic sublimity, a "lovely and picturesque sight" (1978, 80). When she arrived by buggy to observe the roundup of 20,000 cattle, though, her attention became focused on fear of the animals and disgust over their treatment: "I could not help thinking that were the whole thing done more quietly and gently much time might be saved, as the cowboys so terrify the wretched beasts that they become like mad things" (1978, 77–78).

Like Longworth's and Kingsley's references to the crude American sport of buffalo-hunting, in this passage Pender contrasted her genteel, upper-class sensibilities against uncouth American modes of cattle rustling. Her feminine imagining of quiet and gentle treatment of the animals recalls the English upper-class discourse of "the lady." Pender went on to clarify that "I did not like the cowboys; they impressed me as brutal and cowardly, besides being utterly devoid of manners or good feeling"— not a single one of them offered to help her stake up her tent (1978, 78–79). Thus a complex array of capitalist business interests, a sense of feminist liberation in "roughing it" outdoors, upper-class admonitions toward proper cattle-raising techniques, romantic expressions of picturesque scenery, as well as a feminine arrogance toward the cowboys' poor treatment of the cattle and, by extension, Pender herself, all combine in her narrative.

Beyond those with personal business interests, other British women positively portrayed large-scale, capitalist-improving development of the region. Emily Pfeiffer, refreshed from lunch and a good cup of tea, closed her chapters on the American West thus reflecting: "The sun is shining; the world is in progress; the end is still hopeful if God is its Guide" (1885, 261). Travelers often advocated large-scale development of land that was represented as "useless" (such as the central grasslands) but at the same time advocated the preservation and protection of other resources, especially picturesque or aesthetically pleasing land, such as mountains and forests, from invasive, large-scale, polluting forms of civilization such as the railroad. Emily Faithful, for instance, represented progress as something good so long as the place undergoing progress was not beautiful or picturesque or worth preserving in its "natural" state. She lamented the invasion of the railroad in the Colorado Rockies:

> The giant of the nineteenth century—the ogre who, while he brings these lovely places within ordinary reach, spoils their picturesqueness and destroys their solitude—is gradually asserting his sway throughout this wild district . . . disturbing the serenity of the eagles, hawks, and coyotes. (1884, 145–46)

Mrs. Vincent expresses similar displeasure on her subsequent journey to Pike's Peak (1885, 1: 80). These travelers' positions resonate well with the late nineteenth-century preservationist and protectionist rhetoric of John Muir, which stood in opposition to more conservation-minded, "wise-use" arguments about management of western resources articulated by Gifford Pinchot (Gottlieb 1993, 26–29). To the preservation-minded, the monumental aspect of sublime nature, such as that found in rugged mountains, held value in particular as a scenic resource; deserts, semiarid valleys, and prairies held little interest as natural or scenic environments to be protected.

Faithful and Vincent, then, expressed a romantic nostalgia for the sublime aspects of mountainous landscapes that were to be destroyed by the invasive forces of civilization. Yet, these and other writers also asserted that the railroad would positively impact the prairies and plains. Faithful, for instance, was pleased with the "peace and order" that the railroad brought to the 1880's prairie landscape in Kansas:

> Peace and order now prevail; schoolhouses abound, and prosperity has been insured by the Atchison, Topeka, and Santa Fe Railroad, which brought civilization into the heart of this rich country. This dry plains and the prairie grass have been transformed into fields of corn, and today Kansas stands to the front among the agricultural States. (1884, 258)

Faithful effused that "immigration to Kansas means prosperity . . . for those who are prepared to take proper advantage of the resources America affords cannot fail to command success" (1884, 258–59). Although these excerpts focused on Faithful's belief in the transformative power of capitalism on physical land, her narrative continued by extolling the fruitful outcomes of capitalism on Kansas culture and society (1884, 261). Other travelers similarly centered their writing on the benefits of capitalism and especially the ability of the railroad to positively transform the region (e.g., Pfeiffer 1885, 117, 120). Seen out of scarcity rather than density of meaning, the central grasslands, lacking primarily in aesthetic appeal, held little value without the improving hand of capitalism.

Conclusion

In this chapter I have argued that one key influence upon late nineteenth-century British women's travel writing about the American grasslands is mode of transport; travelers' responses to the prairies depended to a large degree on how they experienced them in terms of type of transport and level of engagement with the land. Women riding trains straight through the region viewed an aggregated, grand-scale version of the grasslands in which one scene may have appeared like any other. Those writers often turned their attention inward, to the interior train compartments themselves, appropriately domestic or domesticated women's spaces. A recurring theme in this chapter has also been the dual gender and class construction of the proper English lady and how this version of womanhood was affirmed and imposed on others, especially within the confines of the trains.

Turning their attention outward, these travelers were often bored with what appeared to be the uninterrupted horizons of the prairies and plains. Much of this chapter has focused on the influence of romanticism on Victorian women's travel texts, specifically examining the complementarity and discontinuity between nineteenth-century conventions for the beautiful and the sublime and the possibilities for deploying those qualities onto the landscapes of the American interior. I have examined the aesthetic appeal that the grasslands held (or failed to hold) for these travelers, finding that most of them treated the landscape as aesthetically disappointing. They represented the grasslands as lacking in attributes found in other places (such as trees, vegetation, and picturesqueness). I have argued that they textually completed this landscape through discussions of wildlife, flowers, and notable features of the skies. In their capacities as travel writers the women searched for the unique and discovered ample qualities of the region worth reporting. Positive responses to some aspects of the grasslands conform to the travel writer's ability (and need) to find value in strange and unfamiliar scenes. I have also argued that other positive interpretations of the prairies appeared in the text of Rose Pender, a woman who experienced more intimate engagement with the land on her cattle roundup. Pender's domestic orientation combined with her sense of freedom and well-being in the open country complements but also contrasts with dominant social norms for women in Victorian England.

Some writers focused their texts on the future development of agriculture for the region. The rhetoric of large-scale, capital-improving progress for the grasslands occurs in some of their narratives alongside that of a more protectionist perspective on other regions of the west. Although travelers such as Emily Faithful and Mrs. Vincent advocated turning the "useless" land of the central plains into productive agriculture, they and other writers were ambivalent over the inevitable despoliation and destruction of aesthetically pleasing environments (such as the Rocky Mountains) that resulted from such development. The central interior of the continent was thus constructed as a place of profitable capitalist development: a place primarily envisioned for what it could become rather than what it was.

❧ 3 ❦

Peak Practices

*Englishwomen's Heroic Adventures
in the Nineteenth-Century American West*

How time has slipped by I do not know. This is a glorious region,
and the air and life are intoxicating. I live mainly out of doors and
on horseback, wear my half-threadbare Hawaiian dress, sleep sometimes under the stars on a bed of pine boughs, ride on a Mexican
saddle, and hear once more rise low music of my Mexican spurs. . . .
[Estes Park] is surely one of the most entrancing spots on earth.
            —Isabella Bird, *A Lady's Life in the
            Rocky Mountains* (1969, 102, 116)

I was invited to go on the cow-catcher, with which every American
engine is armed. It is a kind of nose of iron bars sharply pointed,
which sweeps any obstacle from the track; and on the top there is
just room for three people to sit with their feet hanging down close
to the rails. But though in my secret heart I wished just to feel what
it was like for once, [my brother] Maurice told me that it was really
such a risk that I resisted the temptation; and we settled ourselves
comfortably on the back platform.
            —Rose Kingsley, *South by West or Winter in the
            Rocky Mountains and Spring in Mexico* (1874, 106)

IN THE FIRST EPIGRAPH, the renowned explorer Isabella L. Bird, during her first solo trip abroad at age forty, discovered, embraced, and eloquently described the rugged outdoor life of early 1870s Colorado. In much

of *A Lady's Life in the Rocky Mountains* (1969) Bird represents herself as strengthened by the outdoors, overcoming or "conquering" her own frailty through arduous hiking or horseback riding in difficult mountainous terrain. By contrast, Rose Kingsley emphasizes a much different image of Victorian womanhood in her *South by West or Winter in the Rocky Mountains and Spring in Mexico* (1874). During a rail excursion into the Rocky Mountains in 1871, Kingsley recounts her repressed desire for risk and adventure. She presents herself as properly controlled and deferential to her male protector, a brother she was visiting in Colorado Springs. Bird's and Kingsley's and other Englishwomen's narratives about hiking, horseback riding, taking rail or stage excursions, or in other ways experiencing mountainous landscapes of the American West in the late nineteenth century exhibit highly complex, ambiguous, and often contradictory or paradoxical representations of themselves as gendered individuals.

The multifaceted and multipositioned figure of the Victorian "Englishwoman abroad"[1] has received considerable attention over the past two decades from geographers, historians, literary critics, and others (e.g., Callaway 1987; Birkett 1989; Foster 1990; Mills 1991, 1996; Strobel 1991; Chaudhuri and Strobel 1992; Ware 1992; Sharpe 1993; A. Blunt 1994; Blunt and Rose 1994; Burton 1994; McEwan 1996). As these scholars have shown, middle- and upper-class British women who traveled abroad in the late nineteenth century as missionaries, wives of colonial administrators or military men, professional travel writers, reporters, or leisure-class tourists wrote of their gender identities in myriad ways. They represented themselves as the intrepid adventuress defying racial and sexual boundaries; the duty-bound domestic servant enacting self-sacrifice for family, community, and nation; the devoted Protestant missionary saving her benighted sisters in the colonies;

---

1. Although I will refer to the women travelers in this study as both English and British, they were in fact Englishwomen, though Scotland became Isabella Bird's adopted homeland. The terms English and British were often used interchangeably during the period, with "British" often referring culturally to English, and thus privileging English identity over Welsh, Scots, or Irish. (See Sharpe 1993 for further discussion.) I also use British here because it was the British empire the women travelers represented and because the feminist movement was also primarily a British phenomenon (Burton 1994, 5).

4. Isabella Bird Bishop at the time of her marriage in 1881. Reproduced courtesy of the Royal Geographical Society.

the vulnerable lady upholding hegemonic versions of femininity associated with gentility and class privilege; and the suffragist advocating nineteenth-century liberal feminist social reforms (adapted from Ware 1992).

Much of this literature has focused on British women's uneasy relationships with British colonialism and imperialism, especially the ways in which imperial discourses on race, class, and nation combined with Victorian domestic ideologies in both the maintenance of feminine codes of behavior and contestations of these codes in notions of female liberation. Little work, however, has focused on the complex intersections between British imperialism and gendered subjectivity for "Englishwomen abroad" in the mountainous landscapes in the late nineteenth-century American West.

In this chapter, I explore Englishwomen's travel writing about the Rocky Mountains and Yosemite Valley, two important side excursions off the transcontinental railroad journey during the 1870s, 1880s, and 1890s. I examine narratives about both the indoor spaces of western tourism and the outdoor mountainous landscapes of the West and problematize notions of feminine codes of behavior, early first-wave feminism, and their convergence with British imperialism outside the context of its formal empire. My concern in this chapter is to examine gendered subjectivity in the texts and to show how discourses of gender worked alongside and through imperialist, nationalist, and class discourses. I am concerned to show, for example, that attention to geographical context unsettles what other scholars (such as Pratt 1992 and Mills 1991) have identified as "imperialist language" in British Victorian women's travel writing about the conquest of mountain peaks. Women climbers claiming western places as their "own" demonstrate not triumph or domination over place but a particular kind of triumph over self and emotive attachment to place.

In the following discussion, I identify the main tropes of mountain adventure in the women's writing, which range from actively "conquering" mountain peaks to passively waiting for the men to do so; from fearing danger and fatigue to ridiculing the incompetency of local (male) guides; and from resisting adventure to expressing female empowerment and abandonment in it. I am not necessarily seeking common characteristics of all the travelogues (even though common characteristics do, in fact, appear), nor is my concern to demonstrate the individuality of each traveler by highlighting the contradictions inherent in treating them all as a homogenous group. My emphasis, rather, is on the production of gendered subjectivity emerging out of a particular nexus of British imperialism, discourses about gender, and early foreign travel in the American West. It will become clear that in many ways the women reinscribed themselves as feminine, domestic subjects in wilderness environments, yet they also explored and contested the powerful inscriptions of domesticity that arose out of hegemonic (masculinist) versions of Victorian femininity. In so doing, they articulated with, and thereby perhaps even can be seen to have reconstituted, hegemonic ideologies about femininity, domesticity, and more contestatory versions of Victorian womanhood.

Much of the scholarship dealing with British women travelers abroad has emphasized women's participation in European colonial and imperial exploitation of Asian and African people, land, and resources. As such, this body of work contrasts considerably with earlier scholarship on Victorian women travelers (e.g., Middleton 1965; Russell 1986) that valorized Victorian women for breaking out of repressive social norms through travel, but, in so doing, ignored their racism, classism, and sexism. Also problematical, however, is that works such as Mills (1991), Blunt and Rose (1994), and others paid little attention to emerging feminist discourses of the late nineteenth century that challenged and transgressed normative gender roles for traveling bourgeois women. Thus, needing further attention is how British women travelers engaged with the tropes of early "first-wave" feminism and its interconnections with imperialist ideologies such as genteel-class chauvinism and worldwide expansionism.

The heterogeneous ways that colonial women's positions as white, middle- or upper-class Protestants have intersected with the rhetorics of female liberation and emerging feminism have been taken up by several authors not concerned specifically with travel writing or spatiality (e.g., Ware 1992; Burton 1994; Sharpe 1993). Resonances between early British feminist movements and imperial politics can be found in works concerned with rescuing underprivileged women in the colonies. Burton argues that feminists claimed a place in empire by "enlisting empire" and its values in arguments over female emancipation, and as such, they should be counted among the "shapers of imperial rhetoric and imperial ideologies" (1994, 5). British first-wave feminism, like its counterparts elsewhere, was a movement primarily focused on (white) women's suffrage, but it also engaged a number of other legislative and social reforms: improved educational and employment opportunities for women, marriage and property law reform, abolitionism, and more generally the uplift of the socially dispossessed both at home and throughout empire. As such it called for white women's inclusion in the imperial state and in the service of a healthy imperial state. Feminists thus represented the success of their causes as bringing Britain itself to the apex of civilization, arguing that women's exclusion would threaten the superior status of Britain. As both Ware (1992, 119–66) and Burton (1994, 1–32) point out, it was again women's moral authority that gave British feminists justification to speak against the "uncivilized" patriarchal practices of other countries, such as Indian sati.

Women travelers to the American West articulated with other British feminists in their desires to save their downtrodden Native American sisters, a subject I discuss in chapter 6. In the present chapter I explore other resonances with female liberation in the women's texts, particularly those of self-empowerment. These women travelers were advancing into the public sphere, traveling, collecting ethnographic data, hiking and mountaineering, and writing and publishing books. The ways that such expressions of self-empowerment and self-improvement worked through the impulses of empire in the mountains is an important question, especially in the ways that such rhetoric articulated with class and national identity.

Not surprisingly, the signifying practices of the Victorian bourgeoisie remain at the forefront of these narratives—writing, sketching, and embracing and taking pleasure in domestic tasks that servants normally performed at home—all helped align these women's mountain experiences with both a superior English identity and genteel femininity. And certainly mountain excursions lend themselves to an analysis of the gendering of British adventure stories and their specific relationships to empire, especially outside of the context of British colonial settings. These women helped rewrite the terms of the Victorian adventure tale, but on their own terms; they at once asserted their genteel femininity by counterposing themselves against their more active and adventurous male partners and, at the same time, reconstituted where white, British bourgeois women might feel at home in the American mountains—even to the extent of guiding the mountain guides out of dangerous situations. Such narratives of adventure, not incidentally, also articulated with a growing American tourism industry that catered to such wealthy international travelers.

In several ways, then, British women travelers collaborated in and reinforced the ideological work of imperialism, and yet their expressions of self-empowerment are unlike the more familiar tropes of colonial and imperial discourses.

I begin untangling these issues by first situating the women in the nineteenth-century mountainous West. My discussion then proceeds with a discussion of appropriate styles of dress and other domestic concerns of travel, such as what the women wrote about their western accommodations. Following that, I analyze several tropes of women's mountaineering experiences and conclude by asking whether and how anything these travelers wrote in the mountains might be construed as "liberatory politics" (after Ware 1992, 163).

Traveling the Mountainous West

The seven travelers whose narratives I examine here all journeyed to the American West in the last three decades of the nineteenth century and typically visited Yosemite or the Colorado Rockies as part of a larger grand tour of North America (they include Isabella Bird and a subset of six of those introduced in chapter 2). The women describe their mountain experiences in Yosemite and Colorado in as few as several pages, but most devote several chapters to the mountains, and one (Bird 1969), an entire volume. Isabella Bird's and Rose Kingsley's (1874) texts focus on the Colorado Rockies, and Thérèse Longworth's mountain experiences were primarily in Yosemite (1974, 2: 21–24, 58–90). The books by Lady Theodora Guest (1895, 59–77, 119–48), Emily Pfeiffer (1885, 120–37, 205–61), Rose Pender (1978, 23–35, 53–61), and Lady Howard (1897, 28–46, 76–100) cover travel in both locations. Only Isabella Bird traveled alone; Lady Howard and Rose Kingsley were accompanied by their brothers, Thérèse Longworth by her male secretary, and Emily Pfeiffer, Lady Theodora Guest, and Rose Pender by their husbands.

The Rocky Mountains of Colorado and California's Yosemite Valley were important destinations on the itineraries of many British men and women who toured the western United States in the late nineteenth century. New and improved transportation and accommodations enabled unprecedented numbers of British travelers and tourists to experience for themselves these "monumental" natural wonders of the West. Tourist guidebooks on America, such as *Crofutt's Trans-continental Tourist's Guide* (see page 37), were important commercial influences on British popular opinion of these and other sites in western America. The main source of tourist information about western America, however, as noted in chapter 2, was provided by the major railroad companies. The Colorado Rockies and Yosemite Valley were among the best advertised destinations off the Union Pacific–Central Pacific Railroad's route from Chicago to San Francisco. The railroads not only enabled these forested mountain landscapes to become attractive destinations for wealthy tourists, but, in seeking passengers, actually promoted their use (White 1991, 410–11; Milner, O'Connor, and Sandweiss 1994, 628–29).

Yosemite's reputation as a popular tourist attraction began as early as the 1850s. Congress set it aside and under the control of California with the 1864 Yosemite Act. Helped along by the completion of the transcontinental railroad, Yosemite grew into a "fashionable pleasure resort" in the 1870s and 1880s, for foreign and American visitors alike. The park finally came under federal control by 1890 (Demars 1991, 10–27). After an arduous, sometimes several-day staging into the valley from Raymond or other towns, tourist itineraries in the park followed established patterns, typically including day excursions into the valley's principal attractions, such as Yosemite Fall, Bridalveil Fall, Mirror Lake, and, for a panoramic view of the valley, a trip to the top of Glacier Point (Demars 1991, 35–36). Thérèse Longworth wrote that Yosemite "has recently become quite the fashion," adding that "everyone in San Francisco says that Yosemite is *the* big thing in the world just now" (1974, 2: 58–60, her italics).

American and British imperialisms reached a particular nexus at Yosemite during the period. As tumultuous Native American genocide and virtual enslavement proceeded apace throughout the region (Trigger and Washburn 1996, 57–115; White 1991, 337–40), the setting aside of wilderness areas such as Yosemite as a social space where the wealthy could distinguish themselves as arbiters of a leisure-class lifestyle likewise advanced. The creation of Yosemite Park, achieved by state and federal governments, well-spoken preservation-minded environmentalists such as John Muir, and landscape architects such as Frederick Law Olmsted, among scores of other interested parties, ensured a place where the negative effects of American urbanization could be countered; Yosemite became a place of recreation and "rejuvenation" for those who had benefited most from urban-industrial capitalism, among them eastern American bureaucrats and wealthy international travelers (Demars 1991, 9–22; Milner, O'Connor, and Sandweiss 1994, 628; Cronon 1995, 78).

Likewise, a particular nexus of American and British imperialism was evident in the Rocky Mountain region of Colorado. The healthful climate and myriad sporting and recreational activities made the region an especially attractive destination for health seekers and foreign tourists (Farrar-

Hyde 1990, 147–90). Many transcontinental travelers took side excursions from Denver to Colorado Springs and Manitou Springs, site of one of the principal tourist attractions of the region, the 14,000-foot Pike's Peak. Colorado was also home to many wealthy British investors, titled remittance men, and retired colonels, and the large numbers of Britishers who had settled in the Rockies provided focal points for some travelers' journeys (Rose Kingsley's, for instance). In addition, extensive investment opportunities, particularly in mining, cattle ranching, and railroad development attracted British visitors (Athearn 1962, 116–25; Mulvey 1983, 1990; White 1991, 260–63; Rico 1998). Athearn reports that Colorado "was almost an English reserve," with one of every three ranches in Colorado in the later nineteenth century belonging to Englishmen. "Any capitalist could then come," continues Athearn, "enjoy the delightful climate, and live comfortably" off his invested income that returned 10 to 18 percent on loans (1962, 118, 120). British investments helped finance capitalist ventures such as the development of the Denver and Rio Grande Railroad (Beebe and Clegg 1958; see chapter 5), which facilitated Colorado's deepening entry into the global economy. And clearly such expansion into the region depended upon drastic reductions in the Native American populations by warfare, disease, near extinction of the buffalo, and nearly complete alienation from their former lands through the reservation and then allotment process imposed by the U.S. government, discussed in depth elsewhere (e.g., White 1991).

Setting Out: What to Wear?

Attention to western train travel, accommodations, food, and clothing during their mountain journeys were key features in Englishwomen's travel writing. These travelers paid considerable attention to the closed, intimate home-like interiors of trains as they journeyed westward, as discussed in chapter 2. Their focus on social life aboard the trains, quality of food, lack of privacy, and complaints about American travelers and railroad personnel were consistent with a feminine voice of travelers who derived much of their textual authority from discussing appropriately domestic topics and who aligned their femininity with their aristocratic class and superior English identity. Many of the women's representations of their own clothing in mountain environs achieved a similar discursive end, associating their ladylike behaviors and mores with the English upper classes, yet at the same time contesting dominant constructions of Victorian femininity.

Guidebooks such as Lillias Campbell Davidson's *Hints to Lady Travellers* (1889) served as "conduct literature" or advice manuals on proper travel etiquette and behavior for privileged women travelers. Davidson explained how to buy a railroad ticket, what to take on a journey, and why not to take one's maid along (they are "a great nuisance"). Davidson also suggested how to pack: "with 'liberal use of tissue paper,' each gown in a tray to itself and a monogrammed wrap for each pair of shoes" (as quoted in Middleton 1965, 7; also see Mills 1991, 100–2). To Davidson, appropriate travel apparel was necessary for safety reasons; dresses just above the ankle (for mountaineering) would help the traveler maintain an aura of respectability necessary to ward off men's unwanted sexual advances (Mills 1991, 102). This advice appears in considerable contrast to the way Isabella Bird (1969) dressed and, as Middleton (1965, 7–8) has observed, the way she packed her belongings in a luggage roll on the back of her saddle while trekking through the Rocky Mountains on horseback.

Bird describes her riding costume as "thoroughly serviceable." An experienced horsewoman, she preferred to ride astride, arguing that she adopted the trousers and divided skirt for practical reasons, to allow more freedom of movement: "I could not ride any distance in the conventional mode," she wrote (1969, 10). While apparently opposing the clothing conventions of her gendered class position and ignoring the Lillias Campbell Davidsons of the time, Bird simultaneously emphasized the femininity of the outfit:

> For the benefit of other lady travelers, I wish to explain that my "Hawaiian riding dress" is the "American Lady's Mountain Dress," a half-fitting jacket, a skirt reaching to the ankles, and full Turkish trousers gathered into frills falling over the boots—a thoroughly serviceable and feminine costume for mountaineering and other rough traveling. (1969, 10, fn. 3)

When the *London Times* described her as riding in the Rockies in "male habiliments," she reportedly told her publisher John Murray "that as she had neither father nor brother to defend her reputation, she expected him personally to horse-whip the *Times* correspondent" (Middleton 1968, 8). Bird returns often in her text to the apparent ambivalences of her mode of riding and dress. Although she claimed to "submit to the restraints of civilization" by riding side-saddle to meet Colorado's Governor Hunt in Denver, she stressed her forgetfulness in failing to remove her riding dress and spurs before making social calls (1969, 139–51). In the riding dress, Bird "shrank" from the public eye, and from her own reputation for skilled equestrianism, upon leaving a hotel in Estes Park, yet was "exhilarated with delightful motion" on the ride that followed (1969, 74). Thus, while Bird appears to contest convention in dress and behavior for women, her ambivalence effectively sustains her close tether to more proper and conventional dress for women of her social station. And in fact, Bird more explicitly positioned herself against clothing reform in a later book about her travels in Japan, in which she claimed not to be tempted by the clothing reformers (as discussed in Mills 1991, 105). Western America served as a useful location for such an ambivalent gendered subjectivity. Bird portrayed western America as "blissful" in allowing her freedom to ride in her own fashion, yet its service to her unconventionality also proved it to be a place lacking in civilization: men were unastonished at her abilities or dresswear, for instance (1969, 10–11).

Several of the travelers reported that hotel personnel provided them divided skirts for mule or horseback excursions into Yosemite. Lady Howard addressed the subject of "male habiliments" during her stay at Yosemite in 1894. Although the "balloon-shaped divided skirt" that she was provided for a journey up to Glacier Point seemed "absurd," she acknowledged that it was the "universal fashion all over the west" because it was much safer for horseback riding (1897, 86). Lady Theodora Guest similarly reported that the "divided . . . very much divided" skirt made her feel "ridiculous," even if it was the vogue on the city streets of San Francisco (1895, 151–52, 134–35). Thérèse Longworth, in her description of preparations for a two-day Yosemite excursion, took the trope further by ridiculing in detail her riding companions' "knickerbockers" and the determination of a group of unidentified fellow travelers to ride astride when they lacked the skills necessary to even mount their horses. Longworth mocked the foolish outfits and the ensuing theatrics: "Chairs, and stools, and grooms, and high rails were all put in requisition. . . . More than one lady, in spite of all the assistance so rendered, mounted on the wrong side and found herself with her face tailwards!" (1974, 2: 64–66). Guest, Howard, and Longworth all present images of the proper English lady appropriately above western, and feminist, clothing reform, yet they are willing to acknowledge its benefits. Longworth in particular, at the above scene's end, ultimately, if equivocally, "speaks for" feminist reform by recounting her traveling companions' position on the clothing issue:

> I must do the ladies the justice to say that they rode astride on principle, being fully convinced that side-saddles were diabolical inventions of the tyrant man, to drag woman lop-sided through the world, and that the only reason why woman did nor excel in equestrian feats was the simple one of the malicious awkwardness of her "fixings." (1974, 2:66)

The equivocal statements made by Bird and Longworth about proper dress worked both with and against the hegemonic feminine ideal of genteel-class British chauvinism. To these writers, feminist challenges to appropriate dresswear were an American invention; thus travelers' alignments with such challenges also called into question Britain's role as a world leader in social reform (cf. Burton 1994). Yet while Isabella Bird may "go native" for a time in western America, she and the other travelers maintained and thus helped to reconstitute the association between more feminine styles of dress and their gentility.

Western Fare and Domestic Class Relations

> I never dreamt how really essential a piece of bread is to one's comfort before. (Pender 1978, 23)

> We are all among the snow heads in Colorado, eleven thousand feet above the level of the sea, and we have had our tea brought and laid our upon a table in our section of the car, and have laughed at our comfortable bourgeois attitude in the midst of such thrilling scenes. (Pfeiffer 1885, 137)

British women travelers to Colorado and Yosemite devoted considerable portions of their texts to detailing the quality of western hotels, inns, and other accommodations, what they ate and how it tasted, and their daily domestic routines—making toilet for special occasions, tidying up their rooms, and occasionally performing domestic tasks to which they were unaccustomed, such as washing their clothes.

All of the travelers to Yosemite commented upon the hotel accommodations throughout the region, which Demars (1991, 27–54) describes in some detail. Travelers' responses were varied. Some described "excellent suppers" of venison cutlets and tea at Clerk's hotel (Pfeiffer 1885, 2–16) and the occasional "capital" luncheon at stage stopping places (Guest 1895, 122). But complaints about the deficiencies of hotels were more common. Rose Pender declared that all the hotels in the region were "bad," "dreadful," "fly ridden places" (1978, 34, 35). Emily Pfeiffer reported her "deepening disappointment" at opening the "disgusting" provisions, "this worse than Barmicide feast" supplied for a day's stage journey. The food at Bernard's hotel was "absolutely rebutting to a dainty palate," and her meal at a "vile" inn near Yosemite was "execrable" (1885, 209, 246, 255). Stereotyped western·violence was bound to erupt over the food at the inn, as Pfeiffer's husband complained about it, and the cook, a "giant functionary," appeared, wielding a knife. Pfeiffer concludes the passage by asserting that "these things are among the chances of western travel" (1885, 256).

Emily Pfeiffer further complained that lack of good service, and especially servants, were serious detractions from what might have otherwise been enjoyable western travel. At Clerk's hotel in Yosemite, she complained that "attendance is nil in America" and her room lacked "the requirements of civilization" (1885, 216). Pfeiffer's protestations over bad food and service mark her as in need of servants to enact proper domesticity, which the apparently servant-less West inhibited. Although this trope was common in aristocratic British women's (and men's) travel writing about the American West (also see Longworth 1974; Guest 1895; Athearn 1962; M. Allen 1987), more complicated ways in which gendered subjectivity intersected with domestic class relations can be read in the texts of women who established their own housekeeping in the mountainous West for longer periods of time, such as Rose Kingsley and Isabella Bird in Colorado and Rose Pender in Wyoming and Nebraska.

Kingsley, Bird, and Pender portrayed themselves as enjoying the "freedom" to perform domestic duties by themselves, often in outdoor settings. Pender's experiences are described in chapter 2. Kingsley lived in a temporary wooden "shanty" with her brother in Colorado Springs while more permanent accommodations were being prepared for her. She depicted herself as thoroughly enjoying and taking pride in the primitive conditions and in the "fun" of improvising furniture and decorations.[2] The shanty became "quite habitable" after, for instance, her brother "found an old wooden stool, which had been used for mixing paints upon, tacked a bit of coloured calico over it, deposited upon it a tin basin, and there was an impromptu wash-hand-stand" (1874, 48). Kingsley describes herself as turning into "quite a good laundress" under these conditions, and in fact she helped others, such as new English immigrants, learn about "the mysteries of soaping, boiling, rinsing, starching, and ironing" (1874, 66, 117).

Early upon arrival in Colorado, Isabella Bird stayed with a family named Chalmers while trying to organize an expedition to Estes Park. Holes in the roof of the cabin, unchinked logs, the absence of tables, beds, basins, towels, windows, lamps, or candles in her room, and a litany of other deficiencies of the dwelling and property proved to Bird that Mr. and Mrs. Chalmers were ignorant, inept, and inefficient, even after nine years of attempted homesteading on their 160 acres (1969, 45). Chalmers frequently ridiculed the English, and Bird writes that her host trusted "to live to see the downfall of the British monarchy and the disintegration of the empire." Their lives were "moral, hard, unloving, unlovely, unrelieved, unbeautified, [and] grinding" (1969, 46, 50). Bird's daily routine at their place consisted of drawing water from the river, sweeping, washing garments by hand ("taking care that there [were] no witnesses" to her inexperience), knitting, writing, and "various odds and ends which arise when one has to do all for oneself" (1969, 40–43).

Bird presents herself as equally at ease killing rattlesnakes outside the cabin or helping an emigrant who had just given birth (1969, 42–43). And

2. Kingsley also may have not complained about the arrangements so as to not offend her hosts, the owners of the railroad company whom she would later accompany on a reconnaissance mission in Mexico (see chapter 5).

5. *My Home in the Rocky Mountains.* From Isabella L. Bird, *A Lady's Life in the Rocky Mountains* (Norman: Univ. of Oklahoma Press, 1969), 91. (Orig. pub. 1879, London: John Murray.) Reproduced courtesy of Oklahoma University Press.

in fact, while at the home of her more refined neighbors, the Hugheses, she writes of helping out by baking bread, washing dishes, and working in the fields, though preferring "field work to the scouring of greasy pans and to the wash rub, and both to either sewing or writing" (1969, 69). Bird was pleased with the log cabin she finally moved into alone. She claimed that "it is quite comfortable—in the fashion I like," and takes only "about five minutes to 'do,' and you could eat off the floor" (1969, 73, 124).

A nexus of gendered subjectivities operates in these narratives. Kingsley's and Bird's western displacement, on one hand, appears to offer the women a sense of prideful self-sufficiency in the simple circumstances of the shanty or log cabin. Bird distances herself from the domestic realm in her narratives about killing rattlesnakes and performing hard physical labor in the fields. But rather than casting off their domestic selves altogether, to become heroic adventurers (à la Middleton 1965; Birkett 1989; Foster 1990), Bird and Kingsley here represent themselves as embracing the domestic tasks, which presumably their own servants normally performed at home, and becoming empowered by them. They are, for perhaps the first time in their lives, taking care of themselves. Bird declared: "I really need nothing more than this log cabin offers" (1969, 124). Bird's discovery of self here, though, must be considered in light of her privileged social status and the fact that her survival in the cabin was never in question. Kingsley especially tends to represent herself in an almost childlike role, playing house as it were, and both narratives start to resemble tours of the working class.

Both Kingsley and Bird represent themselves as appropriately unfamiliar with and unaccustomed to unpleasant domestic work. When Bird offered to wash some plates, Mrs. Chalmers replied that her hands "aint no good; never done nothing, I guess. Then to her awkward daughter: 'This woman says she'll wash up! Ha! ha! look at her arms and hands!'" (1969, 44–45). Thus while Bird enacts domesticity, she simultaneously maintains her own version of true femininity by presenting herself ill-prepared and too delicate for work other than knitting and sewing. Although she claims that her own hands are "very brown and coarse" (1969, 45), it is Mrs. Chalmers who frequently appears manly and with whom Bird contrasts herself. Mrs. C. "is never idle for one minute, is severe and hard, and despises everything but work," she reports (1969, 47). Mrs. Chalmers's unceasing work and heavy manual labor does not approximate the role of the proper bourgeois woman embedded in English Victorian patriarchal discourse: while bourgeois men were judged by their success at entering and competing in the commercial sphere, the women "proved" the success of their men by their idleness and leisure-time activities—enabled through the domestic labor that servants performed—and which Bird herself carefully maintained by activities such as writing (but see Langland's 1995 view of bourgeois women as influential household employers).

Rhetorically distanced from the manliness and hard labor of working women, both Kingsley and Bird assert that class distinctions, and servants, do not inhere in uncivilized places like Colorado. Though, as noted, Bird submits that "I really need nothing more than this log cabin offers," she also contends that "elsewhere one must have a house and servants" (1969, 124). Kingsley similarly complains about the lack of servants in Colorado. It is a "very serious difficulty," she submits, "one it seems almost impossible to overcome. They are simply not to be had, whatever you pay them" (1874, 126–27). According to Kingsley, the only hope for places like Colorado was importations of Chinese from California (1874, 127). Thus, while these travelers may represent themselves as empowered by their newfound self-sufficiency and the pleasures that domestic works brings, the gendered subjectivity of Bird and Kingsley also does not stray too far afield from the "helpless" femininity of Emily Pfeiffer. For these writers, the mountainous dwellings of the American West provide a venue for the testing of new forms of gendered subjectivity, which rest on highlighting national differences in the employment of proper class relations. And it must be noted that both writers ignore the extent to which the class structure and labor relations of the West, particularly in regard to the domestic labor of Chicanas in the mountainous West, differed little from their "ideal" (see Deutsch 1987, 33, 87–106, 127–61; Glenn 1994, 409–11).

Heroic Adventures and Incompetent Local Guides

As British women narrate their outdoor excursions into the mountains, by foot, horse, mule, stage, or train, interesting connections can be detected among the rhetorics of emergent feminist empowerment, more hegemonic expressions of femininity, and British nationalism and imperialism. One common literary device obvious in these women's travel writing is the signifying of local guides on mountain excursions as incompetent, and the woman traveler, through the prized Victorian values of resourcefulness, perseverance, and intelligence, in some way saves herself and other travelers from indeterminate ends. This trope resonated well with the Victorian literary heroine who, as long as she retained her purity and proper manners, could be admired for her fortitude in the face of adversity (Reynolds and Humble 1993; R. Phillips 1997).

Rose Pender (1978) and a group of international travelers rode mules and hiked to the top of Pike's Peak, Colorado in 1883. When the party reached the snow line, Pender reported that the "guides were loud in their protests that we should not be able to get to the top, the snow was so deep," yet she and the others were determined to continue (1978, 58). "Our first climb," she writes, was very severe, and nearly stopped our breath; but after a bit we got better, and went along at a good pace, till we reached the last crown of the Peak. The snow was very deep and not hard, and often I slipped through up to my waist, struggling out as best I could. (1978, 58)

At this stage, their guide became exhausted, and as Pender reported, he was "no help to anyone, and at last threw himself down and declared he was done" (1978, 58). Only biscuits and brandy from Pender's satchel helped revive him and several of the others, and eventually the group made it to the lookout tower at the top, but not without repeatedly sinking waist-deep into snow and suffering excruciating headaches from the 14,000-foot altitude. In describing their return to their hotel, Pender wrote:

Great was the excitement at the little hotel to know how we had got on, and great was the surprise expressed when, after a good hot bath and fresh apparel, I took my place at the *table d'hôte* as fresh as if I had done nothing out of the way. Poor Mr. B—— suffered terribly from sun-scorching. His face and neck were severely blistered, and he was burnt a real scarlet; glycerine and rose-water gave him a little relief, but it was many days before he recovered from the effects of the sun and snow combined. The poor guide was snow-blind for some days, and the two Americans went about wearing dark glasses, and declared themselves quite knocked up. Thanks to the precaution of wearing a thick veil and neckerchief, I did not suffer in the least; indeed, I enjoyed the whole thing thoroughly, and like to shut my eyes now to recall the grand view and the marvellous colouring. (1978, 61)

In other words, Pender was the only one to come out of the ordeal unscathed. One might read a feminist discourse of female empowerment intersecting with Pender's nationalism in this passage. Pender succeeded in ways that the guide, her husband, and the other men did not, and she further claimed her English superiority at the expense of the Americans (one from New York and the other Brazil). Pender appears to claim mastery over the event (and view) with little effort.

When Lady Howard (1897) and Lady Guest (1895) toured the Pike's Peak area, they described experiences matching Pender's. Howard rode a cog-wheel train up to the summit, and once there, announced "here we alight; one or two fainting dead away, unable to bear the rarefaction of the air. Fortunately there was a doctor among the passengers who at once attended to them" (1897, 34–35). She then described recommending to her fellow travelers (and readers) Peru's coca leaves for endurance against the bitter cold and rarefied air, asserting that "travellers and particularly mountain climbers would do well to provide themselves with this easily-carried and most efficient specific" (1897, 34–35). (She does not say whether she herself took some.)

Theodora Guest likewise took the train to the summit of Pike's Peak. At the top, Guest noted that she was 7,000 feet above Manitou Springs, Colorado, and 14,147 feet above the sea. She exclaimed:

> The effect of the rarefied atmosphere was such that on getting out of the train one man fainted dead away, and was only revived by his companions rubbing snow on his face. M., expecting to feel very bad also, watched all his symptoms, and considered himself giddy. H. N. looked very bad, and felt so; so did most of the fellow travellers, some twenty-four in number.
>
> I could not discover any sensations whatever, so at once sat down on a structure of old sleepers, which lifted me out of the snow, and in a small sketch-book tried to convey a reminiscence of the most enormous landscape I ever saw in my life. (1895, 68)

As these women represent themselves as the only ones successfully enduring the hardships of travel, their texts point toward a particularly exaggerated version of the heroic Victorian adventure tale.

The Victorian adventure tale was a deeply gendered myth about a male hero who was courageous, strong, and persistent, in search of gold, land, or other "imperial dreams," and who, directly or indirectly, promoted British overseas investment or immigration (R. Phillips 1997, 68–69; Kearns 1997). Given the particular educational, religious, and administrative context of masculinities in Victorian Britain, colonial work itself was often constructed as an adventure for male colonial administrators, travelers, capitalist developers, or imperial military officers. Although the identity politics of colonialism often involved adventure for men, it was not as available to colonial women, who were often placed within the domestic sphere and whose jobs were to articulate with and maintain proper British households in the colonies (Callaway 1987; Strobel 1991; Chaudhuri and Strobel 1992).

When elite British women traveled to the American West, however, the context was quite different. British women traveled to the West as professional writers or tourists or with husbands or male relatives who were involved in capitalistic ventures with American entrepreneurs (the obvious cases including Kingsley and Pender; see chapter 2). This requires then a much different reading of the relationships between gendered subjectivities, adventure, and empire, specifically in the ways that transgressive feminist empowerment can be read as uniquely intersecting with rhetorics of British imperialism.

Isabella Bird took the trope of the incompetent (male) guide to the extreme as she described a failed attempt to reach Estes Park guided by the "useless" Mr. Chalmers. An accomplished horsewoman, Bird wrote much of her text as a heroic adventure tale, as she trailblazed to mountaintops and other destinations despite blizzards, incompetent guides such as Chalmers, and logistical obstacles. In one section of Letter V titled, "Nameless Region, Rocky Mountains" (1969, 53–60), Bird described her couple of days' frustration near the beginning of her stay in Colorado, following Chalmers through the St. Vrain Canyon in search of Estes Park. After immediately getting lost after lunch on the first day, she complained:

> For four weary hours we searched hither and thither along every indentation of the ground which might be supposed to slope towards the Big Thompson River, which we knew had to be forded. Still, as the quest grew more tedious, Long's Peak stood before us as a landmark in purple glory. . . . Chalmers, who had started confident, bumptious, blatant, was ever becoming more bewildered, and his wife's thin voice more piping and disconcerted, and my stumbling horse more insecure, and I more determined (as I am at this moment) that somehow or other I would reach that blue hollow, and even stand on Long's Peak where the snow was glittering. Affairs were becoming serious, and Chalmers's incompetence a source of real peril. (1969, 58)

They and their horses and mules eventually fell into a gulch, mistakenly having followed a bear trail. Recovering from that, and with no remaining provisions, Chalmers, his wife, and Bird camped out the night. In the morning, to her horror, all the horses had escaped, because, according to Bird, they had been improperly secured by Chalmers the night before. In resignation, Bird reported that they finally decided to return home, and dejected, wrote that "we never reached Estes Park" (1969, 60). In what she represented as a "last resort," Bird demanded control of the doomed expedition:

> Vainly I pointed out to him that we were going northeast when we should have gone south-west, and that we were ascending instead of descending. . . . He then confessed that he was lost, and that he could not find his way back. His wife sat down on the ground and cried bitterly. We ate some dry bread, and then I said I had had much experience in traveling, and would take the control of the party, which was agreed to, and began the long descent. (1969, 62)

Bird probably did have more traveling experience than Chalmers, and it might also be argued that travelers had access to some resources that local people did not, such as maps, but Bird would not likely have depended upon Chalmers had she known the route to Estes Park. In the end, she compares her own (superior) knowledge of mountaineering to that of a local (man), and by stressing the failings of others (Chalmers and his wife) in comparison to her own leadership abilities and mental toughness, she guarantees her own heroine status in the narrative.

Many scholars of British women's travel writing have noted the extent to which travelers represented themselves *as women* undertaking particular activities, especially transgressive ones (Russell 1986; Birkett 1989). The trope of women's heroic adventures challenged and transgressed dominant ideologies of gender roles and relations. Privileged women, emphasizing attributes of courage, strength, and persistence, directly challenged ideologies of self-sacrificing, duty-bound Victorian mothers and wives. In that sense, they helped rewrite the terms of the Victorian adventure tale itself and without relinquishing their femininity to do so. These are strong women, yet women who apply their "feminine" knowledge and skills to their activities, such as their knowledge about proper attire and supplies needed for mountaineering (e.g., Pender's veil and neckerchief). These women's adventure tales, then, can be read as confirming hegemonic ideologies of gender roles and relations but also challenging and transgressing them, as Richard Phillips (1997, 98–110) has shown in another context.

These travelers actively created space for women outside the domestic sphere, in this case, in the mountains of Colorado, reconstituting where bourgeois women might feel "at home." As outdoor Rocky Mountain landscapes were portrayed as a plausible destination for women, one might read their narratives as extending British influence—a particularly progressive form of women's advancement—in Colorado. They thus might also be read as extending both American and British imperialisms in the region by encouraging further tourism there. And Colorado was already home to many British immigrants and investors; these additional "mappings," particularly in successful and "heroic" narratives, may have reinscribed it as an appropriate place for British assistance in American empire building, especially in mining, cattle, and railroad enterprises (White 1991, 260–63).

Women Travelers as Resistant Adventurers

The diversity of gendered subjectivities written into these travelers' texts cannot be overstated. In contrast to the heroic narratives of Isabella Bird and Thérèse Longworth (below), women traveling with their husbands or male relatives often represented themselves as content to engage in more "feminine" pursuits or passively watch the men's mountaineering adventures. They typically represented their men as protective, keeping them out of harm's way (as in Kingsley's excerpt in the epigraph to this chapter). Lady Guest, for instance, referred to the men of her party as her "protectors," whose duties safeguarding her in Yosemite included holding an umbrella over her to keep the sun off (1895, 131).

Many of the women described themselves as preferring their rooms and the local environs of the hotels, and activities associated with them, to mountains and forests. Lady Howard wrote that one day in Glenwood Springs, Colorado, while her brother climbed a mountain, she sat "out in the sunny garden for the delightful luxury of a whole afternoon of quiet sketching and reading" (1897, 43). Similarly, Emily Pfeiffer reported that, rather than explore the area in Yosemite, she saw her "better part in remaining among the satisfying surroundings of the Hotel Bernard, and letting the lovely environment soak into me" (1885, 242). Although these women were active sewing, sketching, collecting flowers, and especially writing at the hotels—all which may be considered signifying practices of the Victorian bourgeoisie—they also explicitly located themselves in their narratives as passive, and sometimes distressed, observers of men's more "dangerous" activities in the mountains. During her stay at the Cliff House Hotel in Manitou Springs, Colorado, Pfeiffer describes her efforts at writing in her sitting room, yet distractedly absorbed with the whereabouts of her husband, who was making an ascent of Pike's Peak. In her account, Pfeiffer anxiously and continually watched the clouding over of the peak from her room, noting when her husband should have reached the top (1885, 123–24). A few pages on, she announced that, "By this time, half past three, E—— should be well on his way down from the peak, which for the last hour and a half has been clear of clouds. I am going to the Iron Springs, there to sit and wait until he comes" (1885, 126). As Pfeiffer took her "lonely walk" up the glen to wait with "anxious expectancy of E——'s return," she wrote of her thoughts returning to home, especially to the birthday of a loved one (1885, 126).

Pfeiffer's narrative here appears in considerable contrast to the heroic adventuring of other women who themselves took the excursion to Pike's Peak (Guest, Howard, Pender). Her account of a trip to see a waterfall near Cheyenne Canyon reaches the same rhetorical conclusion (1885, 133). In these excerpts, Pfeiffer "domesticates" the Colorado wilderness by demonstrating her feminine concern for her husband and the child left behind at home. Mills (1991, 94–107) argues that such discourses of femininity served to socialize women into domestic roles as caregivers and helpmeets who were primarily concerned with family and relationships. In that sense, Pfeiffer's text complicates the gendered subjectivities of British women in mountains. Her engagement with the scenery appears detached and primarily visual, witnessed from the confines of her room. She is most "at home" in the interior (and indoor) spaces of travel, what Mary Louise Pratt has referred to as women's "room sized empires" (1992, 159–60), even if she is also "at home" very publicly traveling and writing as a member of the international elite.

Many of the women were not quite as "resistant" adventurers as Emily Pfeiffer; they hiked in the mountains, but only with the help of men. Rose Kingsley chronicles many mountain excursions with her brother, further inscribing him in her text by drawing him standing near some rocks in Monument Park, Colorado. She explains how he helped her across streams and other dangerous spots on several mountain excursions (e.g., 1874, 71). On one "great 'exploring expedition'" with her brother (1874, 120), in search of a route from Manitou to Glen Eyrie, Colorado, a distance of about four miles, she reported that "the sides [of the hill] were too steep that M. had to slide down to the bottom, and catch me in his arms as I came down after him" (1874, 121). Also with her brother, Lady Howard took a five-mile hike through the redwood forests near Yosemite, succeeding in maneuvering along a railroad track at a "dizzying height" and a trestle bridge over a deep ravine only by holding on to her brother's umbrella and following him (1897, 77, 78).

These texts suggest highly ambivalent subject positions for women travelers; they at once locate the women in the domestic environments of the hotels and rooms as well as in the outdoors (Howard 1897, 43; also see the previous discussion of R. Kingsley 1874, 46–48). These texts, moreover, suggest a particular rhetorical "duty" to their male relatives. In these excerpts, the women's resistance to adventure serves as a feminine standard against which their husband's or brother's active and adventurous male identities can be counterposed. Their articulations with motherhood, femininity, and bourgeois pastimes coincide with those discussed by Ware (1992) and Davin (1978) as conducted in the service of empire. Inscribing themselves as conventional bourgeois subjects with appropriate leisure-class interests combined with other, more transgressive modes of gendered subjectivity, such as in the promotion of tourism. After all, expansive hotels were built to cater to such "refined" foreign clientele (Farrar-Hyde 1990, 147–90, 244–95; Demars 1991). Western America serves here, then, as the scene for extending a particularly conventional, masculinist version of gendered subjectivities for both women and men, realigning British men with the spaces of adventure, and in so doing demonstrating the heterogeneity of imperial discourse.

The Ambivalence of "Imperial" Conquest

Many of the travel writers seem to have been concerned to defy Victorian femininity by portraying themselves as strengthened by rugged western environments, as independent, adventurous women heroically "conquering" the destinations of their travels, even becoming protective of other females. And yet, they also emphasized specifically feminine aspects of travel writing, such as in downplaying the adventurousness of their journeys, complaining about how emotionally or physically difficult the journeys had become, and representing themselves as passive, weak, and in need of men's help. This ambivalence is played out most significantly within the narrative trope of conquest of mountain peaks, which also often serves as the peak literary moment in the narratives more generally. Therefore, in this last section of the chapter, I turn in some detail to a discussion of some intersections among gendered subjectivities, imperialism, and mountain peaks.

Isabella Bird's narrative about her four-month stay in the Estes Park region of Colorado in the autumn and early winter of 1873 seems to offer, again, an opportunity for interrogating the tensions and ambivalences between women's gendered subjectivities and mountainous landscapes. Writing about Estes Park for the first time, Bird exclaimed:

> Such as it is, Estes Park is mine. It is unsurveyed, "no man's land," and mine by right of love, appropriation, and appreciation; by the seizure of its peerless sunrises and sunsets, its glorious afterglow, its blazing noons, its hurricanes sharp and furious, its wild aroras, its glories of mountain and forest, of canyon, lake, and river, and the stereotyping them all in my memory. (1969, 104)

One of the principal excursions Bird describes in her *A Lady's Life* is her ascent of Long's Peak (the summit of which is along the North American continental divide), with "Rocky Mountain Jim" and two student trappers (1969, 83–101).[3] Her description of the panoramic view from the top contains many of the markers of heroic achievement:

---

3. Much has been made of Bird's romantic association with the "notorious" Jim Nugent. See Birkett (1989, 55–58), J. Robinson (1990, 81–82), and Barr (1970, 60–99).

> At last the Peak was won. . . . From the summit were seen in unrivalled combination all the views which had rejoiced our eyes during the ascent. It was something at last to stand upon . . . this lonely sentinel of the Rocky Range, on one of the mightiest of the vertebrae of the backbone of the North American continent, and to see the waters start for both oceans. (1969, 98)

Much of Thérèse Longworth's descriptions of horseback riding in Yosemite reads comparably. Longworth claimed she was the "first white woman who scaled [the] rugged fastnesses" of the Little Yosemite Valley, 6,000 feet above the great Yosemite Valley (itself 4,060 feet above sea level). In a peak literary moment, Longworth described going through "the necessary formula of planting my stick and throwing up my hat, which gives me a claim to several hundred acres of land" (1974, 2: 81). The mood set by Longworth's narrative is not unlike the victorious moment recorded in Fiske's famous photographs of women of the period atop Glacier Point, Yosemite (a version of which is depicted on this book's cover; see figs. 6–7). All the authors at some point describe their rapture and amazement over similar peak experiences. Rose Kingsley describes "the whole panorama . . . stretched beneath us" on the top of Mount Washington in Colorado (1874, 46), and Lady Howard exclaims that the "whole panorama" at the top of Pike's Peak was "indescribably grand" (1897, 35).

These excerpts illustrate what Pratt (1992) argues is one of the most distinguishing features of "imperialistic" Victorian travel writing, that is, what she terms the "monarch-of-all-I-survey" trope. To Pratt, the trope described peak moments at which geographical "discoveries" were "won" for England (1992, 201). In this "discourse of discovery," the imperial travel writer conquered the landscape and heroically claimed dominance and authority over it. Pratt characterizes the monarch-of-all-I-survey genre as deeply gendered masculine, whereby male explorers were able to render "momentously significant what is, especially from a narrative point of view, practically a nonevent"—with the help of local guides "you pretend to conquer" what they already knew, and thus convert local knowledge into "European national and continental knowledges . . . and relations of power" (1992, 201–2). Following Pratt, Mills adds that the very act of

6. Overhanging Rock, Glacier Point, Yosemite. Photograph by George Fiske (ca. 1890). Reproduced courtesy of The Bancroft Library, University of California, Berkeley.

describing a panoramic scene is also mastering or colonizing it (1991, 78–79; also see Kearns 1997, 457–59). What is actually just a passive experience of "seeing" becomes momentous when the traveler brings the information home, puts it on a map, and lectures about it at Sunday afternoon geographical society meetings.

Although Pratt claims that promontory descriptions are very common in romantic and Victorian writing of all kinds, she notes that women do not spend a lot of time on promontories "nor are they entitled to" (1992, 213) because the masculine heroic discourse of discovery is not readily available to women. Evidence that women often remained near hotels and places "below" does seem evident in these texts. For example, Lady Howard reported that, in Yosemite, her brother set off for the "difficult climb to

7. Peak practices of Victorian women (Kitty Tatch and Katherine Hazelstine), on Overhanging Rock, Glacier Point, Yosemite. Reproduced courtesy of the National Park Service, Yosemite National Park. Cat. no. YM-5252. Photograph by George Fiske (ca. 1890).

the top of Eagle Peak," while she spent "the most enchanting of days wandering in the happy valley" (1897, 93). Similar to Pratt's contention that Mary Kingsley more comfortably inhabited swamps than mountain peaks during her explorations of West Africa (1992, 213–14), Howard remains below, viewing the beauty and glory of Yosemite "from within," in contrast to the summits above.

Nevertheless, Bird and Longworth do seem to have recreated such peak "imperial" moments—claiming mastery and ownership of Estes Park and Yosemite—for home audiences in much the same way as male travel writers did and in a context very unlike the colonial settings of much British travel writing. With greater attention to gendered subjectivity than

Pratt (1992), Mills (1991) and Alison Blunt (1994) argue that peak imperial moments do occur in women's travel writing, but because particular kinds of ambivalences inhere in them, ambivalence toward imperialism itself is produced in the narratives. Alison Blunt's very different reading of Mary Kingsley's landscape descriptions of West Africa serve as a useful example (1994, 63–67). Blunt reads Mary Kingsley's ascent of Mount Cameroon as marking her within the patriarchal and imperial tradition of exploration, but also outside of it. Because Kingsley could appreciate the value of a view obstructed by mist, her position relative to the landscape ultimately was aesthetic, not "strategic" or resting on a relationship of domination.

That women's "heroic" voices could be undermined by a feminine discourse simultaneously available to them seems evident. Bird's text turns out to be much like those of the "resistant adventurer's" already discussed. She made her way to the top of Long's Peak guided by Jim Nugent and in fact roped to him, and on the way down followed him, so that his "powerful shoulders" could help steady her (1969, 99). In contrast to Mr. Chalmers, Jim is an intelligent and necessary guide to Bird's discoveries and achievements. And while her description of her ascent to the continental divide emphasized heroic achievement, on her descent of the mountain, her narrative voice became uncertain as she admitted to experiencing fear, danger, and especially fatigue and exhaustion. She wrote about crawling most of the way down the mountain, losing courage and strength and finally on approach of the horses wrote that "with great difficulty and much assistance I recrossed the lava beds, was carried to the horse and lifted upon him, and when we reached the camping ground I was lifted off him and laid on the ground wrapped up in blankets, a humiliating termination of great exploit" (1969, 100). Although travelers are much less likely to be as enthusiastic on the return journey, Bird's admissions of frailty clearly do not fit within the heroic discourse of discovery or adventure.

Though Mills (1991) might argue that women writers had special access to the feminine discursive spaces of cowardice, mistakes, and defeat in the face of danger, it must be noted that men, too, described the suffering, fatigue, danger, and even death involved in exploration and adventure (Martin and James 1993; R. Phillips 1997). Both women and men, by accentuating the difficulties connected with their achievements, in a sense, improved upon them. Overcoming obstacles made the achievement that much more heroic and proved how much personal credit was due them in managing the ascent or discovery. All the writers discussed here emphasized the dangers of western mountainous regions, particularly emphasizing the danger of travel itself, such as in the staging into Yosemite (R. Kingsley 1874, 96; Pender 1978, 3, 34; Guest 1895, 120–24, 145; Howard 1897, 32, 84). Thus, in addition to the stock requisite features of western travel narratives—evidence of dramatic feats of engineering and "exotic" animals and people (Farrar-Hyde 1990, 120–30)—one might include imaginings of the West itself as a place of danger for women. Even if travelers also assured their readers that the rough trips are "also quite practicable for ladies" (e.g., R. Kingsley 1874, 57)—because after all, to admit otherwise would be to compromise their "rationality"—their emphasis on danger shores up the women's courage, strength, and toughness in addition to creating points of interest in the narratives.

For women especially, though, mountaineering permitted a particular form of mental control over the body, and collapsing on the way down illustrated the physical demands of the ascent. This might be especially true of Isabella Bird, who traveled to escape her spinal complaints (which only seemed to surface when she was at home). This type of willed control of the body to perform exceptional deeds contrasts with a more traditionally feminine way of controlling the body through sickness, anorexia, neurasthenia, or even wearing corsets. The medical discourses of the Victorian period, which "proved" women's weaker bodily structure and their resulting limited intellectual capacities (Vicinus 1972; Callaway 1987), feminized suffering itself, to the extent that overcoming suffering through arduous mountaineering might have had more discursive purchase for women climbers than men.

Thus I would argue that women's exaltations over achieving a grand view, such as Isabella Bird's claiming Estes Park as her "own," may be best analyzed as a mastering of the *self* rather than Estes Park. In the context of travel in the American empire, Bird's claim that "Estes Park is mine . . . by love, appropriation, and appreciation" (1969, 104) more than anything else seems to mark Bird's emotional attachment to place and conquest of her own frailty. Bird frequently located herself emotionally within Rocky Mountain landscapes. She wrote about horseback riding from the St. Vrain Canyon to Longmont, Colorado, through a snowstorm:

> It was simply fearful. It was twilight from the thick snow, and I faced a furious east wind loaded with fine, hard-frozen crystals, which literally made my face bleed. I could only see a very short distance anywhere; the drifts were often two feet deep. . . . I had wrapped up my face, but the sharp, hard snow beat on my eyes—the only exposed part—bringing tears into them which froze and closed up my eyelids at once. You cannot imagine what that was, I had to take off one glove to pick one eye open, for as the other, the storm beat so savagely against it that I left it frozen, and drew over it the double piece of flannel which protected my face. I could hardly keep the other open by picking the ice from it constantly with my numb fingers. . . . It was truly awful at the time. (1969, 233–34)

Bird's triumph over adversity seems to constitute a position of self-empowerment here, which contrasts with both imperial conquest of place and the image of the "angel in the house" Victorian matron. In this passage Bird emphasized her pain and suffering but most of all her own endurance. It is *her* eye that she is picking open, which again calls to mind Bird's health problems and a newfound sense of self control over her body in the mountains.

Women travelers seem to have emphasized the dangers and fatigues of travel for quite distinctive purposes. Thérèse Longworth devoted several pages of her *Teresina in America* (1974) to a night spent alone in Yosemite—in a hollow tree. Intending on catching up with a group of fellow travelers on horseback, Longworth found herself caught in rain, then hail, and then a blinding snowstorm. She reported that finally the snow enveloped her "like the white pall thrown over an infant corpse. I could not see my horse's head or my own hand a yard before me" (1974, 2: 84). Completely lost and disoriented, Longworth detailed how she spent the night in a hollow tree, "with the horse's head close to me so as to profit by the warmth of his nostrils." The next morning, as she attempted to maneuver out of three feet of snow, Longworth heard the sound of panting which she thought indicated the presence of another horse. Raising her voice "in delirium," she cried out for help:

> [The noise] came from the other side of a high granite crag. . . . I rounded the corner with a beating heart and exultant hope, and found myself face to face with a—*grizzly bear*—so near that our eyes actually met; and I shall carry the memory of his expression to my dying day. I do believe that the beast saw the agony of my soul when this horrible crisis of my fate assailed me. He never attempted to touch me. He never moved the almost pitying eyes with which he regarded me. (1974, 2: 89)

Longworth reported that she ran from the bear, lost consciousness, and finally was found the following day by a hunter, "frozen and insensible" (1974, 2: 86–90). In this passage, her achievement is rather ambiguous. Like Bird on Long's Peak, she does not conclude her story by discovering a grand view or even by saving herself. Rather, her achievement was simply in surviving a dangerous ordeal. Her final exaltations were about surviving two days in the wilderness and overcoming the "spectre of death" (1974, 2: 87). The climax of her text, then, is a scene of conquest: not conquest of a mountain peak but conquest over herself.

Englishwomen's "peak practices" in the American West, then, might be read as signifying an emotive attachment to place or personal empowerment through rugged physical exercise and the overcoming of fear. The tropes of imperial conquest may be present in the texts, but they are not largely cast in the empire-building terms of "domination over" the land (or people). In fact, many of the writers describe monumental views as enabled only through crawling to "peek" over precipices, rather than viewing them from a standing position (e.g., Longworth 1974, 2: 75). It seems important, then, to acknowledge that the mountainous West provided a particular kind of relationship to the landscape for British women travelers. I have not been concerned here with landscape description per se, but it seems clear that a study of gendered subjectivity appearing in colonial discourse, through or outside of landscape description, obviously cannot proceed without close attention to geographical context.

A much different reading of the imperial tropes of adventure and empire emerges from women's travel literature about peak experiences in the American West. The West appears in these narratives as a dangerous place for women, lacking in more civilized modes of behavior and transport, tropes that are nonetheless necessary for travelers to enact transgressive modes of gendered subjectivity. "There's nothing Western folk admire so much as pluck in a woman," claimed Isabella Bird (1969, 19). At the close of her book, Emily Pfeiffer comes to the same conclusion when she writes that "the assumption that a woman was not sufficient to herself would here be considered the reverse of a compliment" (1885, 258). The West serves for these travelers as the site of expansive roles for women, usurping, perhaps, Britain's hegemonic role in advancing feminist causes (Burton 1994), and yet again proves its own lack of civilization in the process. The figure of the British imperialist-feminist amid the lesser "empire" emerges in the last analysis.

Conclusion

Vron Ware, in her work on the early feminist reformer Josephine Butler, questions whether it was possible in the nineteenth century "to be a feminist and simultaneously to have an alternative view of popular imperialism" (1992, 163). Although she basically concludes it was not—British feminists did not contribute to the downfall of empire and the liberation of colonized people—there was a "glimmer of light" on the question at the turn of century, in women who connected women's status with the emerging (Indian) nationalist movement. Ware goes on to say that "it was not until the issue of women's suffrage had transformed feminism in the Mother Country that women there could really begin to take part in the political emancipation of the colonies" (1992, 164).

I find Ware's comments useful for situating imperial women's travel writing within discourses of early (western) feminism, and within historical geography of the American West more generally. The authors of the texts examined here did not explicitly align themselves on either side of the debates about first-wave feminist reforms. (Though Longworth did positively portray the benefits of women's suffrage [1974, 2: 28–29] during her visit to Wyoming, the first territory to grant women the vote in the United States, in 1869.) While Birkett (1989, 197) and others assert that Victorian women travelers such as Isabella Bird were mostly concerned to present themselves as vehemently against the "new woman" image, many seemed to implicitly embrace it. Thérèse Longworth refers to herself as a "subject of scandal" (1974, 2: 68) for her risky and audacious activities in Yosemite. Thus, while these women did not explicitly position themselves as feminists, all of them in one sense or another created new social spaces for traveling bourgeois women, marking in personal ways the transformative effects of travel and mountaineering.

Not incidentally of course, they meanwhile inserted more conventional discourses of femininity into their texts, weaving both gendered subjectivities through multiple individual interpretations of their class and national identities. Class privilege allowed these women access to travel, and the travel narrative in turn gave them a venue for disclosing proper ladylike behaviors in a foreign context. Ultimately the travel narrative provided a forum for them to consolidate their positions as members of the ruling classes of the world's most powerful empire. Important relationships appear here among the women's feminisms, imperialist proclivities, and class positions as they discussed proper dress for women, proper domestic relations, their heroic adventures, and their "conquest" of their own personal physical limitations.

From the perspective of early twenty-first-century feminism(s), which defines itself as concerned with multiple forms of oppression, Englishwomen such as these made good imperialists more than anything else, as many theorists of women's travel writing have been (rightly) concerned to show. And yet, it seems important also to remember with Ware (1992, 164) that it was only through the passage of political reforms advocated by first-wave feminism, with which these women's texts must be aligned, that a critique of empire from women within it would eventually emerge.

4

Gender, Nature, Empire

Women Naturalists in Nineteenth-Century British Women's Travel Literature

WITH JEANNE KAY GUELKE

NINETEENTH-CENTURY TRAVELERS' and explorers' narratives generated considerable interest within British geography during the 1990s, as feminists and postmodernists sought to extend the scope of the discipline's historiography, particularly in deploying travel narratives to critique empire and patriarchy (Barnett 1998; A. Blunt 1994; Livingstone 1992). Expanded attention to Victorian women travelers and writers still engages debates about whether such women are properly "in" or "out" of particular scripts of geographical traditions and, if "in," how they are to be characterized. Within the mainstream or outside the margins (Domosh 1991a; Stoddart 1991)? As plucky protofeminists (Birkett 1989), as victims of sexism (McEwan 1998a), as agents of empire simultaneously negotiating respectable femininity (Blunt and Rose 1994; Kearns 1997), or even as virginal spinsters to be contrasted with sexually liberated males (Gregory 1995)?

Gillian Rose (1995) reminds us that such alternate versions of geography's history basically reflect debates about the nature of the discipline today. Disciplinary history continues to exhibit problems of presentism, in which "the writing of certain kinds of pasts is legitimated by, and legitimates only certain kinds of presents." Rose (1995, 414) argues that it is important for geographers to extend their historiography beyond today's accepted disciplinary boundaries and "paternal lines of descent" (see chap. 1); "Writing [geographical] histories without considering what has been constructed as not-geography is to tell only half the story. It is also to replicate the erasure of geography's others." She argues against the notion of geography as transparent intellectual territory, and for a "focus on the boundaries at which difference is constituted" (1995, 416).

Working from Rose's insights, in this chapter we examine some "near-geographies"—the naturalist and botanical writings and artwork of three aristocratic British women who traveled to California in the late nineteenth century. California, with its giant sequoias and redwoods, scenic Yosemite Valley and Sierra Nevada, and the Mediterranean flora of the southern coasts, especially attracted travelers with a naturalist orientation. Constance (C.G.) Gordon Cumming and Marianne North were well-known world travelers and nature artists during their lifetimes; Theodora Guest, sister of the Duke of Westminster, was more obscure.[1]

Our case study of the California naturalist writings of Cumming, North, and Guest is undertaken with the primary question of whether they produced an identifiable "women's knowledge." We ask how their gendered subjectivities affected how they produced natural history. We do not undertake this task in some sort of naive essentialism (Women and Geography Study Group of the RGS/IBG [WGSG] 1997, 20–21). To the contrary, we circumscribe our subjects in terms of their learned culture and situated knowledge: ethnicity (British), class (upper), period (late Victorian), and education (natural history, discussed in detail below.) Natural history and overseas travel lend themselves easily to the concept of negotiated discourse, involving specific practices such as field sketching, collecting, train travel, and language. Nor do we attempt to discover naturalist "foremothers" and intellectual lineages; for we view Cumming, North, and Guest simply as participants in larger popular

---

1. Yosemite was among the most well-advertised scenic attractions of the transcontinental railroad journey, and many British women travelers, as discussed in chapter 3, described their experiences there. Thérèse Longworth also published a fictional account of her experiences in Yosemite, *Zanita: A Tale of the Yo-semite* (1872), that featured a strong likeness of John Muir as principal protagonist.

projects, rather than as founders of them or as educators of subsequent generations of students.

In that sense, we are not attempting to describe Cumming, North, and Guest as representative of the larger cohort of British women who traveled, wrote, and often collected or sketched, such as the better-known Mary Kingsley and Isabella Bird. Rather, we focus upon a selection of the three women's travel and botanical experiences primarily as a means of understanding the heterogeneity of geography's history and the "situated knowledges" that comprise it (even if we also implicitly place importance on incorporating analyses of women's narratives into our discipline). As the WGSG (1997, 20) explains:

> Here history is being written not in terms of understanding contemporary circumstances, but in terms of forgotten or erased knowledges, of lines of writing and analysis which were marginalised, overlooked or bypassed by other (masculine) lines of enquiry. Such strategies of writing history then provide ample testimony to the heterogeneity (as opposed to homogeneity) of geographical knowledges and to the legitimacy of non-hegemonic geographical knowledges today.

Part of this project must necessarily address the problem of narratorial authority for women (S. Morgan 1990; Morin and Guelke 1998), of how their communications about nature reveal the rhetoric of women's efforts to be taken seriously by the public. We believe that how Victorian women described nature or how they discussed their landscape paintings is more than the sum of their empirical observations, situated knowledges, disassociation from imperialism (Pratt 1992), or the physicality of their voyages (Kearns 1997). In addition to these, women chose particular tropes in order to be recognized as credible experts.

In this chapter we ask about the types of records female naturalists produced within the venues that were available to them. Although our focus on nineteenth-century natural history suggests potential pedigrees for today's environmental geography and biogeography, the writings of our three subjects relate more closely to nonresearch endeavors that nevertheless engage many geographers today, namely, the rationales behind liberal education, ecotourism, nature writing, and environmentalism.

The landscape and botanical painting and sketching of the three women can be classed among the "forgotten" or "erased" knowledges or skills (WGSG 1997, 20) important to geographers of an era of primitive photographic technologies. Although these endeavors have been defined out of today's empirical geography, they share an obvious common focus on spatial distributions and the earth's living surface.

But we interrogate more recent postcolonial versions of disciplinary history, as well. Beyond Victorian travel writers' emphasis on geographical concepts such as place, landforms, and foreign areas, the broadly inclusive theme of nature overlaps today's disciplinary boundaries. As discussed below, we do not find the three naturalists to be disingenuously "innocent" of colonialism; indeed, they often explicitly supported it. Rather than demonstrating how these women exemplified imperialism or femininity in British colonies where power relations were institutionalized, we study them in the more sociopolitically ambiguous terrain of California. Although California was part of an independent republic, British capital, investment, and tourism signified a modified or informal imperial presence there and in other parts of the American West (White 1991, 258–263; Rico 1998; Farrar-Hyde 1990).

We provide an alternative to the argument that the quintessential knowledge-producing imperial subject was male and middle class (McEwan 1998a; Kearns 1997, 451) by examining wealthy women from privileged, well-connected backgrounds. These upper-class women had different expectations and constraints than those influencing middle class British women, for whom the ideologies of domesticity and respectability were more prominent (Mulvey 1990).

In order to address these themes we begin with overviews of Cumming, North, and Guest and their contributions. To contextualize their work, we then summarize the milieu of Victorian British natural history with attention both to cultural artifacts, such as species names, collections, and botanical illustrations, and to colonial power relations, such as the mercantilist agenda of Kew Gardens and the destruction by lumbermen of California's sequoias and redwoods. Disciplinary ambiguity and erasure of distinctive borders between science and popular culture were hallmarks of British natural history, particularly before 1880, a discursive space that women such as Cumming, North, and Guest could and did exploit. We conclude with some implications of our research for interpreting "fathers" of academic geography such as Alexander von Humboldt and for extending the scope of histories of geography beyond the confines of academic research lineages to include its more pedagogical and popular forms.

Brief Biographical Sketches

Constance Gordon Cumming (1837–1924) traveled and published extensively throughout her life, enabled through her aristocratic, wealthy Scottish background.[2] Cumming visited San Francisco and Yosemite Valley in 1878, and published, along with seven other travel books during her career, *Granite Crags of California* (1886) out of her experiences. She was also an accomplished watercolorist, exhibiting some of her 1,000 paintings and sketches throughout Britain and self-illustrating her books, including *Granite Crags*.[3] Cumming has been recognized as an artist of the American West. Thirteen of her water colors are listed in the Smithsonian's inventory; one of her paintings, *Father of the Grove (Calaveras Grove)*, is in the Kahn Collection in the Oakland Museum (Thurin 1997, 81), and

2. Cumming's parents died in her youth, though not before her mother imparted in her an extensive knowledge of and appreciation for botany, zoology, and geology (Cumming 1904, 34–38). She noted, for instance, that she "had access to all the books and periodicals on gardening" (1904, 35). Unmarried and with few familial or other responsibilities, she began her travels in 1868, when she toured India with her sister and brother-in-law. In 1872 she traveled to Ceylon, later to Fiji, followed by California in spring 1878. In all Cumming authored eight books about her global travels, on South Asia, the South Pacific, California, China, and Ceylon, and also produced an autobiography late in life (Adams 1883; J. Robinson 1990, 93–95; Birkett 1989; Cumming 1904; Thurin 1997).

3. Cumming's painting and sketches appeared in the Indian and Colonial exhibitions in London and subsequently in Liverpool and Glasgow; others were exhibited to support missionary work. *Granite Crags* contains eight of the fifty drawings and watercolors she made of the Yosemite area. Given Cumming's (and North's) subsequent exhibitions of their paintings, we assume a British (and American, in Cumming's case) public's taste for viewing this form of botanical and other naturalist representation.

8. Constance Gordon Cumming as she appears
in her autobiography, *Memories* (Edinburgh:
Blackwood, 1904), 196. Photograph by W. Crooke.
Reproduced courtesy of the Collection of The Public Library of Cincinnati and Hamilton County.

others are held by the National Park Service, Yosemite National Park, and
the California Historical Society.[4]

Granite Crags of California (1886), written as letters to Cumming's
brother and sister, mostly describes the forests, trees, shrubs, flowers,
parks, and gardens of central California and her experiences exploring
and painting the Yosemite Valley. Cumming devotes entire chapters to

4. In her lifetime, however, Cumming lamented her lack of recognition for her artwork; that it brought her "no advantage whatever, beyond receiving a couple of medals"
(as quoted in Birkett 1989, 228).

individual gardens and especially the forests of the Sierra Nevadas, high-lighting species previously unknown to her. Cities as well are brought under a naturalist gaze as Cumming's narration of them focuses nearly entirely on the biota of their gardens and parks, such as Golden Gate Park and Woodward's Garden in San Francisco.

Marianne North's (1830–1890) posthumously published travel writ-ings, the two-volume *Recollections of a Happy Life: Being the Autobiogra-phy of Marianne North* (1892), describe her two trips to North America in 1875 and 1881.[5] The project that North made her life's work, on the advice of her friend Joseph D. Hooker, Kew Gardens's director, was to paint as much of the world's flowers and vegetation in their natural habi-tats as she could manage (Brenan 1980; S. Morgan 1996; Ponsonby 1990; Middleton 1965). North accordingly spent nearly fifteen years of her life traveling around the globe, collecting natural objects, painting flow-ers and scenes of natural vegetation. As a wealthy Victorian in an era when most women of her class were educated at home, North had little serious artistic or scientific training. What she did possess, like Cum-ming, however, were sufficient private funds to pay for her own travels and sufficient personal connections to travel with influential letters of introduction to botanical gardens, colonial administrators, and influen-tial citizens wherever she went. A wealthy single woman from a well-con-nected family, North donated funds to Kew Gardens to build a gallery to house over eight hundred of her paintings, together with panels of wood sampled from trees of the various places she visited, including those of Yosemite.[6]

5. After North's death, her voluminous correspondence and travel diaries were edited and posthumously published by her sister (North 1892).

6. Within the North Gallery, Marianne North arranged the rooms to house col-lections sorted by continent, with groups of paintings organized by country of origin (Brenan 1980; Mabey 1988, 177; North 1892; Ponsonby 1990). The North Gallery thus became a kind of symbolic, carefully organized microcosm of world plant bioregions. After retiring from active travel, she designed gardens around her country house with a similar continental plan.

9. Marianne North at her easel. Photograph reproduced courtesy of the Director, Royal Botanical Gardens, Kew.

Lady Theodora Guest (ca. 1840–1924) toured North America in 1894 by private train car.[7] Her *A Round Trip in North America* (1895) details her seven-week, 11,000-mile criss-cross journey of North America both through narrative description and her own illustrations. As the latest of the three naturalists considered for this study, Lady Guest most firmly belongs in the category of tourist; in her *Round Trip*, Guest, more so than either North or Cumming, commented on American social life, major cultural or scenic attractions, and tourist accommodations. Yet Guest equally represents the archetypal "amateur naturalist" figure of the late

7. Guest traveled in comfort with her husband and a male friend in a private railroad car arranged by an American friend, Frank Thomson, general manager of the Pennsylvania Railway, and attended by a manservant (Lawrence) and her (nameless) lady's maid. She made a point of visiting American botanical gardens, notably the Missouri Botanical Gardens in St. Louis, and in California the private grounds of widowed Mrs. Leland Stanford (with letters of introduction).

nineteenth century that we characterize below. Flowers, gardens, trees, seashells, insects, and wildlife most capture Guest's interest during her North American journey, and descriptions of the quality of her lodgings, restaurant meals, transportation, and porter arrangements frequently intertwine with her naturalist writing.

Traditions of British Natural History

In order to address our basic research questions of whether or how our suite of British female naturalists expressed a gendered knowledge or an imperialist agenda through their writings, it is important to delineate some of the attributes of Victorian natural history and science as competing sets of cultural practices, and of British women's opportunities within them. We position gender and class issues centrally within our analysis. For instance, attainment of the career of "scientist" or "geographer" either requires birth into a privileged class as a prerequisite or else it is the corollary of the attainment of an academic post (Berman 1975; Rupke 1994, 55–62); in the nineteenth century it usually required maleness, as well.

Several different intellectual traditions also pertain to female naturalists in Britain. One of the most visible was scientific botany, especially as it came to be defined after about 1870, and as professional botanists would define their field today (Shteir 1996; Creese 1998; Gates 1998). Together with various branches of zoology, Victorian natural science emphasized classifying, collecting, and preserving specimens. David E. Allen (1976) defined a second tradition as natural history, which encompassed both taxonomy as well as a range of protoscientific ideas and practices that either yielded to, or uneasily coexisted alongside, natural science. An example might be an amateur plant collector who identified several new species and possibly wrote up these discoveries for the journal of a scholarly society, all the while adhering to a belief in natural theology: that collecting plant specimens encouraged appreciation of their Creator.

A third even more extensive category that is far too polyglot conceptually to encompass some very different fields (as defined today) might be called "nature studies," a term specifically coined in the late nineteenth century. It is Barber's (1980), Merrill's (1989), Shteir's (1996) and Gates's

(1998) more extensive scope for natural history, comparable to Germany's *Naturphilosophie* (Koerner 1993, 472).[8] It would include scientific botany, horticulture and gardening, environmental education, poetry about nature, as well as paintings of plants within the humanities and fine arts traditions. Both the more concise and inclusive delineations of natural history pertain to endeavors that were wildly popular in Victorian Britain (see, for example, Carruthers 1879; Lowe 1874; Scourse 1983; Sparrow 1905; Turner 1893; Yonge 1887).

But the value of the more conceptually inchoate scope of nature study is that it provides a catchment area for everything relating to nature that does not currently take as its reference point presentist contemporary natural science. It also is a way to comprehend artifacts that overlap out of science into other more popular or creative endeavors. For example, Victorians were fond of cataloging specimens and displaying them in glass cases in their parlors, thus blurring the distinction between taxonomy and home decor.

The distinction between the amateur and the scientist, the tourist versus the scholar, probably registered seriously in Britain only after 1870, with traces of the older undifferentiated thinking patterns persisting for decades afterward (Rupke 1994, 59–60; Livingstone 1992, 212–13). For context, recall that no British universities offered natural science degrees before 1861. In the 1870s when North and Cumming began their voyages, Britain's leading scientific societies normally were run by gentleman amateurs (D. Allen 1976, 56–57, 184; Livingstone 1992, 158–60).

Indeed, Charles Darwin would be considered an amateur by today's definition of scientist. He never held an academic appointment, had no advanced degree, and did most of his writing at home on the Wedgwood estate. Much of the deference accorded to him by the scientists of his era apparently rested on his privileged family connections (Berman 1975; Brockway 1979; Rupke 1994).

Part of the reason for this state of affairs was Britain's tradition of the independently secure gentleman scholar, for whom education in natural

8. "Nature studies" took on a concise meaning at the turn of the century as a reaction against scientism and as a program of environmental education for children (D. Allen 1976, 203, 227).

science was an expression of self-improvement. Shteir (1987; 1996, 174) termed this context "polite botany," botany at the breakfast table. The purpose of studying botany was to improve and polish the gentleman or lady as much as it was to advance knowledge, particularly with the justification of natural theology. Indeed, a diagnostic feature of the elite was their prerogative to separate learning from the need to apply it to earn a living; a belief with major implications for the advancement of natural science, given Britain's hegemonic class system.

Amateur-based natural history did create space for women to study natural phenomena on the equivalent moral grounds of self-improvement. Within the conceptual framework of the doctrine of separate spheres (Cott 1977, 197–205; Smith-Rosenberg 1985), Victorian natural history operated far more in the private domestic sphere than did the professionalized scientific experimental botany and zoology that replaced it. Even within the strictures of middle class Victorian social norms, women's naturalized affiliation with the private sphere permitted them access to learning natural history along with most of its practices: membership in most field clubs, development of specialized private botanical gardens and greenhouses, correspondence with other naturalists, preservation of specimens, authorship of books and papers, and botanical illustration (Phillips 1990; Creese 1998). If the most prestigious London natural science societies were based on the gentleman's private dining club model and consequently excluded women (along with working class, ethnic, and religious minority men), many of the regional and local societies were mixed by both gender and class.

Several environmental historians, geographers, and literary critics have analyzed the ways in which elite Euro-American women in particular inhabited the naturalist figure in the nineteenth century, principally through botany and travel writing (Norwood 1993; McEwan 1998a; Shteir 1996; Meyers 1989; Gates 1998; Gould 1997; Losano 1997). Norwood (1993) argues that botany's association with a feminine aesthetic tradition led to its becoming a popular hobby for privileged women, including for leisure-class travelers. McEwan (1998a, 219) calls botany the "feminine science par excellence" in the nineteenth century, "unmanly and ornamental." Women's exclusion from postgraduate education and professional science throughout most of the nineteenth century turned Britain's amateur approach to nature study into women's preserve (Gates 1998; Shteir 1987, 1996). With the garden considered an extension of the domestic sphere, interest in flora especially complemented women's restricted mobility. The study of botany encouraged women to be outdoors and engage in a limited intellectual pursuit. Norwood (1993, 54–97) argues that this was reinforced through women's participation in botanical drawing and flower painting. Women excluded from university posts found outlets in writing natural history texts for elementary schools and children (Meyers 1989). Some British social commentators argued, regarding genteel young ladies on country estates, that botanizing and floral painting would distract them from idleness and turn them toward natural theology (McEwan 1998a; Shteir 1987, 1996). Moreover, taken out of the realm of artifact and into the realm of social norms and motives, botanical illustration could provide a rationale for leisured women to imbue their travels with wholly acceptable Victorian impulses toward nature study, dissemination of information, self-improvement, and cataloguing the natural world.

As recently as 1905, a British art historian could argue that few female artists were attracted to landscape painting (Sparrow 1905, 69), suggesting that women "are more held by the personal than the abstract." This splitting of nature may reflect Edmund Burke's (1757) widely accepted division of feminine and masculine aesthetics. Gould (1997, 35–36) argued that female naturalists' language tended to emphasize the beautiful concepts deemed suitable for women by Burke's division of aesthetics into the beautiful and the sublime. To women belong descriptions of the petite, delicate, and colorful, in contrast to appropriate male emphases on grand, vast, awe-inspiring, or mysterious entities.

Wealthy, privileged Victorian women like Guest, North, and Cumming with a taste for natural history therefore could and did exploit venues open to them. The figure of the wealthy, indomitable English dowager comes to mind: self-confident, socially active and adept, an absolute arbiter of taste, and often outspoken. Tourism might also suit her tastes, as it did for many Victorians who could afford to travel. Victorians enamored of natural history planned to collect, sketch, or paint specimens and scenes during their holidays. Ornamental gardening or even private botanical gardens could be developed as an adjunct of domesticity or the showplace grounds of a country house. The noblesse oblige ideology of social reform could also extend to environmental protection. But because few British women received a systematic university education before 1900 (Creese 1998), many of their writings today suggest a more idiosyncratic, reflexive, eclectic, and fluid tone than the discrete fixed hierarchical categories and theories beloved of university men (Lawrence 1994, 21). If excluded from histories of natural science on one hand and academic humanities and fine arts on the other, Victorian women naturalists were strongly affiliated with the vanishing fields of natural history or nature study that could be claimed by neither or both. Theirs was a catholic, eclectic world.

Although their interests generally turn to the recovery of neglected authors or female naturalists' rhetoric or self-expression, the problem of how Victorian women signified narratorial authority engages scholars of female naturalists as well (Shteir 1987, 1996; Gates 1998). Susan Morgan (1996) and Antonia Losano (1997), in focusing on Marianne North, argue that she moved beyond the rhetoric of a woman engaged in a naturalized feminine pursuit of flowers to deploy a sense of personal emancipation and professionalism in her journal writings about her floral paintings. In our readings of travelers' texts (below) we find that their attempts to establish themselves as authorities on botany and other sciences emerge in a number of ways. Among many other strategies, they submitted their paintings to public display; they provided Latin names and Linnaean terminology for the different species of plants and animals they encountered; they drew on the expertise of male authorities they met, such as John Muir, when it suited their arguments (e.g., Cumming 1886, 325–31); and they collected biological specimens, sometimes for public collections. North, Guest, and Cumming also compared the natural landscapes of California to that of other places around the globe, based on their own earlier travels, establishing their credentials as seasoned world travelers.

Mary Louise Pratt (1992) posits male European naturalists abroad as disingenuously ignoring the colonialism of which they are agents, for instance in their textual erasure of indigenous people. In considering female naturalists in British colonies, McEwan (1998a, 219) argues:

It is no coincidence that the participation of middle-class British women in field natural history corresponded with the expansion of the British empire and the increased opportunities for travel abroad ... botanical study was very often the legitimating factor for women travellers' otherwise transgressive presence in imperial spaces.

Mary Kingsley, for instance, justified her presence in colonial West Africa by claiming that she traveled simply to collect botanical specimens (A. Blunt 1994). Drawing on the work of Pratt (1992), McEwan goes on to argue that there "was a close relationship between natural history, cartography, and the geographical enterprise of naming, which were central to the emergence of Europe's 'planetary consciousness' and the construction of global-scale meaning. Travel writing, and the observational enterprise of documenting geography, flora and fauna, was fundamental to this" (1998a, 219). Yet we question whether wealthy and evidently self-confident women considered themselves to be either transgressive or "innocent" of British imperialism—they often fully supported it.

Women's "Naturalist Knowledge"

Botanical Illustrations, Landscape Painting

Constance Gordon Cumming, Marianne North, and Theodora Guest all sketched and painted on their travels. But to define their artwork only in the context of a suitably feminine, ladylike pursuit is to overlook the multiple and much more extensive set of discourses in which their work appeared. To relegate botanical illustration just to the "breakfast room" or other feminine sphere, for example, is to overlook the multiple utilities of this type of artifact. Highly detailed exact line drawings of flowers, left plain or colored, were extremely useful to the plant taxonomy of the Victorian period, as any amateur can attest who has tried to identify a plant species using one of the older unillustrated and highly specialized plant keys. Precise botanical drawings were invaluable to plant taxonomists who worked with taxa that could not be readily dried and pressed into herbarium sheets, such as cacti. Botanical illustrations occurred along several social continuums, moreover. The more scientific were specifically crafted to display flower stamens and pistils for systematic analyses;

the more lavish and appealing, to sell horticultural products or to subsidize botanical research; the more dilettantish, to grace parlor walls (W. Blunt 1950; Buchanan 1979; Mabey 1988; Scourse 1983). Thus, the notion of discrete categories of what is scientific, protoscientific, or popular, commercial, or fine art erodes in the example of Victorian botanical illustrations.

Nor were Victorian women's contributions to botanical illustrations restricted to ladies of (too much) leisure (P. Phillips 1990; Creese 1998). Notable female and male botanical illustrators also came from the families of trades people, such as publishers, engravers, and nurserymen, who had a strong business interest in high-quality reproductions (Weathers n.d.; W. Blunt 1950; Buchanan 1979; Mabey 1988; Shteir 1996). A few women produced museum-caliber floral still-life paintings or incorporated accurately rendered flowers within paintings of human subjects (Sparrow 1905). It would also be mistaken to view women as uniquely restricted within the field of botanical illustration: men contributed to this field, ranging from amateurs to the dean of Victorian botany, Kew Gardens's director Joseph Hooker.

Lady Theodora Guest often contradicts tidy feminine categories in her artistic creations. Guest illustrated *A Round Trip in North America* herself, primarily with landscape sketches of California coasts, scenic waterfalls and rock outcrops in Yosemite, and other western mountainous scenery. But she also sketched a simple flower, *Cyclobothra,* as her book's cover design. Her interest in natural history and botany come to the text's forefront in a number of such ways. At train depots, rural villages, cities, beaches, and other scenic attractions Guest describes and names the hundreds of botanical and other specimens. She narrates and sketches sublime scenery when it suits her purpose, but also takes closer looks at flowers. She delighted equally in both wild and cultivated flowers, at a time when many cultivars had only recently been grown commercially from their wild progenitors (Brockway 1979; Coats 1969). Guest also emerges as a feminine, "polite" naturalist in the practice of her vocation. She frequently mentions male members of her travel party picking flowers for her to sketch or holding an umbrella over her head to keep off the sun while she sketched (1895, 131).

Marianne North devoted much of her life to a project intended to support the Hookers' mercantilist agenda at Kew Gardens: to represent by means of plant specimens Her Majesty's entire empire (Brockway 1979; Rupke 1994, 80–84; Ritvo 1987, 205). Both North and Hooker justified her vocation to paint the world's flowers and vegetation as a way to record rare and beautiful flowers that were rapidly disappearing under human impact. Her vivid colors contrasted sharply with the dried, often faded herbarium specimens, black-and-white etchings, and primitive photography that typically portrayed flora during her era (Brenan 1980; Mabey 1988; Ponsonby 1990).

If it is difficult to place North as a botanist or more scientific type of naturalist,[9] it is also difficult to place her as an artist. From a fine art perspective, North's technique is not strong; the novelty of her subjects is what principally engages the viewer. She cannot be classified as a scientific illustrator: most of her flowers are insufficiently detailed to permit exact taxonomic analyses. She did not appear to consider selling any of her paintings at a time when opulent botanical illustrations were used to market ornamental garden plants and even serious scholarly botany books.

Several critics cryptically term North's flowers as unpleasant or even frightening (W. Blunt 1950, 237; Merrill 1989, 168). From a creative perspective, however, such negative comments suggest that North unsettled and then engaged the viewer in an alternative way of seeing the natural world. Indeed, in her best paintings, such as those of California carnivorous plants, North shares a talent with Georgia O'Keefe for "pulling" the viewer into the plants: they begin to appear as wholly other, as exotic, and sometimes as erotic female (Losano 1997, 443–44) or male. Her painting of a fallen, decaying California sequoia also exhibits these characteristics: it is not skillfully executed, but her focus on the interior of the rotting trunk begins to pull the viewer into its dark recesses. And perhaps the amateurish quality to many of North's paintings is also the point: encouraged to be a decorative but not a serious professional artist, it is what a wealthy woman of her generation *would* have produced.

---

9. Other botanists named a genus plus three new species after her, an honor usually reserved for titled colonial administrators or respected botanists.

C. G. Cumming sketched landscape scenes most days while in Yosemite. She described her daily routine as beginning at 5:00 A.M., with male chaperones, porters, or carriages carting her art supplies to the day's designated location (e.g. 1886, 204, 242–44). Cumming's descriptions of her sketching and painting expeditions in Yosemite produce her as an authoritative, purposeful traveler and naturalist (cf. Losano 1997). What Cumming considered her systematic and comprehensive method of exploring and painting Yosemite (1886, 189–90) would ensure her status as one with expert, reliable knowledge of the region. And in fact, Cumming became known for the "accuracy" of her landscape paintings. She wrote of friends' insistence that she exhibit her Yosemite work in a grand show before leaving the Valley (1886, 282–83). She had finished twenty-five drawings during her time there and began another twenty-five; most of which she considered large for watercolor sketches (thirty by twenty inches). The enthusiastic band of supporters at the art show gratified her, "as they recognized all their favourite points of view, and vouched for the rigid accuracy of each" (1886, 282).

On her last expedition through the park, Cumming took the opportunity to further emphasize that these attributes of expert, authoritative knowledge via naturalist art belonged squarely in the feminine domain, at least for those with genteel, if informal British educations and backgrounds. One (female) visitor claimed Cumming must be a man to produce such artistic creations: "Why, I do believe you are a man! Come now, do tell me, aren't you a man really?" In response, Cumming wrote:

> Why my poor little water-colour paint-box should be considered masculine I cannot say, but it attracted great notice in the valley as something quite unknown, even to most of the tourists, the artist masculine, armed with cumbersome oil-paints, being the only specimen of the genus known in the Sierras. (1886, 289)[10]

---

10. Ogden (1990) identifies the best known of Yosemite artists as Albert Bierstadt, famous for his "monumental" large canvasses and Hudson River School style. Ogden identifies no female artists of the Yosemite Valley, yet Cumming ought to be counted among them.

Cumming perhaps disturbed Yosemite visitors by painting grand vistas in primitive settings versus dainty close-up flowers, the former encoded as masculine in Burke's aesthetics (Gould 1997, 35–36). While poking fun at the implied manliness of oil paints versus the more feminine watercolors in the above excerpt, in a larger sense Cumming here, though, seems to be subverting these compartmentalizations.

Nature Aesthetics

Hotel developers, railroad companies, the federal government, and other entities interested in promoting tourism principally directed attention to sublime nature in the American West, especially available at such monumental, scenic attractions as Yosemite. But Cumming presents herself as much more than a mere tourist; she occupies a rhetorical space of a travel writer with a keen sense of duty to provide measurable data and other statistical information about California's mountain ranges and the waterfalls, trees, and rock formations in Yosemite Valley (1886, 216ff). And yet the genre of travel writing also gave Cumming an opportunity to express what might be called a "naturalist-aesthetic" more so than a "scientific management" style of naturalist knowledge. In fact, she includes the latter only to support her expressed love of nature, or, alternatively, the aesthetic unlovability of certain aspects of Yosemite scenery. Providing heights and measurements of rock formations in Yosemite served, then, an aesthetic purpose for Cumming. "I give you the altitude of all these grand crags and mountains," she wrote, "because I know no better way of conveying to you some standard of their glory; and yet how utterly useless figures really are to enable any one to realize such subjects!" (1886, 124–25).

Cumming's romantic and aesthetic language places her beyond the pale of natural science by focusing on the author's subjectivity and on meaning and value of nature beyond the lab or herbarium. Cumming devotes more text in *Granite Crags of California* to describing trees than any other natural feature, and it is in her descriptions of trees that her aesthetic language gains its full rhetorical force. Much of the text focuses on the well-known groves of the giant redwoods and sequoias (e.g., 1886, 77–81), highlighting their numbers; sizes—one tree was 132 feet in circumference; and ages—some as old as 2,000–3,000 years. Though duly

10. *The Sentinel Rock*. From Constance Gordon Cumming, *Granite Crags of California* (Edinburgh: Blackwood, 1886), frontispiece. Reproduced courtesy of the Collection of The Public Library of Cincinnati and Hamilton County.

impressed by their characteristic features, Cumming finds little attraction to the giant trees: "There is nothing lovable about a Sequoia. It is so gigantic that I feel overawed by it" (1886, 76). In reflecting on a day's outing near Clark's Ranch outside of Yosemite, she wrote: "We have spent a long day of delight in the most magnificent forest it is possible to imagine; and I have realized an altogether new sensation. . . . They are wonderful—they are stupendous! But as to beauty—no. They shall never tempt me to swerve from my allegiance to my true tree-love, the glorious Deodara forests of the Himalaya" (1886, 75).

While drawing on and gaining authority from her extensive prior traveling experience, Cumming here applies the standards of art criticism to nature, as opposed to more scientific standards. She prefers the Himalayan trees to the unlovable giant sequoias, although she concedes that in Yosemite the "queen of beauty" is the sugar pine, *Pinus lambertiana*: "So exquisite is the grace of its tall tapering spire and slender branches, each following the most perfect double curve of the true line of beauty" (1886, 79). Although interested in classifying and providing taxonomic descriptions and names to the scores of varieties outlined in a chapter on forests of the Sierras (1886, 322ff)—the pines, firs, spruces, and cedars—in the end Cumming ranks them according to their beauty and other aesthetic qualities, such as shape, proportionality, and color. In this way Cumming seeks to deflect attention from the grandeur of the big trees, toward an appreciation for the subtler qualities of the less-noticeable varieties.

North's published memoirs regarding California also place her well within the aesthetic side of the Victorian naturalist tradition (S. Morgan 1996, 1: 202–12, 2: 191–201). She rates various sites as beautiful or ugly depending on whether wildflowers are in bloom or shriveled in dust: the latter a common occurrence as she visited California in summer. North spends "lovely" days painting intriguing vegetation. Views and sunshine are "magnificent" (North 1892, 2: 195). In North's discussions of scenery and flowers, however, the rhetoric of establishing her authority may also be glimpsed. She compares Yosemite Valley with Switzerland, the Dolomites, the mountains of Brazil, and the Tyrolean Alps, thus establishing her credentials as a knowledgeable world traveler. Garden plants in California are "nothing new" but familiar to her from India, Brazil, and Australia.

So long as equally important variables of ethnicity (Britishness) and class (privileged) are included, it seems clear that by the final quarter of the nineteenth century, Burke's division of sublime men and beautiful women no longer held: these writers adopted the long view when it suited them, either in paintings, sketches, or written texts.

11. Marianne North's North American carnivorous plant painted in England. Behind, on the left, is a Californian pitcher plant (*Darlingtonia californica*), with in front a common pitcher plant (*Sarracenia purpurea*); on the right is a yellow pitcher plant (*S. flava*) with in front a Venus flytrap (*Dionaea muscipula*). Reproduced courtesy of the Director, Royal Botanical Gardens, Kew.

Collecting and Cataloguing

Victorian women contributed to scientific botany as it was defined in their day, based on published scientific papers indexed by the Royal Society (Shteir 1996; Creese 1998; Gates 1998). Sometimes contributions were based on discoveries of new species or careful descriptions of taxa. Even for naturalists who did not write up their investigations, women's (and men's) collections of natural objects, when donated to research herbariums and museums, formed the material basis for researchers' scientific taxonomy and systematics. Although this branch of biology has receded to a minor subfield today, it comprised a significant share of the discipline during the nineteenth century (D. Allen 1976; Barber 1980; Harvey-Gibson 1919; Merrill 1989) and remains the foundation for much biogeographical and ecological research. North, Cumming, and Guest also collected specimens during their travels. Encouraged by friends (including Charles Darwin) to pursue her interests in botany, Marianne North's primary goal of painting the world's tropical plants and flowers was seconded by collecting and donating her samples of tropical woods to Kew Gardens (Ponsonby 1990; J. Robinson 1990, 146–47).

Lady Theodora Guest collected specimens throughout the journey and recorded her findings at each day's end (though does not say what she intended on doing with them back in England). Returning to the train car after a day's outing along the coast at Monterey, California, she wrote: "I hastened to my press, made of blotting-paper and an enormous atlas, to dry the many new wild flowers; and deposit our cones and shells in the various nets that hang round the car for such purposes" (1895, 113). Guest expresses frequent pleasure in finding and collecting various species in their native habitats:

> We drove on to the beach, where I had hoped to make a sketch, and sat down on the rocks for the purpose. But there was too little sun and too much wind, so . . . I joined the others, who were doing better in Venus's ear shells, or "Abelones," [*sic*] as they are called by the natives. It was very difficult, amusing, scrambling in the rocks, especially impeded as I was by a variety of wraps . . . but it was worth a struggle to pick up with one's own hands some of these grand shells one had admired from childhood . . . it takes a great pull to get them out, they stick so fast in the rocks, and some of them have the abelones still in them, which is more than one bargains for. We made a really good haul at last of big ones, in their glorious colours; all the curls of the semicircular edge of the shell turning the same way . . . those in the China seas turning the other. (1895, 115–16)

Guest's text reads much like that of today's African photo-safari tourists on first encountering "zoo animals" about their own business in the wild. Guest was equally blissfully unaware as are most tourists of any ecological impacts of their trophy-seeking, which included shells of large, living abalone. This excerpt exhibits a variety of Victorian nature themes, including the difficulties of feminine attire for collecting specimens.

Binomial Nomenclature

We previously noted how collecting, both specimens and observations, was important to all of these writers. This acquisitive quality to botanizing and landscape painting seems akin to hunting: nature is not just admired, but as some sort of trophy a sketch, a watercolor, a pressed specimen, a written description is obtained and brought back home (Losano 1997). And just as trophy hunting was reserved principally for upper-class English men, so botanizing requires upper-class women's informal education, refinement, and sensitivity.

Bruno Latour (1987, 215–45) and David Miller (1996) offer a more explicit interpretation of naturalists overseas, as individuals who knowingly transfer geographical and biological information back home to "centres of calculation" such as London's scientific and military institutions. A "cycle of accumulation" then follows, in which useful information stored at the center is utilized by subsequent voyagers who contribute new information back to it in turn, often in the belief of future economic or political gain such as exploitable crop species or advantageous trade routes.

For new data to be truly useful at the center, however, systems of classification—such as binomial nomenclature—and protocols for naming new phenomena are highly desirable. Foucault, in his *The Order of Things* (1970, 125–65), details one archaeology of scientific classifying discourses that developed in natural history. He argues that beginning in late seventeenth-century Europe, this involved matching up visual attributes of natural phenomena with their representations ("things and words"). The end purpose of these classification systems and cycles of accumulation was amassing of political and economic power at the center of calculation (Gregory 1994).

Caution is required in making these connections, however. It should be remembered that Carl Linnaeus's first purpose, for example, was not to support global colonization but to enable European botanists to communicate about local species, presumably in support of the natural theology he firmly upheld (W. Blunt 1971). Stated differently, binomial nomenclature is only partially implicated in colonial expansion or ecological imperialism, which have proved themselves entirely capable of classifications of foreign areas and devastating conquests without it. Common English names of plants are equally up to the task of Europeanizing the tropics, for example, so long as botanists of different languages do not need to communicate with one another.[11]

Tracing the overlay of the scientific European mind upon the planet to Linnaeus's development of binomial nomenclature in the eighteenth century indeed traces "paternal lines of descent" (Rose 1995, 415), but it can ignore the intervening decades before this type of revolution was sufficiently complete to assume the naturalized status now accorded them. For example, Linnaeus's own "sexual" system of species identification was based on flowers' number and arrangement of stamens and pistils. It rapidly collapsed under various competing natural systems that expanded the plant taxonomist's task to examine seeds, leaves, buds, etc. (Stafleu 1971; Meyers 1989; Koerner 1996). The sometimes acrimonious debates between proponents of newer and better systems took decades to sort out, leaving Linnaeus principally remembered as the semantic founder of the genus-species Latin name and secondarily remembered as proponent of a thoroughly discredited system for actual plant identification. Compendia of plant species will often print lengthy lists of the various Latin names by which they have been known, together with the names of the botanists who proposed or used the various Latin names in their research: mute evidence of the indeterminacy (if not occasional disarray) of nomenclature within its community of practitioners.

Other forms of expression, other idioms addressing the natural world, have proven themselves equally capable of verbally Europeanizing the rest of the globe, ranging from the Catholic Church to Goethe's and von Humboldt's mystical belief in the unity of nature (Koerner 1993; Dettelbach 1996). During the natural history fad of the Victorian period, western idioms ranging from binomial nomenclature to aestheticism and the romantic impulse to natural theology were widely applied to overseas environments and cultures (Livingstone 1992, 130–33). Victorian travel

11. Recall that the genus *Pinus* means pine, *Lilum* means lily; species names *vulgaris*, *borealis*, and *foliosum* mean common, northern, and leafy, respectively. *Rosaceae* is the rose family.

writers and naturalists proved dexterous in deploying these different styles to suit their rhetorical purposes. It is in the interplay between, and selection of, various terms to describe nature that their agendas can be discerned.

The texts by North, Guest, and Cumming are rich and detailed in their observation of flora and use of binomial nomenclature. If Lady Theodora Guest was not always accurate (confusing, for example, California live oak, *Quercus,* with holly, *Ilex*) (1895, 122), she seems to make a serious effort to use Latin names for flora. Marianne North gives genus names for many plants, but seldom species names, and common names often serve (e.g., North 1892, 2: 197). She gives no taxonomic analysis or speculation on her observations. She sometimes prefers ornamental gardeners' idioms, such as whether wild or cultivated flowers are massed and in monochrome or multicolored groupings. Cummings' tree examples cited above display a mixture of botanizing with a wholly romantic impulse to reflect on nature's impacts on her emotions.

The use of Latin names by North, Guest, and Cumming thus becomes a way to affiliate the traveler with the ranks of learned botanists, rather than the common herd. Their frequent use of genus or family names only, however, suggests that some did not make the effort to identify the species they observed, placing them more in the category of the tourist than of the professional botanist. As a cultural practice, binomial nomenclature becomes a way for them to establish narratorial authority rather than to supplement scientific advances.

Naturalists and Empire

Particular naming procedures, as a form of collecting little-known places via travel texts and other written genres, may not straightforwardly support imperial agendas. But attempts by women travelers to acquire and disseminate botanical observations and specimens in other ways did more explicitly serve larger imperial purposes, even as the biographies of North, Cumming, and Guest suggest quite different impulses for travel. When reading their "ladylike" naturalist pursuits against the development of American and British imperialisms in the American West region, this may occur at several scales.

For instance, C. G. Cumming positions herself as "scientific manager" when discussing agricultural production of the San Joaquin Valley of California, pointing out the extent of cultivation, farming procedures, fertility of the soil, and general outputs. She gushes over potentialities for future European immigrants, especially with the aid of irrigation (1886, 59–65, 349–57). In this way Cumming serves as an adjunct promoter of American imperialism via British expansion overseas, encouraging European immigration to California and thus continuing displacement of Native peoples and a turn to a cash economy.

Shteir (1987, 1996), Gates (1998), Susan Morgan (1996), and Losano (1997) are mindful of naturalists as purveyors of their home society's mores as well as their mercantile agenda. This relationship is perhaps most applicable to the case of Marianne North and Hooker's project for Kew Gardens, as he sought new exotic plant species with commercial potential for British consumers (Brockway 1979, 103–39; Frost 1996; Ronald King 1985, 205; S. Morgan 1996, 117). Although potential tropical plantation crops generated the keenest interest, the Victorians also imported thousands of exotic plant species for ornamental gardening (Webber 1968; Martin 1988). Ideally living plants from overseas that could be propagated were sought for the Kew Gardens, but dried herbarium specimens and sketches from both male and female donors were also archived. Thus, British women's travel books that reported on botanizing and overseas gardens—those by North as well as Cumming and Guest—had at least the potential to stimulate British consumers' appetites for wild and cultivated exotic species.

North apparently supported the Kew Gardens project of mercantile botany. She painted economically useful species that had previously been collected and developed by male botanists. We uncovered one example of a commercial plant hunter in Sarawak who based his quest to export a rare pitcher plant (*Nepenthes northiana*) upon one of North's paintings (Coats 1969, 209). Marianne North's donation of funds to build the North Gallery at Kew Gardens to house her paintings suggests her desire to contribute to its project. Yet Cumming and Guest seemingly wrote and sketched outside this type of explicit mercantile agenda. North also painted species that could not be cultivated commercially in the colonies or in English gardens or hothouses specifically to show what these little-known wild species were like.

Environmental Rhetorics and Imperial Ambivalence

Complaints about rampant American deforestation and lumbering also surfaced in the women's texts as a form of naturalist knowledge. Their rhetorics do not stem from mercantilism or scientific ecology but can be traced to an alternative romantic or aesthetic tradition that measured the effects of deforestation by standards of beauty or ugliness. Like many other commentators who engaged in the emerging environmentalist debates, these writers supported the preservation or conservation of picturesque or aesthetically pleasing landscapes such as forests while advocating the large-scale development of land that was considered otherwise useless, such as the central American grasslands (see chapter 2). Such emerging environmentalist aesthetics, aligned with John Muir, John Ruskin, Henry David Thoreau, and others, positioned itself against the ignorance and greed of the American government, American businessmen, and working-class lumberers. Both Cumming and North politicized environmentalist concerns in this way.

Marianne North's narrative places her firmly within European traditions of imperialism, ethnocentrism, and femininity (Blunt and Rose 1994). North easily erases the local, particularly indigenous inhabitants, a trait in common with Pratt's (1992) depiction of European naturalists overseas such as Alexander von Humboldt. North, too, pursues nature, not people, except insofar as they are knowledgeable naturalists themselves. Yet North's inability to identify strongly with people in preference for vegetation permits an "anti-conquest" (Pratt 1992) of a different type. North displays a moral environmentalist sensitivity in her criticisms of loggers, who by 1880 had already decimated many stands of California's big trees. In one passage, for instance, she reports:

> My host took me some miles up a side valley to see some [redwood trees] which were fifteen feet in diameter, and nearly 300 feet high. They were gradually sawing them up for firewood, and the tree would soon be extinct . . . it is invaluable for many purposes, and it broke one's

heart to think of man, the civiliser, wasting treasures in a few years to which savages and animals had done no harm for centuries. (1892, 2: 211–12)

North condemned the commercialism of California clear-cutting practices. Although British people of North's class benefited from logging under Britain's development of American natural resources (White 1991, 260–63), criticism of environmental despoliation provided one means of positioning one's aesthetic sensitivities in a morally superior position. Cumming's environmental politics also emerges on the subject of deforestation. "Well would it be for California," she asserts, "if her human inhabitants would give some heed to the future of her timber, instead of so ruthlessly destroying it to meet the requirements of the moment" (1886, 319). Cumming raises a number of troubling issues related to destruction of the California forests, including species extermination, wasteful practices (such as cutting down trees solely for their bark), ineffectual and "worthless" California lumbering laws, the ruthless greed of (working class) lumberers, and crass appropriation of nature by business for capitalistic ends (1886, 43, 319–20, 341). Of the depletion of the redwoods she complains:

> Formerly many of the hills near San Francisco were clothed with the beautiful redwood; but it was found . . . valuable for building purposes, . . . it is a favourite wood with the builders; and so the forests near San Francisco now exist only in the form of houses or railroad timber. And still the work of destruction goes on, and north and south the lumberers are busy felling the beautiful growth of centuries, to be turned to common use. (1886, 43)

And of the giant sequoias she laments: "It is really pathetic to hear of the wholesale destruction of these grand forests, which year by year are mowed down wholesale by lumberers—men whose one thought in connection with trees is, how many feet of timber they will yield" (1886, 45–46). Even when destruction arose from scientific advancement rather than commercial lumbering—as in the following case, when she witnessed the felling of a tree whose wood and bark was to be distributed to various parts of the world—Cumming questioned the justness of the "murder":

One of the noblest trees was felled, an operation which kept five men hard at work for twenty two days, boring through the tree with pump-augers. Even after the poor giant had been sawn in two, it refused to fall, and its murderers had to work for three days more, driving in wedges on one side, till they succeeded in tilting it over; and great was the fall of it. (1886, 311)

The critiques of deforestation from both Cumming and North seem principally to derive from their naturalist-aesthetic impulse rather than from a more scientific or ecological one. To them, deforestation is bad because crass Yankee materialism motivates it and because it leaves ugly scars on the landscape. The narratorial authority that both North and Cumming exert on environmental issues also seems to derive from their feminine, upper-class gentility. As women, they were positioned to articulate heightened sensitivity to natural beauty. Such feminine, upper-class women were by their gender excluded from and by their wealth and class insulated from the world of business; thus, they were situated in a position from which to critique lumbering practices. However, their class positioned them to benefit from the world of business, even if they could not personally own property. Thus, these texts demonstrate an uneasy association between naturalist-aesthetic knowledge and advancing capitalist-imperialism development in the region.

Discussion

Alexander von Humboldt's inclusion in geography's "paternal lines of descent" is seldom questioned. He nevertheless drew inspiration from Goethe and Schiller, and with them he believed in the unity of nature, the primacy of art, the personal emancipation of travel (Pratt 1992; Koerner 1993; Dettelbach 1996; Nicolson 1990). Yet these aspects of his thought lie excluded from most presentist contemporary accounts of his contributions to geography and natural science. Although postcolonialists might interrogate the "innocence" of von Humboldt's romantic impulses (Pratt 1992), they might equally support scholarship on him that extends beyond conservative tropes of Man the Scientist and that links him to the larger social and cultural movements of his day.

Like Alexander von Humboldt, the Victorian women naturalists discussed in this chapter equally revered grand scenery, quoted poets, and expressed their landscape ideas through artistic sensitivities. They belong to a forgotten tradition of inquiry about the earth's surface that was not science or much like contemporary geography, but it had a highly distinguished pedigree in western thought nonetheless (Gates 1998, 253). Indeed, a cursory look through any British poetry anthology will reveal how closely attuned to nature Britain's canonized Victorian poets were, and some of their poetry contains the kind of detailed, precise observations of organisms that would today be ascribed to ethologists or plant ecologists.

Merrill's (1989) view of natural history includes a range of cultural practices that were subsequently written out of both natural science and the historiography of protoscience as well as out of humanities and the fine arts into the indeterminate zone of popular culture.[12] Both he and Allen (1976) argued that the Victorians blurred many disciplinary categories and distinctions that are taken for granted today or, put differently, that many of today's western taken-for-granted classifications had not yet developed. Consequently, from a presentist perspective, scientific advances appear today to have been more clear-cut and uncontested than they actually were at the time and also to have changed society's thinking far more rapidly than is often the case.

There is no need to interpret nature poetry, prose nature writings, travel diaries, or botanical sketches as "bad science" or "un-geography." Rather, it makes sense to view Victorian naturalists as partaking of a large, inchoate tradition with diverse sources of inspiration that only began seriously to diverge into separate subjects in the 1870s, with the emergence of modern university disciplines. But the lineages that did not become natural science research nevertheless extended the liberal arts tradition in American university teaching, in today's popular, aesthetically based

12. See, for example, Lowe's (1874) book *Our Native Ferns*. It mixes taxonomy, ecology, aesthetics, and horticulture. The author acknowledges the contributions of numerous amateur collectors to his knowledge of various species.

environmentalism,[13] in landscape paintings, and in nature writing. Guest, North, and Cumming indicate through their texts and paintings something of what Victorian natural history was like with all of its attendant imperialism and situated knowledges. Victorian naturalists, particularly women, were often self-described (and subsequently criticized) as amateurs. The root of amateur is *amare*—to love. Before about 1870, this passion was eclectic and meant simply that one studied nature for love of the subject, not because one needed it to earn a living. As such, to be an amateur was a mark of class privilege. That Victorian women tended to produce particular types of naturalist knowledge speaks eloquently to the masculinization of academic knowledge and the power relations that intimidated most women from advanced educations and academic careers. A Great Men (or even Great Women) linear historiographic tradition (Livingstone 1992; Stoddart 1986) cannot include much of what women produced; a cultural history approach can question *why* female naturalists produced what they did (Shteir 1987, 43) from within the venues open to them.

In the hands of women naturalists, naturalist travel writing indeed displays some very subversive opportunities to rethink geography today from the sidelines of "not-geography" (Rose 1995, 414) or "erased knowledges" (WGSG 1997, 20). The figure of the Victorian female naturalist writing from the eclectic natural history or nature studies tradition subverts masculinist classifications and narrative structures of scientific botany and regional geography. Lawrence (1994, 21) in fact claims that indeterminacy and flexibility of language and subject matter was a hallmark of travel writing generally and women's travel writing particularly. The Victorian model of amateur curiosity-based learning, and learning that leads primarily to better-informed human beings, finds little place

13. The liberal arts tradition in undergraduate education is a cornerstone of the curriculum in a comprehensive American university, as their catalogues will attest. As a Swede, Linnaeus had no hope of fostering colonies in a political sense. He did, however, encourage his peripatetic students to bring back live plant specimens to Sweden in the hope of growing them commercially at home (Koerner 1996), a goal that failed in Sweden's dark winters.

today in geography's research-based lines of descent historiography, but it is difficult to argue against the value of intellectual enrichment in the artistic creativity, environmentalism, or ecotourism which it fostered. In short, there may be something rather threatening in what the outlook of a Cumming, North, or Guest represents to the professionalized middle-class natural science and geographic establishment, both today and during the Victorian period.

Did our three naturalists exhibit a kind of "women's knowledge"—not as essentialized but as reflective of their ethnicity, family status, and class, which in turn permitted them to pursue their own interests in the natural world and in travel? There were feminine aspects to their practices, such as Cumming's and Guest's acceptance of chivalrous males who picked their flowers or carried their belongings. Although none of the women considered themselves to be feminists, it is hard not to read a certain amount of personal emancipation and the desire to be taken seriously in their texts. This is not to cast Guest, Cumming, or North as heroines, however: their Victorian prejudices against poorer classes and people of color offend today's sensitivities. Perhaps it is best to interpret their gendered knowledges as in a state of negotiation, as when Cumming paints heroic landscapes but demurely refers to her "poor little paint box," or when North speaks out against male lumbering practices: from a safe distance.

If much of Victorian women's natural history writing seems boring or forgettable today, it must be remembered that they hold no monopoly over boring or forgettable publications, whether written as natural science or nature studies and within or outside of the academy. For one thing, most readers today will have lost the educated Victorian's facility with a range of nineteenth-century literary and scientific source materials, so that simultaneous allusions to poets and botanists that might have thrilled a Victorian reader have lost their richness of meaning today. We need not simply add in Great Women to a Great Men tradition of naturalist historiography, in any event (Shteir 1987, 33). Rather, we should become cognizant of the ways in which smaller lives and lesser figures explored and utilized the intellectual developments of their period and in some ways foreshadowed ours.

↘ 5 ↙

Surveying Britain's Informal Empire

Rose Kingsley's 1872 Reconnaissance
for the Mexican National Railway

The cry which is now heard throughout the length and breadth of
the country is, "Give us peace and railroads. By the first, we gain
security for the development of our noble country. By the latter we
render that peace more secure, by the increase of power which would
be given to the existing government; and further, they would give us
a ready market for the increased production of our land."

— Rose Kingsley, *South by West or Winter in the
Rocky Mountains and Spring in Mexico* (1874, 411)

MARY KINGSLEY'S LESS-FAMOUS older cousin Rose Kingsley[1] traveled
to Mexico in 1872 as part of a reconnaissance team for the Mexican
National Railway, headed by the American railroad promoter William J.
Palmer. Kingsley detailed her participation in this trip in her travelogue,
South by West or Winter in the Rocky Mountains and Spring in Mexico

1. *South by West* is divided roughly in half between the United States portion of Kingsley's journey (primarily Colorado) and the portion of her travels in Mexico. I discuss only
her travels in Mexico in this chapter. Rose's younger cousin Mary Kingsley became the
popular Victorian traveler best known for her two books about colonial Africa: *Travels in
West Africa* (1897) and *West African Studies* (1899). According to McEwan, the cousins
were "quite close by all accounts" (personal correspondences, May 1993 and May 1998).

(1874). The lasting impact of such reconnaissance trips cannot be over-stated. Six hundred forty kilometers of Mexican railroad had been com-pleted under the governments of Maximilian, Juárez, and Lerdo (spanning the years 1862–1876), consisting almost exclusively of the British-owned Mexican Railway between Mexico City and Veracruz. During the Díaz years (1876–1911) following Kingsley's travels, 20,000 kilometers of rail-way were added, through the native political elite's support for reconnais-sance missions such as Palmer's and through financing by U.S., British, and Dutch entrepreneurs (Sinkin 1979, 174; Coatsworth 1981, 35–41; Bazant 1977, 111–113).

Throughout *South by West* Kingsley made many references to Mexi-co's need for a railroad, as well as the need for opening a trade route from Mexico to the United States. As summarized in the above epigraph, King-sley valorized her journey by claiming that the railroad would bring peace to the country, saving Mexico from its two main problems—the "inertia of the people" and political disturbances. Contact with other nationali-ties through the railway would "stimulate the Mexican to action" and the country could thus "regenerate" itself (1874, 189, 192, 249, 409–11).

What follows is my reading of Rose Kingsley's account of her partici-pation in the development of the Mexican National Railway. It is first an effort to draw attention to Britain's "informal empire" in Mexico and to situate Kingsley as part of the British and American capitalist vanguard there. This requires acknowledging the structure of capitalist develop-ment abroad and its implications for women's travel and the production of imperial travel writing. My second goal for this chapter is to explore ways in which Rose Kingsley's writing about Mexico engaged the narra-tive rhetorics of capitalist development by inscribing herself in the text as both a bourgeois rational capitalist and a genteel, English lady.

Little scholarly attention on imperial discourse and representation has been paid to nineteenth-century British expansionism in Mexico. Although a few scholars have taken up critical studies of mid- to late- nineteenth-century British travel writings about the countries of South America (Pratt 1992; K. Jones 1986, 195–211), similar efforts (in English) do not address British travel writing about Mexico during the same period. The cultural theorist Robert Young asserts that in Britain, work on Latin America tends to function distinctly from much of colonial discourse analysis largely because it was not an area where the English have played any great historical role. Therefore, according to Young, it tends to remain the preserve of Latin Americanists within Hispanic studies (1995, 165).

Yet, nineteenth-century Latin America was part of Britain's informal empire, a relationship greatly stimulated by independence movements that ended the Spanish mercantilist system (J. Smith 1979; R. Miller 1993; Johnston 1992). Latin America became a major field for British financial investments and the recipient of large quantities of Britain's cheap manufactured goods, much of it from the unofficial black market. Latin America, in turn, became a supply field of raw materials and foodstuffs to Britain. British investments gained momentum in the second half of the century in the form of loans to build railways and roads, modernize ports and mines, and develop new industries. Thus, British companies with investments in Latin America burgeoned suddenly on the London Stock Exchange. In Mexico, British interests initially centered on revitalizing the mines abandoned during independence (Sinkin 1979, 15); gold and silver exports accounted for 90 percent of the exchange for manufactured goods. British investors also played an instrumental role in establishing Mexican banking, textiles, manufacturing, and railroad transportation. Financiers such as the London Bank dominated the commercial houses with remarkable impact. Opening its first branch in Mexico City in 1864, the London Bank introduced the circulation of bank notes in Mexico (Bazant 1977, 87).

British travel to Mexico and travel writing about Mexico was largely stimulated by investment opportunities in mining in the early part of the nineteenth century, followed by the commercial interests noted above, especially the building of the Mexican rail lines. Much of the British travel literature throughout the century reads as advance scouting for these capital interests. A search through catalogs of British travel texts on Mexico during the period reveals a significant number of titles in English. These accounts attest to the diplomatic, military, and especially the commercial presence of the British in Mexico after independence. These include

Colonel Bourne's *Notes on the State of Sonora and Sinaloa* (1825); George Francis Lyon's *Residence in Mexico, 1826: Diary of a Tour with a Stay in the Republic of Mexico* (1926); Sir Henry George Ward's (the first British ambassador to independent Mexico) *Mexico in 1827* (1928); and George F. Ruxton's *Adventures in Mexico* (1846). Perhaps the best known of early British women's published travel accounts of Mexico is Frances Erskine Calderon de la Barca's classic *Life in Mexico, During a Residence of Two Years in that Country* (1843). Calderon was the Scottish wife of the first Spanish ambassador to Mexico, a woman whom Rose Kingsley quoted on Spanish colonial history. Lady Emmeline Stuart Wortley and her twelve-year-old daughter Victoria also wrote separate accounts of Mexico during the mid–nineteenth century, in *Travels in the United States, North America, Caribbean, and Peru during 1849 and 1850* (Wortley 1851), and *A Young Traveller's Journal of a Tour in North and South America During the Year 1850* (Welby 1852). When the railroad lines made the western and southwestern portions of the United States more accessible to foreign travelers, Mexico was also added to the itineraries of many Britishers on grand tours of North America later in the century. These include Lady Winefred Howard of Glossop (1897), Mrs. E. H. Carbutt (1889), and Rose Kingsley (1874). A published account of an Englishwoman in Guanajuato in the late nineteenth century can also be found in Annie Poole's *Mexicans at Home in the Interior* (1884). Clearly British investors and industrialists made significant "contributions" toward the management of Mexican resources and its national economy. Thus, I would call attention to the need to expand our interpretations of "British colonial discourses" into the arena of the informal, noncolonized territories of the empire, referring instead to such discourses and rhetorics as imperialist or neoimperialist.

Situating Kingsley's *South by West*

Over her lifetime, Rose Kingsley would write books on French art, rose cultivation, and English history. Her best known work, *The Order of St. John of Jerusalem (Past and Present)*, published in 1918, is a history of Malta in the Middle Ages. At a much earlier stage in her writing career, however, she narrated personal experiences in the travelogue *South by West*. Kingsley had come to North America in the autumn of 1871, unmarried and twenty-six years old, accompanying the Dean of Chester as a representative of the Episcopal Church of England to a convention in Baltimore. Her father, the Reverend Charles Kingsley, was an accomplished English novelist and social commentator, among other things.[2] *South by West,* written as letters—probably to her father and mother—and as journal entries, began after the convention when Rose rode the transcontinental railroad across the United States to visit her brother Maurice who worked as secretary for the Denver and Rio Grande Railway in Colorado Springs, Colorado (see chapter 3; Athearn 1962, 194). During her four-month stay in Colorado, Rose helped Maurice keep books for the company, writing out agreements for lots and memberships.

While in Colorado, Rose was invited to join her friends, whom she referred to as "General and Mrs. P," on the General's important business in Mexico.[3] The general was the U.S. railroad entrepreneur William Jackson Palmer, founder of the Denver and Rio Grande and the Mexican National Railway companies (Pletcher 1958, 47–50). The business involved a reconnaissance trip through Mexico for the Mexican National Railway. In March 1872 the threesome traveled by steamship from San Francisco to Manzanillo, on the Pacific Coast of Mexico, and then crossed the width of central Mexico to Veracruz on the Gulf of Mexico. From Manzanillo, they traveled by stagecoach through Colima, Guadalajara, Querétaro, and Mexico City, and then traveled by train from Mexico City to Veracruz. Her brother,

2. Charles Kingsley was chaplain to Queen Victoria (1859), professor of modern history at Cambridge (1860–69), and canon of Westminster (1837). He was one of England's first churchmen to support Darwin's theories and to seek reconciliation between modern science and Christian doctrine. As such, he was known for his "Christian progressivism" through social programs such as improved education and sanitation. Widely read in England, Kingsley's 1863 novel *Water Babies* was inspired by his thoughts on evolution. He also wrote *Westward Ho!* (published in 1855), and *American Notes: Letters from a Lecture Tour* (reprinted in 1958).

3. Although General Palmer was associated with the railway, Mrs. P. had started a school in Colorado for colonialists' children. Rose apparently already knew the couple before meeting them in Colorado. Rose made many references to visiting Palmer's acclaimed home in Glen Eyrie, near Colorado Springs, and she lived in accommodations provided by the Denver and Rio Grande Railway Company during her stay in Colorado.

Maurice, and a party of engineers took the overland route from the United States to explore the more northern portions of the proposed rail route and eventually met up with Rose's party in Querétaro and Mexico City.

As head of Kingsley's expedition, General Palmer's American and British connections made his, and therefore Rose's, journey an especially blended version of an advance guard for American and British capital in Mexico. Palmer was an American educated in England. He learned about narrow gauge railway technology in England from the engineer George Stevenson, and, after an apprenticeship with the Pennsylvania railroad, became the first to build a railroad using that technology in the United States. Being well adapted to the mountain terrain of Colorado, the technology proved particularly appropriate for the Denver and Rio Grande Railway (Beebe and Clegg 1958).[4]

Like the Denver and Rio Grande, the Mexican National Railway (*Ferrocarril Nacional Mexicano*) was Palmer's initiative but largely funded by British, American, and Dutch capital. The relationship between Britain and the United States, through Palmer and his associates, was thus as international collaborators in the capitalist development of Mexico. The Mexican National Railway was initially paid for by stocks and bonds issued by London firms and later assisted by Mexican subsidies (Pletcher 1958, 47). British capital had also been used to fund the first Mexican railroad, from Mexico to Veracruz. During the "Restored Republic" of President Juárez, discussed below, the British had difficulties in completing the Mexico City–Veracruz line, due to Mexico's uneasy diplomatic relations with countries that aided in the French intervention of the 1860s.

Nevertheless, Juárez was anxious for the railroad to be completed, and he actively sought funds and congressional approval for the completion of

---

4. Colorado was home to many wealthy British health seekers and investors, titled remittance men, and retired colonels, and with the help of them, Palmer's million-dollar bond issue to inaugurate his Colorado railroad succeeded with $700,000 from England and $300,000 from a construction company in his native Philadelphia. His Denver and Rio Grande Railway opened for business in 1871, and was eventually extended from Denver to Ogden, Utah, in 1884. As Beebe and Clegg (1958) assert, Palmer had admiration for all things English, to the extent that his Colorado Springs home, which Rose Kingsley visited many times, was modeled after the home of the Duke of Marlborough.

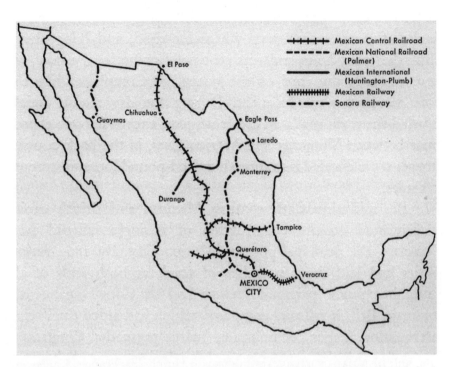

12. Northern railroad lines in operation about 1895. Reprinted from David M. Pletcher, *Rails, Mines, and Progress: Seven American Promoters in Mexico, 1867–1911*, 24. Copyright © 1958 by American History Association. Used by permission of the publisher, Cornell University Press.

the line by 1873. Between 1867 and 1873 a large contingent of American railroad promoters, including Palmer, appeared on the Mexican scene, petitioning Congress for concessions to build rail lines, and particularly those connecting the United States and Mexico City. Palmer's ambition was to build a railroad connecting Denver to Mexico City via El Paso, Texas, and a branch line from the main line at Acambara to Guadalajara, Colima, and the Pacific seaport of Manzanillo.

With his expedition completed in May 1872, Palmer left Mexico having secured promises for the first 300 kilometers of the Mexican National Railway. After much negotiation, Palmer's company eventually won only a concession to build a line from Mexico City to Laredo, Texas in 1880. The railroad was opened for business in 1888 (Pletcher 1958, 48; Best 1968).

Palmer's 1,287 kilometer (800 mile) line represented the shortest route from the Mexican capital to the United States border. Mexico eventually purchased the line in 1908.

Mexican Travel and "Gendered Imperialism"

Describing her Mexican travels, Kingsley repeated several topics treated in the Colorado portion of her book (see chapter 3). She wrote about Mexican domestic life and Mexican society—especially of the wealthy landowners who hosted her party at haciendas stretching from Manzanillo to Mexico City. The contemporary political situation also provided an important theme as she wrote of both the Juárez regime and the "rebellious" *pronunciatos* who threatened attack of the stage coaches she was riding. She also devoted much attention to what she envisioned as the future economic prosperity of the country as it was linked to the development of the railway. *South by West* gained authority through several forms of support. Kingsley illustrated the text with her own drawings and interspersed her narrative with long quotations by other travelers, observers, and historians such as Alexander von Humboldt, Frances Calderon del la Barca, and William H. Prescott. Her father wrote the book's preface and brother, Maurice, lent further credentials by contributing an entire chapter to the book, "A Reconnaissance in the Southern Tierra Caliente" (1874, 357–81).

Mary Louise Pratt (1992), Jean Franco (1989), and others have identified a particular narrative category, "capitalist vanguard writing," in colonial and postcolonial Latin America.[5] As Pratt argues: "Far from mystifying European expansionist designs in their writings, the capitalist

---

5. Pratt focuses here on European travel literature about South America in the early decades of the nineteenth century. Alexander von Humboldt's *Political Essays on Mexico*, though, produced during his year there in 1803–1804, does not fit the narrative conventions of capital vanguardism. Pratt reports that von Humboldt spent most of his time in Mexico City, among scholars and in libraries and among scientific communities, the outcome of which was a representation of Mexico as ahistorical, cultivated antiquity, and as both primal culture and nature.

vanguard tended to thematize them—indeed, consecrate them." Pratt contends that Spanish American society itself was mainly encoded as a logistical obstacle to the forward movement of the Europeans, with the journey of the capitalist-vanguard traveler-writer allegorizing the lust for progress (1992, 131–36, 146–55; quote from 148).

Although it is important to recognize both the discursive and material constraints on the production of women's texts and the unique kinds of geographical knowledges they produced, it is equally important not to fall into essentialized categorizations about women travelers' motivations, interests, and travel experiences. "British women travelers" are as diverse as the destinations of their travels, even if they were similarly subordinated in patriarchal hierarchies of power. Moreover, as Stoler and others argue, subjectivities of colonizing bourgeois Europeans were influenced by the manner in which they came in contact with people in the colonies (1995, 98–116; Ashcroft, Griffiths, and Tiffen 1995; Mohanty 1988, 65–88). In that sense, the European subject-author emerged only through engagement with specific peoples in specific material circumstances. Below, I draw attention to a number of ways that locations through which Kingsley traveled were gendered, classed, and racialized. This worked against her constructing a singular, collective "Mexican" identity in her text. Rather, she produced a particular gendered and classed version of British imperialistic ideologies and modes of thought while in Mexico, which in the villages, on rural roads, and in homes of wealthy landowners were made and played out in different ways, producing multiple, complex others in her text.

Though so much of Rose Kingsley's rhetoric has all the markings of masculinist capitalist vanguardism—she frequently engaged the tropes of progress, efficiency, authority, and paternalism—what comprised the contact zones of her travels were materially and discursively different from those of General Palmer, Maurice Kingsley, and the other men and women with whom she associated in Mexico. Thus, a reading of her text helps draw out the complex ways in which the discourses of imperialism, in its many guises, chronicled and facilitated foreign entrepreneurial missions in nineteenth-century Mexico.

Reconnaissance for the Mexican National Railroad

Statistical Reconnaissance

Throughout her Mexican travels, but primarily during her stagecoach journey between Manzanillo and Mexico City, Kingsley reported extensively on the mineral, agricultural, industrial, and labor resources of the region and of particular haciendas she visited. She listed and described a range of economic activities. These included the exports of Manzanillo (coffee, rice, and wood); the goods entering Mexico City by canal; the annual yield of salt works near Colima; soap manufacture in Zapotlán; pottery making in Guadalajara; the workings of a sugar plantation in San Marcos; cotton and flour mills—the "very poetry of manufacturing," using machinery from England, of course—near Querétaro and other places; wheat growing near Querétaro; and the output of pulque plantations west of Mexico City (1874, 188–92, 204–14, 222, 241–45, 268–69, 295, 384).

Kingsley also assessed the potential outputs of the land, including the potential for wine making in the Lerma Valley; the cost of land in comparison to potentially irrigated fields of sugar and cotton near Colima; and the value of irrigation near Guadalajara (1874, 195, 209, 251, 258, 279). Near Colima she stopped to consider the possibilities of preempting a vein of white marble, which was "quite unnoticed" by the Mexicans (1874, 195). Kingsley ended her book with a chapter entitled "Mexico and Its Resources," which described the topography and climate of the three zones of Mexico, their mineral and agricultural products, costs of labor and land, and estimates of the value of mines awaiting development (1874, 399–411). (Kingsley would have gone to Querétaro and Guanajuato as important mining centers, although her travels took place after the most prodigious mining stage of these areas.)

Kingsley's narration in these passages captured the essence of capital control. She gained legitimacy as a woman writing and traveling within the context of British and North American patriarchal social relations by positioning herself as an informed, authoritative, and patrician holder of such statistical, managerial, and scientific knowledge. Kingsley adopted an objective mode in her presentation of the survey and measurement results. She positioned herself as an authoritative source of information and presented data as simple fact or truth rather than as subjective observation. Many of her descriptions of Mexico appeared in what seemed to be deliberate and self-consciously antiaesthetic, pragmatic, and economistic language, characterized by a modernizing "industrial reverie" (Pratt 1992, 149). Even though she never explicitly disclosed the larger purpose of her travels or explained whether she was hired by Palmer or took the trip at her own initiative, she clearly situated herself as an indispensable member of the reconnaissance team. Kingsley portrayed her duties along the route as essential to the success of the venture. "My special department," she wrote, "is to keep notes at each rise or halting place, of the elevation from the two barometers; besides general notes, as all the others do, of the produce and trade of each place we pass." Throughout the text Kingsley additionally counted the number of mules and wagons they passed, and the contents and quantities of goods being moved by them (1874, 254, 284, 215).

The Politics of Prosperity

As evidenced in the epigraph to this chapter, on the last page of her narrative Rose Kingsley quoted (nonspecific) Mexicans who cried "throughout the length and breadth of the country" to "give us peace and railroads." She claimed that the railroad would save the country from its two biggest problems—the inertia of the people and political disturbances. Kingsley's father, in the preface to the volume, echoed this sentiment, writing:

> The time for developing the vast resources of th[e] country is surely close at hand. It possesses every earthly gift, save—for the present at least the power of using them. . . . We must hope that her government will so conduct itself toward foreign statesmen as to re-enter honorably the comity of Nations; and toward foreign capitalists, so as to attract the wealth— American, Dutch, and English—which is ready to flow into and fertilize and pacify the whole country. . . . [I hope that] ruffianism. . . . retreats before that most potent of civilizers, the railroad, as it pours in, from the distant regions of the old States, a perpetual reinforcement of the good, to drive the bad further and further into yet more desolate wilderness. (1874, vii–ix)

Both daughter and father contended that massive economic development of the country would stabilize Mexico's turbulent political scene, which at the same time was largely the product of liberal reforms advocated by President Benito Juárez. Kingsley's travels in 1871–1872 occurred during the time of the "Restored Republic" (1867–1876), when attempts to establish the republican, liberal tenets of the 1857 constitution were once again resumed after the fail of Maximilian in 1867. Juárez's reforms attacked the Catholic Church, the military, the power of the economic guilds, and Indian communities. With the seizure of both church property and Indian communal lands, his regime anticipated the formation of a new class of yeoman farmers (Sinkin 1979, 25, 170). However, the liberal leaders themselves and the large landowners were the only ones who could afford to buy the newly confiscated land. This period was thus marked by a large increase in the growth of the haciendas and the centralization of power in the hands of landowners and a small group of merchants and professionals. In central Mexico, where Kingsley traveled, a well-defined conflict arose between hacienda owners, rancheros (small farmers) and village ejido, or Indian communal property holders. Hacienda owners bought out Indian lands and were supported by the power of judgeships in boundary disputes (Franco 1989; Calvert 1973; Sinkin 1979; Bazant 1977).

Within this political climate, the patriarchal and influential voice of Charles Kingsley in the preface to the volume lent validity and legitimacy to the views of his daughter. He explicitly gender-coded Mexico as feminine and capital as masculine (to "fertilize and pacify"), a trope frequently employed in the justification of British imperial expansionism, particularly in the colonies where passive and active principles came to stand for national or racial difference itself (Young 1995, 159–182). Charles's liberal position on social and economic progress leading from natural selection helps bring into focus his statements on the responsibilities of western specialists in the civilizing of Mexico. Associating peace with railroads demonstrated the civilizing mission of British and American capital in its full rhetorical bloom: increased commercialization would bring about nothing less than political stability of the governing party.

Rose's rhetoric as she traveled amid the political unrest must be understood within the context of the immediate justification that she and her fellow travelers sought for the development of the Mexican railroad, as well as the specific representations of Mexican society on which that development depended. Rose's statement that "everywhere as yet the idea of a railroad has been received with acclamation" was undoubtedly influenced by the wealthy Germans who hosted her in Guadalajara, as well as the political and military elite surrounding her (1874, 232), all of whom would have shared the aspirations of the capitalist vanguard.

Thus, Rose Kingsley's position on the development of Mexico's railroads and resources was undoubtedly as much influenced by the Mexican elite's attempts to consolidate their power and construct new hegemonies for themselves under the liberal reforms, as it was by the personal stake Kingsley's friends and family might have had in it. Rose herself, of course, as a woman, would not have had the legal, economic, or political rights to personally gain from such capitalist endeavors. Through her family's class membership, however, she would have been assured of the benefits accruing from them (Hall 1988, 94–107). This raises the question of who, then, Kingsley came to encode as "inert" and in need of European redemption. To answer this it is necessary to take a closer look at the social relations inherent in many contact zones of Kingsley's travels. In the remainder of this chapter, I explore how Kingsley's "politics of difference" was produced out of encounters with heterogeneous numbers of Mexican people, encounters that ultimately enabled her to deploy the message that the construction of the railroad was necessary to save Mexico from its political maelstrom.

Gendered and Racialized Divisions of Labor

Rose Kingsley often claimed that Mexicans in general suffered from inertia and were apathetic and politically troubled. The worn stereotypes she adopted served to classify Mexicans as logistical obstacles to the forward movement of European and American capitalists in Mexico (1874, 409–41). Yet, Kingsley encountered and wrote about diverse individuals and groups of Mexicans during her travels, including governmental dignitaries, political "rebels," wealthy landowners, field and factory workers, Catholic priests, rural Indians, tradespeople, inn keepers, servants, and mule drivers. She related conversations with some of her hosts and lengthily quoted others. Thus, the voices of many people she described—unnamed villagers, workers, and beggars—remained silent in her text. Yet certain stereotypes common in her travel narrative that I discuss below were undermined by a distinct range of representations of Mexican people in highly gendered, classed, and racialized ways that emerged out of different social-spatial contexts.

Rose Kingsley often attributed Mexico's underdevelopment to the laziness and incompetence of its people. "In Mexico," she said, "people always seem to have time" (1874, 315, 401–2). As Skeels notes, the image of Mexicans as dirty, lazy, dishonest, lecherous, and politically unstable was a "familiar refrain in American images of its southern neighbor" in the early decades of the twentieth century, constructed as the negative half of the United States/Mexico opposition (Skeels 1993, 169; also see C. Robinson 1977). Such rhetoric about the lower classes was also common, of course, among the nineteenth-century bourgeois who employed the principles of social Darwinism to serve the interests of British empire building. In this perspective, social stratification generally arose out of inherited genetic qualities (Callaway 1987; Jones 1980).[6] However, Kingsley represented only particular groups of Mexicans as lazy and incompetent: mestizo and Indian males of the "lower orders." Traveling from 20 March to 1 May 1872, through the mountains, canyons, and valleys between Manzanillo and Mexico City, Kingsley and her party stopped at many small villages and haciendas to eat, change mules, and sleep for the night. In many of the villages, Kingsley described groups of men resting and gossiping under trees. She concluded that the men of Mexico, especially the ones "more Indian than Spanish," were inefficient in their agricultural practices and lazy in general. She asserted that "rather than rid their country of robbers they laze around" (1874, 185, 199, 234).

Kingsley further portrayed servants, mule drivers, guards, and other workers throughout the journey as untrustworthy, "intensely stupid,"

6. This intersected with Victorian patriarchy, which postulated that women's biological functions limited their intellectual ones, as well as scientific racism, which inferred social and moral attributes from physical traits such as cranial capacity, skin color, and facial features. The "white man's burden" of imperialism found literary expression in the works of many authors of the day, including those of Charles Kingsley.

and incompetent. She claimed that one driver, while "hideously moaning," took special pleasure in driving over stumps just to annoy passengers (1874, 189, 191–92, 206–8). She likewise depicted the guards who accompanied their stagecoaches as untrustworthy and cruel. After witnessing their gratuitous shooting of a dog, Kingsley declared that she was more afraid of her guards than the robbers from whom they supposedly were protecting her (1874, 273–74). Though male servants were also depicted as intensely stupid people who contrived to misunderstand foreigners, Kingsley had more positive things to say about servants who gave her gifts or who displayed courteous and chivalrous behavior. "I really believe," she said of one "old soldier of the lower orders," that "it is a pleasure to them to be asked to do one any little favour" (1874, 212–13, 296, 323, 355). She portrayed mill and factory workers at haciendas along the route as beasts of burden. They were happy, healthy, and hard-working only if the owners "kept an eye on them" (1874, 204, 270).

These excerpts point to a number of social sites through which Kingsley and the Mexican men in the villages clashed along the lines of gender, class, and racial difference. Her rhetoric reinforced the superiority of one type of (white) hegemonic masculinity defined by the strictures of manliness, chivalry, rationality, exploitation, and efficient use of resources. Kingsley received indications of potential civilization, such as servants' chivalry, appreciatively. As Pratt observes, the capitalist vanguard's task was to ideologically "invent" Latin America as backward and neglected and encode its noncapitalist physical and cultural landscapes and societies as manifestly in need of the rationalized exploitation that Europeans bring. Characteristics of laziness, incompetence, stupidity, and untrustworthiness, then, ensured the need of foreign intervention to turn village men (particularly those "more Indian than Spanish") into productive commercial workers. Social evolution was possible as long as the "missionary" work of capitalism was allowed to progress unimpeded.

Kingsley's depictions of men of the rural villages can also be understood as "distortions" of larger political-economic changes taking place in Mexico at the time of her trip. Assertions that the men would "laze around" rather than rid their country of robbers must be viewed in relation to both Kingsley's anti-Catholic politics and inattention to the effects of liberal reforms. Those reforms introduced under the regime of President Juárez greatly reduced the land holdings of small farmers and Indians as well as the Catholic Church. At the beginning of her narrative, Kingsley explained that her party took the particular route they did because "for various reasons it must be reconnoitered." However, "the only fear for this route," she continued, was that "we may be troubled by bands of robbers on the road" (1874, 171). The "robbers," many of whom were organized under Porfirio Díaz (who had just lost the election to Juárez in 1871 but would replace him in 1876), were the *pronunciatos,* men who "pronounced against" the government and its reforms (1874, 302). As Sinkin (1979, 20) and Hobsbawm (1969) point out, many of these "bandits," "robbers," and "rebels" would likely have been Indian and mestizo men who left their villages to fight displacement by the liberal reforms.

Throughout her Mexican travels Kingsley argued that the country was "overrun with guerrilla bands" who were levying taxes on innocent hacienda owners and confiscating food and goods if they did not pay. She claimed that the rebels used politics simply as an excuse for robbery (1874, 247, 229). She traveled amid much of the fighting, and since stagecoaches were often the targets of attacks, she focused a good deal of attention on her party's preparations for such attacks, the numbers of guards employed, the local political situations in areas through which they passed, and actual or potential encounters with "robbers." She reported that the revolutionists were giving some trouble between Colima and Guadalajara and had cut the telegraph lines there.[7] Kingsley also recorded the number of arms and guards that constituted her own traveling party, noting for instance that twenty-eight guards accompanied them to Guadalajara (1874, 194, 206, 217–18, 224, 228–29). She personally encountered a group of *pronunciatos* only once. Claiming her party had been watched since the coast, Kingsley described a confrontation that came near Seyula. These men, "a despicable set of ruffians, in any kind of dress over military trousers, wretchedly

---

7. Her entries also referred to an attack on Colima the day after she left; that "the revolution had broken out" near Querétaro; that *pronunciatos* were advancing from all sides at Zapotlán; and, that government troops were marching through Seyula and from the west.

armed with old muzzle-loading carbines, and all drunk" confiscated all of her party's rifles (1874, 224–26).

Kingsley's encounter with this band further illustrates the links between her gender and class politics. She juxtaposed a range of representations of these men, highlighting their leader's chivalrousness and civility but referring to his underlings as a "despicable set of ruffians" who were all drunk. Kingsley referred to the leader as major, quoted him as asking for permission to search their coach for arms, and described how he was disarmingly "embarrassed" to be pilfering their rifles. She noted that he magnanimously promised to accompany their coach to his superior's headquarters to ask for the rifles back (they were not returned). Only the leader's chivalrous, cultivated (albeit romanticized) manhood appears equal to Kingsley's discerning, genteel Englishness. This represents a rhetorical move that can best be understood as favorably positioning Kingsley and other capitalist vanguards with the future regimes of power under which Palmer's railroad would actually be built. It was men such as the major in this scene who were to become the heirs of foreign investments in the railroad when Díaz finally took power in 1876. Foreign and Mexican capital together met the nationalistic agenda of the power elite with the "ruffian" rebels only serving to obstruct progress.

Kingsley's discursive alignment with Juárez's reforms and vehement anti-Catholicism also likely grew out of her Protestant background and participation in the affairs of the Anglican Church. The act of privatizing Catholic Church and corporate property would ultimately increase foreign commerce in Mexico. Thus, Kingsley's Protestant mission and her capitalistic one converge in the act of foreign salvation of Mexico, something about which Charles Kingsley and many other influential social commentators of the time had much to say (Weber 1996).[8]

---

8. In Mexico, Rose met only one Catholic priest she admired, a German who had been Maximilian's confessor (1874, 297), but the rest were vain (1874, 336); engaged mindlessly in revolting practices such as confession (1874, 236); and were criminals, themselves fighting against the liberal reforms, such as in Penjamo (1874, 255). She reported that they scowled at her on numerous occasions for her own religious orientation (1874, 290, 329); were thieves who stole the common people's money for the building of useless buildings,

Depictions of lazy or untrustworthy men of the rural villages must also be considered within the larger Victorian context of relations between the sexes. She often portrayed women of the rural villages in a more positive light than the men. While the women were engaged in productive work, the men "lazed about." Village women typically appear in Kingsley's text preparing and serving meals, making textiles or pottery, picking garden vegetables, or accomplishing a wide variety of other domestic tasks (1874, 187–88, 248, 255, 279). Kingsley reported on the contents, quality, and size of practically every meal she ate and every bed she slept in during her journey. Her focus on food and accommodations and the women who were responsible for them elicited both complimentary and derogatory responses. She described simple meals of beans and tortillas as excellent and the Mexican chocolate and coffee as delicious yet recalled crying over one particularly wretched meal and becoming ill from some eggs fried in candle grease (1874, 187–93, 216, 248–56).

Kingsley's attention to domestic matters can be easily understood as stemming from women's material and discursive positioning that gave them legitimate access to insights centered in the female experience of the home, family, manners and fashions (see chapters 2 and 3). In addition, her recurring obsession with cleanliness circulated widely among nineteenth-century bourgeois Europeans and represented a "God-given sign of Britain's evolutionary superiority" (McClintock 1995, 207–14). The rhetoric of domestic cleanliness would find an easy outlet in the work of women writers such as Rose Kingsley whose own racial and national rankings measured progress and civilization at least partly within the domestic realm.

Furthermore, Kingsley's constructions of Mexican village women's productive labor juxtaposed to men's idleness must be viewed in relation to its affront to the properly gendered division of labor within the bourgeois Victorian household. Earlier in her travelogue, Kingsley complained

---

while the people's huts were not fit for pigs (1874, 261, 304); and were frauds (1874, 300). Kingsley declared that the Virgin of Guadalupe was a "fraudulent," "disgusting," and "absurd" story. Rose's deep Anglican roots, anti-Catholicism, and Christian progressivism maps onto her father's work rather well.

13. *Woman Making Tortillas*. From Rose Kingsley, *South by West or Winter in the Rocky Mountains and Spring in Mexico* (London: W. Isbister and Co., 1874), 187. Reproduced courtesy of The Johns Hopkins University.

that the Indian women of Colorado seemed to be virtual slaves to their husbands. They appeared to perform all of the work of the tribe including the hauling of heavy loads while the men walked alongside them carrying no loads except their guns and bows (see chapter 6). Not comprehending that carrying the loads meant ownership of the dwelling and its contents and therefore power and prestige to the Ute women (Wishart 1995, 509–18; compare to Lerner 1986), Kingsley portrayed these women as an affront to the pious, protected, and domestic ideal of femininity embedded in

British Victorian patriarchal discourse. While bourgeois men were judged by their success at entering the public commercial sphere, the women proved the success of their men by becoming economically idle and therefore feminine (Hall 1988, 62–63).

Kingsley's comparison of Ute society to some transparent norm of civilized gender relations worked in a similar way to her discussions of Mexican villages. Though far from economically idle, the Mexican women were portrayed as perhaps less transgressive to bourgeois women's proper roles because their work was situated within the domestic realm. These Mexican women's labor compared to that of servants' in a bourgeois household. In contrast, both Ute and Mexican men were judged by Kingsley as economically and socially unproductive, thereby unable to approximate Western ideals of the civilized woman whose husband pays for maids. The voice of the capitalist vanguard thus became accessible to women traveling within an imperial context. The dual outcome for Kingsley was to inscribe herself in the text as a bourgeois rational capitalist through her implicit identification as a standard-bearing English lady.

This rhetorical maneuver, to measure the Mexican need for capital-improving modes of work based on the gendered division of labor, reversed itself when Kingsley described the wealthy landowners of the haciendas who hosted her from Manzanillo to Mexico City. Kingsley moved considerably within elite Mexican society throughout her journey, meeting and being hosted by wealthy landowners, political dignitaries such as the president, military men in high positions including Porfirio Díaz himself (1874, 183),[9] and professionals, including "intelligent" and "gentlemen-like" librarians and museum curators. These men of means, but especially the wealthy hacienda owners, received considerably different treatment in

---

9. On the ship from San Francisco to Manzanillo, Kingsley reported that she met "two Mexican gentlemen, who say they are merchants traveling for a house in Guadalajara" (1874, 183), one of whom appears in a footnote as Don Porfirio Díaz, "the leader of the Revolution." She said that the men asked to join their party as far as Colima, which was agreed to, since "two more armed men may be an advantage to our little party." Beyond reporting that the "Revolution . . . flamed up more fiercely than ever" upon Díaz's return to Mexico, Kingsley made no further mention of either of the two men.

the text than the men of the lower classes, disrupting a single stereotyped version of "Mexican people" in the text. Because these men productively maximized the potential of capital accumulation and thus shared the ideals of the American and British capitalist vanguard—partly, one would expect, by forming partnerships with entrepreneurs such as William Palmer—they received praise and affirmation from Kingsley.

She referred to Señor Don Juan F. H. in Colima, owner of a large house and fruit orchard, as "dear old Don Juan" who showed her much kindness and hospitality and "who really seem[ed] to think no trouble too great if it add[ed] to his guests' enjoyment" (1874, 197, 203). Staying at the home of the wealthy landowner Don Ignacio Lagos, west of Colima, Kingsley reported:

> Don Ignacio gave us plenty of information about the country and its products. He owns a large tract of land; and grows sugar, coffee, and rice on it. His handsome wife showed us after breakfast some of her lacework and embroidery, for which the women in this State are famous . . . [it is] much like Greek lace worthy of French work. (1874, 192–94)

Another of her hosts, Don Mauricio G., owner of the large San Marcos sugar plantation, showed flawless civility and kindness. Kingsley explained that the plantation covered 22,000 acres, employed 300 people in the sugarworks and in the fields, and produced 3,000 barrels of rum and 550,000 pounds of sugar each year (1874, 212–13, 252, 307). The lives of such men and their families closely approximated the ideal Anglo-European bourgeois order. As the men accumulated more capital, their wives became increasingly removed from the domestic tasks which servants performed. Kingsley identifies with Don Ignacios and Don Mauricio's wives and daughters who, like her, had servants to fulfill domestic duties, thus affording them time for more leisured-class work such as embroidery, lace making, or writing travel books.

Kingsley praised these men and women not only for their refined hospitality, which increased leisure time allowed, but also for their industry and resourcefulness. Yet she also criticized Mexican men of the lower classes for their backwardness, indolence, and failure to properly exploit resources. Kingsley's rhetoric obviously highlighted the similar class interests she shared with many of the bourgeois Mexican men and women, a social group that she did not distinguish by racial difference in her writings. While a small number of them were likely Spanish "Creole," by the middle of the nineteenth century a sizable mestizo population existed among the educated, landowning elite and political leaders (Franco 1989, 93; Sinkin 1979, 19–20). President Juárez himself was Indian. Racial difference was therefore defined by class and geographical difference for Kingsley. Whereas she described the racial makeup and mixing of Spanish and Indian blood for the "idle" village men, she avoided mention of the racial makeup of the wealthy hacienda owners. This may be partly explained by the fact that in Spanish America, racial difference was almost always "washed out" by economic prowess. This might also be explained by Kingsley's apparent desire to reserve discussion of racial difference only for instances of commercial "failure" (Lavonne Poteet, personal correspondence, November–December 1998; Young 1995).

Conclusion

In this chapter I have drawn attention to a region of Britain's "informal empire" and the narrative rhetorics that sustained foreign capitalist intervention there. Rose Kingsley's imperial geography deployed the narrative rhetoric of American and British capital vanguards in Mexico that was constituted through particular expressions of class, gender, and racial difference. Rose Kingsley justified the need of foreign business intervention in Mexico through her pejorative representations of lower class lazy Mexican men and their hard-laboring female counterparts. To Kingsley, these men and women clearly did not meet the standards of proper gender relations found in bourgeois households which "proved" their capitalist productivity partly through women's idleness.

This chapter has drawn attention to how one member of an influential English family participated in and justified American and British imperial expansion in nineteenth-century Mexico. The lasting impact of such reconnaissance trips for the railroad should be acknowledged. Kingsley's rhetoric was in keeping with that of many Mexican political leaders of the time, who were interested in industrializing the country and attracting foreign wealth. These included leaders on either end of the political spectrum. President Porfirio Díaz asserted that the railway "played a great part in the peace of Mexico," and railroad building and industrialization were goals of his thirty-year dictatorial regime (Bazant 1977, 114). By 1908 Mexico acquired the rights to its railroads from British and American companies, with Díaz's *científicos*[10] regulating their operation in the hopes of keeping Mexico's control over its economy and resources at home while continuing to attract foreign capital (Coatsworth 1981, 186; Pletcher 1958, 14–15, 308; Bazant 1977, 107–8, 120–21; Cockcroft 1968, 17). Not incidentally though, the railroads were also instrumental in Díaz's eventual overthrow as they facilitated the Mexican Revolution that began in 1910 (Coatsworth 1974, 55–57).

Considering that the Mexican railroad network established by 1898 remains basically unchanged today (Bazant 1977, 111), one might reflect on how early U.S. and British investments in Mexican railroads helped set the stage for the uneven trade practices between the countries today, particularly between the United States and Mexico. Eighty-three percent of U.S. investments during Díaz's regime were in rails and mining, and the tonnage carried by Mexican railroads increased a hundredfold between 1873 and 1910. New links between cities and outlying areas were established, the shipping of raw materials to industries greatly expanded domestic markets for finished goods, and the opening of new agricultural lands greatly increased land values.

The United States played a dominant part in the rapid economic development of Mexico between 1867 and 1911, during which time it had secured more of Mexico's trade than all of the European nations together. The railroad links to the United States also enabled Mexican labor migrations northward, allowed easier U.S. and other foreign access to Mexican resources and goods, and consolidated U.S. and other foreign investment and landholdings in Mexico (Cockcroft 1968, 17; Bazant 1977, 87,111; Meyer and Sherman 1983, 444–45; Pletcher 1958, 1–5, 296–311; Calvert 1973, 61). British and American capitalist ventures such as the reconnoitering and building of the Mexican railroad helped facilitate what is today one of the most, if not the most, economically unequal border relationships on the face of the globe.

10. The *científicos* were a group of intellectuals influenced by Auguste Comte's positivist philosophy and its goals of modernization through capitalism and science.

⅞ 6 ⅝

British Women Travelers and Constructions of Racial Difference Across the Nineteenth-Century American West

AS PREVIOUS CHAPTERS have outlined, a particular nexus of British and American empire building coincided in the final decades of the nineteenth century on American land west of the Mississippi River. Much of what British visitors observed during their travels in the American West attested to America's own version of empire building. Encouraged by national expansionist politics and a military presence, Euro-American industrialists, land speculators, miners, settlers, and others rushed to occupy and control western lands, and travelers often described the situation of Native Americans dislocated by this process. With few exceptions, the last decades of the nineteenth century represented a nadir in the historical geography of most western Native Americans, as the U.S. government undertook their wholesale removal onto reservations. Most tribes' land bases were decimated, dependence on government payments and rations was inaugurated, and diseases such as tuberculosis and others caused by poverty ran rampant through their communities (White 1991; Wishart 1994; Berkhofer 1978).

In this chapter, I examine how a group of elite women travel writers wrote about western Native peoples, especially Native women, during encounters with them at sites along the western rail lines 1879–90. Encounters between

British women travelers and western Indians[1] became emblematic of a whole range of social-spatial relationships of domination, subordination, complicity, and resistance. Judgments about racial and gender difference in these texts can be traced to British Victorian colonial discourses, as well as to the social relations inherent in the multiple contact zones within which the encounters took place. Various representations of Native Americans appear in the texts, ranging from revulsion at Native savagery; to romanticization of the primitive but vanishing American; to moralistic, reform-minded concern for the abused "squaw" and her corollary, the Indian Princess; to a recognition of Native peoples' self-definition and self-determination.

In this chapter I explore the many ways in which the contexts for the production of the travel texts were racialized and gendered, and the multiple subjectivities of both women travelers and Native Americans that resulted. I outline particular tropes that were common in the travel narratives, focusing specifically on how these operated within the context of railway travel. I also consider how certain tropes were accessible to or exclusive of women travelers and their ideas of proper female conduct, even if a single gendered or racialized response to western Indians is by no means apparent. Multiple voices and subjectivities appear in these texts, both as authors and as subaltern others.

The twelve women (most already introduced in previous chapters) whose texts I examine in this chapter all discussed train travel and train stations throughout the West in their books. With narratives that generally followed the transect of the railroad, it is significant that the trip from Chicago to San Francisco by railroad would have stopped at approximately 250 stations along the way (Athearn 1962, 17). The women devoted varying amounts of attention to Native Americans in their texts, ranging from single quotations about isolated encounters at train stations or on streets, to abstract logical arguments on their social conditions. Train transportation itself was key to how travelers represented western Native peoples, because

1. Following David Wishart (1994, 1993), I use the term Indians interchangeably with Native Americans and indigenous or Native peoples throughout the chapter. I have noted tribal designations whenever they appear in the travelogues.

it was on the trains or at depots along the railroad routes that travelers and Native Americans most often encountered one another. And again, these meetings took place during what could be considered the worst years for many western Indian nations.

Situating the Contact Zones

Retaining Thomas Jefferson's vision of an empire of liberty comprised of agrarian farmers and traders, American expansionists as early as the 1840s argued that the American manifest destiny was to occupy the entire North American continent (White 1991, 61–84; Limerick 1987, 58, 175; H. Smith 1950). To make room for Euro-American settlers, beginning in the 1830s under the Andrew Jackson administration, the federal government undertook the forced removal of eastern Indians, the inhabitants of the "unpeopled continent." A permanent Indian Territory in the central and southern Great Plains was first envisioned (White 1991, 85–91; Limerick 1987, 191–96), but white encroachment, broken treaties, wars, and a host of inhumane atrocities made this idea short-lived. By the 1850s, Euro-American settlers pushed into this region as well, and the American government continued to sell traditional homelands for unconscionably small payments (Wishart 1994). Native Americans were restricted to smaller and smaller reservations, and in the western United States, even these were engulfed by land-hungry settlers.

Paternalistic reformers and U.S. government officials alike sought a more durable solution to the "Indian problem" after the slavery question was moved to the side of the national political agenda by the Civil War, and a new reservation policy emerged in the 1860s and 1870s. Although the reservation system essentially separated the races, official government discourse articulated it as a policy that would ensure assimilation. It involved attempts to transform indigenous peoples into Christianized farmers and housewives who possessed a concept of private property according to a European pattern. This private property would eventually, after the 1887 General Allotment (Dawes) Act, be imposed in the form of family allotments on reservations. Reservation lands were divided and allocated in (generally) 160-acre quarter sections to individual Indians, and any "surplus" lands were typically sold off. Allotments too were eventually sold (once the government's trust period was ended, or abridged), and the Native Americans' land base was decimated. Estimates are that the allotment process alone reduced Native American landholdings by two-thirds, beginning in 1881.[2] By the late 1870s, all Native peoples were effectively under American sovereignty. The survival of many tribes depended upon government payments from the sale or lease of land and on government rations (White 1991, 108–15). With the exception of some tribes in the Northwest, Southwest, and Oklahoma, by the end of the nineteenth century, most Indian nations could no longer feed or clothe themselves without federal aid.

Train Station Power Politics

The contact zones for nearly all of the encounters between British travelers and Native Americans were the many train depots along the railroad route from Chicago to Denver to Salt Lake City to San Francisco—public spaces in predominantly white settlements. Train stations were their own peculiar kind of contact zones, within which the social and spatial distance between travelers, vendors, onlookers, residents, servants, and others could be fleetingly diminished. Yet train stations themselves embodied imperial relations. They were environments where the spatial frameworks of indigenous peoples uniquely collided with those of both travelers and Euro-American settlers and that cultivated an idealized form of race relations between travelers and residents. The presence of poverty-stricken Native Americans at train stations symbolized the degradation suffered by masses of others, and in particular signaled the failure of the reservation system. Native peoples begging, performing feats of skill, or offering "peeps" at their babies for a nickel or dime at train stations (Athearn 1962, 126) provided ample evidence that federal Indian policies had produced

---

2. Limerick (1987, 198–99) reports that 138 million acres were in the possession of Native Americans in 1887, and that in the next forty-seven years, 60 million of those were declared surplus and sold to whites, and another 27 million left Indian possession through allotment and then as sales to whites. Richard White (1991, 115) notes that, between the years 1881 and 1900 alone, half of the remaining Indian land was lost, the number of acres dwindling from 155,632,312 to 77,865,373.

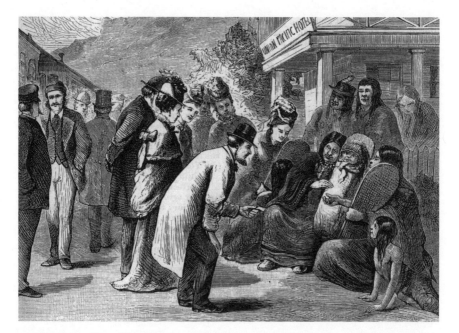

14. *Two Bits to See the Pappoose.* From Henry T. Williams, *The Pacific Tourist* (New York: Henry T. Williams, Publisher, 1876), 195. Reproduced courtesy of the Bancroft Library.

disastrous outcomes. Unfortunately, their presence also served to rein-force popular attitudes about the need for those same policies.

Wishart (1994, 185) asserts that, by 1870, Pawnee Indians of Nebraska were "made to feel like strangers in their own land." He notes that Paw-nees rode the Union Pacific freight cars to Omaha, but that, since passes were required to leave the reservation, Indian agents sent soldiers to bring back Indians who congregated at the rail depots. One Indian agent com-plained that the "'idle and vagrant members of the tribe' who assembled at stops along the Union Pacific line 'gave travellers a bad impression'" (Wishart 1994, 185, 196). But while the Native peoples' presence served to reify the notion that they did not belong in the new settlements—that were, after all, "replacing and expelling 'savagery'"—their continued presence, especially in an impoverished state, was necessary to confirm white cultural and moral superiority (and thus white entitlements to land) (Carter 1993, 155).

Without minimizing the poverty and rootlessness that many Native peoples faced with the onslaught of the Euro-American invasion—the real loss of subsistence, history and identity (Wishart 1994)—it must be acknowledged that a more complex set of social relations took place between Native Americans and whites than the simple oppositional "oppressor–oppressed" model allows. Notions of a power-wielding dominant group (white European or American), which believed in a natural right for white takeover of Native lands, and an essentialized singular group of subordinated others oppressed by this process, emerge from such binary constructions. This model problematically posits two separate, coherent, and stable groups, embodying predetermined collective identities with identical interests or shared oppressions (Mohanty 1988; Ashcroft, Griffiths, and Tiffen 1995, 214), and with consequently limited potential for explaining the range of discourses about Native people that emerged when they came into contact with one another. It further presumes a diffusionist model of European ideologies and modes of thought, which were simply exported around the globe, ignoring how they were played out, received, and modified in various locations (Stoler 1995). Locations of the production of the travel texts were gendered and racialized in a number of ways, and British women took on a number of narratorial voices and positions on Native Americans, thus discursively producing multiple others in their texts. I now turn briefly to British Victorian discourses on race and gender to help situate these multiple and complex discursive positions.

Colonial Discourse and British Women's Travel Writing

Colonial discourse theorists have concentrated considerable attention on the many venues within which Europeans articulated their mission to "save" undeveloped and immature lands and people, at self-proclaimed great cost and effort on the part of the colonizer nations, but for the greater good and progress of the benighted members of other races in the colonies (Said 1978; Young 1995; Ashcroft, Griffiths, and Tiffen 1995; Kaplan and Pease 1993). European public figures and others constructed civilization itself as an evolutionary move from the (feminine) dependent state of primitiveness to an independent (manly) state of civilization with, of course, a racial pecking order built into the process (Hall 1988, 269, 280; Young 1995, 43–54; Stoler 1995). Said's foundational thesis of Orientalism (1978, 113–23) focuses on how the active European observer, or subject, of the eighteenth and nineteenth centuries portrayed, legitimized, and reinforced European expansionism in the colonies, exporting racial and other ideologies from the home country in the process of dominating passive indigenous peoples. Yet, how Europeans' views of themselves were actually produced in the colonies is ignored in an Orientalist framework: colonized peoples are treated as objects of the European gaze and are seldom credited with influencing travelers' opinions. Offering an alternative, Ann Stoler argues for a more relational and contingent model of how various conceptions of racial purity and whiteness were developed and made within particular colonial contexts, involving different sets of people with different class interests (Stoler 1995, 98–99, 301–16).

Many critics have modified and challenged Said's original thesis, considering more specifically time, place, and type of colonial intervention, and, most significantly, challenging the dualistic construction of colonizer and colonized in his model (which Said himself subsequently modified [1983, 1993]). Many feminist scholars of nineteenth-century European women's writing, for instance, convincingly characterized the very complex roles that European white women in the colonies had in their association with imperialistic cultural values (Mills 1991, 1994; Strobel 1991; Chaudhuri and Strobel 1992; Callaway 1987; Blake 1990; McEwan 1994; A. Blunt 1994; Blunt and Rose 1994).

When gender is taken into consideration, a similar slippage in homogenizing Orientalism becomes evident for British women writing within the extra-empire context of the American West. Farrar-Hyde (1990, 110, 125) contends that by the 1870s, European and American tourists expected to see not only evidence of the West as uniquely American, but also dramatic feats of engineering and exotic animals and people, such as Indians. The job of the travel writer was to textualize those features of the place that were most unique and different from home; attention to Native Americans became a stock requisite feature of western travel narratives in the nineteenth century (Athearn 1962; M. Allen 1987; Foster 1990; Georgi-Findlay 1996). Because women travelers' material and discursive positioning gave them legitimate access to insights centered in the female experience, much of what these travelers to the West implicitly defined as the substance of western America was that which revolved around the personal and domestic, morality and religious piety, and women's social roles. Taken together, British women's attention to Native peoples took on special features in the texts, such as displaying a high moral concern for their welfare and paying close attention to their hygiene and appearance. Further complicating the subject position of upper- and middle-class British women were a range of ideologies linked to the themes of civilizing Native women and properly extending charity to those in need. These and other gendered and genteel-class identities were not simply norms or attributes, but sites through which travelers' representations of Native Americans intersected and through which I problematize them.

In addition, I open a discussion here on ways in which the voices and "agency" of Native Americans might begin to be recovered from these texts. Much postcolonial scholarship focuses on retrieving subaltern voices and "reading resistance" from colonial texts (Spivak 1988; Ashcroft, Griffiths, and Tiffen 1995, 85–113; Kaplan and Pease 1993, 365–495). Between and among these women travelers and Native Americans, a host of negotiations and cultural clashes were being played out along multiple lines of difference. A focus on "difference" complicates, but more fully captures, the discursive complexity of the travel narratives than does the simple othering process that Orientalism defined. A focus on difference calls for a more two-sided or multilayered cultural exchange between groups of people, with the terms of difference emerging only out of the encounter itself, as different groups and individuals seek to define the contested zone in their own way (Jehlen 1993). Following Pratt (1992), then, I argue that train stations, moving locations aboard the trains, and other sites across the West were cultural contact zones within which many heterogeneous subjects interacted and exchanged ideas and practices and possessed varying degrees of power to influence the British travel narrative.

Representations of Native Americans

Aesthetic Objects and Vanishing Americans

Many of the women travelers were familiar with and mentioned the novels of James Fenimore Cooper, who, asserts Robert Berkhofer (1978, 93), "more than any other American author. . . . established the Indian as a significant literary type in world literature." Cooper's 1826 novel *The Last of the Mohicans,* for instance, portrayed, among other images, a romanticism and nostalgia for Indians dying out as a result of the onslaught of civilization (Berkhofer 1978, 86–95). But a wide gap existed between Cooper's representations and the impoverished people at western train stations, and travelers sometimes deployed distancing strategies to preserve the literary images intact. Lady Theodora Guest reported that the Indians she met at the train station in Salt Lake City, Utah, had a "stupid, almost idiotic expression of countenance, which quite destroyed any sentiments of chivalry about them, which might have lingered in my mind from the days of Cooper's novels" (1895, 86). When she observed Native peoples from a distance, however, onboard a swiftly moving train, she could retain Cooper's images intact. Later in her journey, crossing a Flathead reservation in the Northwest, Guest noted some Indians riding by, "robed in red blankets on red saddle-cloths, [who] looked very picturesque and effective, as they were not too near" (1895, 170). Such stereotyped images of Native Americans were more easily appropriated in contexts outside the white-dominated towns and settlements, where white racial oppression was more transparent.

At the train station, though, real individuals were rarely matched to stereotyped patterns, displaced as they were by the catastrophic reservation system and by white settlements "replacing and expelling savagery" (Carter 1993). As constructions of racial difference at train stations rested on this contingency (Stoler 1995, 101–16), travelers registered a number of rhetorical disappointments over the Native people that they encountered, such as complaints about their appearance. F. D. Bridges, a world traveler who spent the summer of 1880 in the American West, described seeing her first Indian as she traveled by train east of Oregon. He was dressed as a lumberer, with "calico shirt, baggy trousers and slouch hat." Bridges complained that she expected to behold something "picturesque," but instead saw only an "ugly commonplace individual" (1883, 351). The British suffragist Emily Faithful argued that "[t]he most characteristic Indians ... [were] not in the Far West but at the Indian delegation at Philadelphia" at the Centennial Exposition (1884, 201). Faithful's passage reads more ironically than Bridges's: to her, popular representations are not only artificial, but the most obviously commodified images are the most "characteristic" (to add to which, these characteristic Indians were undoubtedly tribal leaders, dressed in ceremonial garb).

Native women received their own particular defilement in nineteenth-century public discourse; they were represented primarily within the confines of the distorted and antithetical stereotypes of Indian "squaw" and "princess," the logical parallels to the good and bad Indian (Riley 1984, 21–24, 31–33; Berkhofer 1978, 86–95).[3] British women travelers typically portrayed Native women's lives as drudgery, reinforcing representations of the plain, dirty, hardworking but discontented squaw, who was caught in an apparently coercive polygamous relationship. Lady Mary Hardy sarcastically described Ute women at train stations across the Rocky Mountains as "evidently got up for [the] effect" of being seen by railroad passengers:

> The women wore striped blankets pinned round their bodies, and bright handkerchiefs or shawls over their heads. Their long matted hair streamed over their shoulders, sometimes over their eyes; and they had

3. The social construction of Native women as squaws has received considerable attention in western women's histories (e.g., Albers and Medicine 1983; Medicine 1983; Carter 1993). Albers and James (1987) also discuss other stereotypes of Native American women found in pictorial images over the last century. In their study, the Indian princess or maiden has predominated. Since many of the images appeared in such venues as collectible postcards, they often represented the exotic, romantic, and anachronistic, such as women weaving, milling acorns, making arts and crafts, performing for tourists and appearing staged in costumes, roles that did not match the everyday lives of most women. The Indian Princess image rarely appeared in the British travelogues, however, probably because the location of most contact—the train station—offered travelers little in the way of imaginary settings within which poor, displaced people could be transformed into princesses (but see Pender 1978, 66, and Pfeiffer 1885, 183).

added to their natural attractions by blotches of coarse red paint daubed on the dark faces. (L. Hardy 1882, 260)

F. D. Bridges similarly described Native women in train depots across the Rockies, commenting that they "can scarcely be accused of undue regard for [their] appearance—like the hardworking and unpretending hen, [they are] content to leave the 'fine feathers' to the nobler creature" (1883, 401–2).

In these passages, Guest, Faithful, Bridges, and Hardy described Native peoples as primarily visual objects. Whether encountered within the relatively close confines of railway stations, or from a more detached position outside a moving train, Native Americans appear in the texts as aesthetic components of the passing western landscape, racialized in their dress, manner, and hygiene. Aesthetically unpleasing appearances were often used to justify larger imperial processes, even genocide, as when Lady Guest declared that

why the[y] . . . live (or indeed why they *should* live) I cannot conceive. The hair of these Indians is horrible—excessively thick and coarse, black, not reaching more than to the shoulders, and straight and stiff, and their expression absolutely animal. (1895, 89)

The recurring obsession in these travelers' texts with dirt, matted hair, and untidiness can be understood within the larger discourses of racial cleanliness circulating among nineteenth-century bourgeois Europeans: cleanliness was a "God given sign of Britain's evolutionary superiority" (McClintock 1995, 207–14). Part of the European civilizing mission, then, drew on the "commodity racism" of soap to connect the "Victorian poetics of racial hygiene and imperial progress" (McClintock 1995, 209). This type of discourse might find an easy outlet in the work of women writers traveling in an imperial context, whose own racial divide between savagery and civilization would be situated within the domestic realm of home and body.

Even though travelers' concern for Native men's and women's hairstyles, clothing, grooming, and painted faces took on a special similarity and significance in these texts, a diversity of aesthetic representations can, nonetheless, be read from them, suggesting a diversity of Native American lives being lived within the larger context of land dispossession. The recurring theme of the "Vanishing American" also appeared as a common trope in the travelers' texts. While several of the British women did not question whether indigenous peoples "belonged" at sites of white power and dominance in impoverished conditions, other travelers considered them out of context at train stations, displaced from their "real" environments. The magisterial gaze of Iza Hardy at the station in Reno, Nevada, recalled such a displacement:

> At the stations . . . the aborigines hang about the platforms and climb on to the freight-cars . . . We pass through the land of the Piutes into the land of the Shoshonee, but our inexperienced eyes detect no difference in the aspect of these tribes. They all look very dirty; and only through the rose-coloured glasses of romance can one perceive any picturesqueness in them to admire. But we must not fall into the common error of judging the red race by these half-tame specimens who hang about on the fringe of civilisation, left behind by the true Indian, who retreats to his fastnesses before the white man's advance. (1884, 219–20)

Similarly, Lady Howard remarked that the "unattractive" Indians at the depots, "with long lank hair and hideous features," were the "dregs of the once noble 'braves'" (1897, 61). While simply acknowledging that a precontact reality for indigenous peoples had the potential textually to undermine the exploitative practices of the Euro-American invaders, Hardy, Howard, and other travelers instead invoked it as evidence of the Vanishing American. The trope of the Vanishing American recalled a static, antihistorical romantic past, in which noble, picturesque people lived in simple harmony and peace, but were now, because of some immutable racial characteristics, destined for extinction. In this trope, real living people have no place in the present and can only be imagined in relation to a split-off, archaeological past (Pratt 1992, 134).

Rose Pender, who traveled with her husband to the American West in 1881 to inspect the family's investments in the cattle industry (see chapter 2), simultaneously invoked the tropes of "Indian Princess" and "Vanishing American" when she described stopping at a road ranch at Fort

Laramie, Wyoming. She recounted the story of the daughter of the Brule Sioux chief Spotted Tail, who was buried there. Pender clearly invoked the discourse of Indian Princess in describing (the nameless) daughter; she embodied the image of the Native woman who was childlike, naturally innocent, beautiful, inclined toward civilization, and who mediated between whites and Native Americans by siding with the white man (Sherry Smith 1987, 65; Armitage 1987, 14). Pender claimed that Spotted Tail's daughter was the "fairest maiden of the tribe" and fell hopelessly in love with an American officer, "who had made a deep impression upon her young heart." She explained:

> Possibly she mistook the natural courtesy and kindness with which he treated her for a warmer feeling. Indian women are not accustomed to gentle treatment at the hands of their lords and masters. When, at the end of his expedition, the young officer returned to his camp at Fort Laramie he left a desolate heart behind . . . [she] set off on foot in search of her love . . . poor thing! In spite of her efforts she never looked on the loved face; her strength failed, and she fell exhausted on the summit of the small hill overlooking the Fort. (1978, 66)

In her caricature of the noble, suffering maiden, Pender portrayed a woman who was hopelessly ignorant and doomed, a Vanishing American who literally died at the site.

In her *A Lady's life in the Rocky Mountains* (1969) Isabella Bird rarely mentioned Native Americans, though she did assess those whom she observed on a train platform at 1870s Yosemite. She declared that the

> Digger[4] Indians, with their squaws, children, and gear . . . [were] perfect savages, without any aptitude for even aboriginal civilization, and are altogether the most degraded of the ill-fated tribes which are dying out before the white races. (1879, 6)

Bird proceeded to describe in detail their height ("on average five feet one inch"), facial features ("flat noses, wide mouths, long black hair") and

---

4. "Digger" Indian was a derogatory term for people who collected roots for food (Riley 1984, 153).

clothes ("ragged and dirty, with unornamented moccasins"), concluding that they "were all hideous and filthy, and swarming with vermin" (1969, 6). Furthermore, as "only" hunters and gatherers subsisting on fish, game, roots and grasshoppers, these Shoshone and Piute Indians seemed to Bird further down the chain of being than either their more noble ancestors or Euro-American immigrants. While Bird's comments can be understood within the discourses of scientific racism (G. Jones 1980) and the Victorian quest for cleanliness (McClintock 1995), she also introduced the Victorian discourse on "levels" of civilization revolving around relationships between civilization, use of land, and social survival (Young 1995, 31). To Bird, the consequences of contact with whites, with their fixed agriculture and secure title to land, meant the inevitable evaporation of the "lower" forms of subsistence. As they were hopelessly removed from their own aboriginal civilization, they were destined to die out in the face of the white advance, and in fact are revived in the text as already dead.

"Squaws" and Spinsters: Representations of Reform

The civilizing mission of professional Indian reformers (philanthropists, ethnographers, and missionaries) centered on transforming Indian social and cultural life with Christianization, education, and Euro-American domestic ideals. Protestant female reformers' authority to improve the lives of others was based on notions of women as properly pure, pious, self-sacrificing moral guardians, whose virtuous status entitled them to rescue their downtrodden sisters (Pascoe 1990; Armstrong 1987). The role of professional reformer was one of the few accepted careers open to women, and women travelers might well have adopted their rhetoric during their travels to the American West as a way to compensate for their own movements into the public sphere.

Reformers' representations of Native peoples came the closest to challenging the "noble savage" or "bloodthirsty redskin" images (Berkhofer 1978, 27–28, 167) and challenged prevailing attitudes about Indian capabilities and equality with whites. Although resisted by many Native Americans as just another infringement on their self-determination, the works of some white Indian reformers did expose American duplicity and corruption in dealing with Native Americans. Such reformers rejected the notion that Indians were permanently inferior and that they could, by imitating white people, avoid extinction. British women's reformist rhetoric took several forms in these texts: they emphasized the "natural" (positive) qualities of contemporary Native Americans; they articulated a moral concern for their welfare, often by contrasting the scandalous behavior of whites to Natives' reactions to it; and they advocated reform policies intended to help them to adapt to the white advance, such as by conforming to Euro-American gender roles. This rhetoric usually involved highly limiting stereotypes, with travelers failing to recognize cross-cultural differences.

Not surprisingly, once travelers moved beyond the idealized imperial setting of the train station, a specific form of gendered racial discourse emerged in their texts. A few of the women who encountered Native peoples in villages or encampments, typically during excursions into Yosemite, on horseback or by stage, expressed an interest in indigenous women's lives and work that was not obvious from the train station. On reservations and at Indian encampments, the power dynamics of the train station were modified, if for no other reason than that the conditions of many Native Americans deteriorated with proximity to white settlements. Representations of racial difference in the travelers' texts, then, depended on the intrinsically relational and contingent location of the encounter.[5]

The poet Emily Pfeiffer, in her *Flying Leaves from East and West* (1885), simultaneously praised and criticized the work (and life) of a "Digger" Indian she met in Yosemite Valley. The woman exhibited "considerable ingenuity" in her ability to make culinary and other utensils, and as Pfeiffer approached her settlement, she "looked up . . . with a not unkindly glance" (1885, 247–48). Theodora Guest also described Yosemite Indians as living in peace (1895, 138), and F. D. Bridges marveled at the numerous fish caught in a day (40 pounds) with only "bait and crooked pin" (1883, 379). Lady Howard and several other of the writers detailed Indian

5. Kay Schaffer's (1994) analysis of Eliza Frazer's captivity narrative in colonial Australia demonstrates a similar process. Frazer's story underwent several transformations as she described indigenous peoples as increasingly savage and barbarous the farther away in space and time she traveled from them and the scene of her shipwreck.

mythologies of Yosemite (1897, 94). These descriptions of primitive life illustrate the textual necessity for establishing a position against which the writers can define themselves as civilized. Foster (1990, 102) contends, moreover, that representations such as these display an ambivalent attitude toward civilization: while the writer tends to idealize the natural and express what might be a "genuine feeling for the primitive," she does not actually "see" it. That is, the writer appears to place value on the primitive, yet simultaneously codes white culture as superior. To the reform-minded traveler, attributes of quality, refinement, dignity, respectability and even aesthetically white characteristics, signal that reform is possible, while primitiveness and crudity signal that reform is necessary. Thus the "pleasant-looking baby . . . in a birch-bark cradle and gaily-decorated blanket" that is "almost as fair as a European child" represents a hopeful case to Bridges (1883, 402).

Spending a good deal of time on the trains, but with little else to occupy their attention across the long stretches of the plains and deserts of the West, travelers often filled portions of their books with expositions about local Indian-white conflicts. Indians themselves were largely absent from such contact zones, as the British women were detached from the landscapes passing by, "swaddled in [the] Victorian luxury" of the train cars (Farrar-Hyde 1990, 117) and surrounded by other wealthy and leisured travelers. Some writers focused their discussions on economic and political causes for Native peoples' conditions, blaming an inept or corrupt American government or the greed and arrogance of white settlers. Thérèse Longworth stopped at several military forts during her North American journey in 1872–1873. Such sites of concentrated white American power inspired Longworth to reflect on the "clap trap pretence" of the forts: "Ostensibly [they are] for the protection of the few scattered inhabitants, but in reality [they] prevent the Indians from occupying and enjoying their former hunting-grounds" (1976, 2: 23–24). Bridges similarly contemplated the (collapsed) Black Hills treaty as she journeyed near the Yellowstone River region. She explained:

> The hills were granted by treaty as "Indian reservations"; but all promises were scattered to the winds when, a few years ago, gold was discovered

in these parts, and an army of white faces, mad for gain, defied both the federal troops and the Indians, and are still pressing on, in spite of, now and then, terrible massacres by the red men. (1883, 411)

In this passage, Bridges distanced herself from the deceit and wrongfulness of the U.S. government and covetous whites, and as such aligned herself against "civilizing" forces that carry the negative associations of greed and ignorance. Fellow (male) travelers convinced both Emily Pfeiffer and Thérèse Longworth of the unjustness of U.S. actions against Native peoples. A clergyman who had spent much time with the northern and northwestern tribes convinced Pfeiffer, traveling near Cheyenne, Wyoming, that they had been defrauded, and, contrary to popular belief, were "far from dying out under the influences of civilization, ... [they] are increasing at a rate even beyond the normal" (1885, 260–61). In a comparable way, a "cultivated trapper" convinced Longworth on board the train across Nebraska

> that the government had taken the wrong way with them from the first, and that the Indians had suffered cruelly; that their attempts at retalia- tion were trivial in comparison with their wrongs. (1974, 2: 16–17)

These passages not only negatively portray empire building by the United States, but refer to the persistence and even prosperity of Native peoples under the influence of civilization. Treated as a fait accompli, white contact had proven its ability to help Native peoples to avoid an otherwise inevitable extinction, a hallmark of reformist principles. Pfeiffer argued at the end of her narrative that "the ill of ills is that which comes from insufficient virtue of the body politic" in dealing with Indian affairs (1885, 283). Longworth's conversation with a trapper achieved a similar end. Conversely, Theodora Guest, commenting on the Black Hills situation a decade after Bridges (above), aligned herself on the side of the government in U.S.-Indian relations:

> The United States Government is very fair towards them, and does what can be done to educate and maintain them; but restricts them, wisely, to certain reservations, where they are supplied with food, and all they need; and will probably not give much more trouble. (1883, 86)

Taken together, these passages demonstrate the very fluidity of reform rhetoric in terms of what aspects of civilization ostensibly comprised it (i.e., Euro-American expansionism is both evil and desirable). The passages also indicate a willingness to criticize, or at least to appraise, the policies and actions of the U.S. government, transgressing the limits, perhaps, of imperial women's proper discursive domain (Suleri 1992, 75–110). However, it should also be acknowledged that, in the cases of Longworth and Pfeiffer, it was encounters with knowledgeable men on the trains that produced these specific representations of Native American life. Such secondhand evidence allowed them to deflect full responsibility for the arguments off themselves and on to the more authoritative masculine voice.

Another expression of reformist rhetoric in these travelogues revolved around the construction of Native societies as fundamentally sexist. Travelers frequently complained that Native women suffered from (Native) patriarchal oppression. With few exceptions, Native men appear in these texts as barbaric and lazy slave masters.[6] Recall Rose Pender's assertion that "Indian women are not accustomed to gentle treatment at the hands of their lords and masters" (1978, 66). In her 1881 trip that passed through villages in Indian territory by train, Pender also reported that

> the squaws, with their papooses, stared stolidly at us. Here and there we met a (no doubt) great chief, riding, bare-backed, a very little mustang. At one small station we actually saw four "braves" engaged in the exhilarating game of croquet. (1978, 17–18)

To Pender, these Native men (and their horses, for that matter) appear emasculated, engaged in a frivolous game of croquet unfit for a manly

---

6. In one notable exception, though, Isabella Bird recalled being introduced to a Ute Indian chief on a Denver, Colorado, street: "Governor Hunt introduced me to a fine-looking young chief, very well dressed in beaded hide, and bespoke his courtesy for me if I needed it". (1969, 139). This is a very different image of Native American maleness from that of her train station encounter (1969, 6): she recognizes the status difference among the men, and forms an apparent class alliance between herself, the chief, and the governor. As a woman traveling alone, the chief's chivalry also served as a possible source of empathy for Bird (as in Blake's 1990 study of Mary Hall's relationship with African chiefs).

"brave" (and invoking the Eurocentric association of savagery itself with the feminine [Young 1995, 43–54]).

Rose Kingsley, while staying with her brother in Colorado (see chapters 3 and 5), described the Utes in 1870s Colorado Springs as "hideous," the most "revolting specimen[s] of humanity" she had ever seen, the smell of which even horses and mules could not stand (1874, 102, 106). Later, driving alone to shop for supplies between Colorado Springs and Glen Eyrie, Kingsley described what she considered the animal-like behavior of some Ute men:

> Two Indians were outside one of the stores, indulging in such extraordinary antics that I was really afraid to drive past. They ran along like beasts on all-fours; then they tumbled down and rolled over; and they then crouched and pulled their bows. One of the men from the store seeing me, kindly ran and held them till I had passed . . . These Indians are disgusting people; and my terror of them grows greater the more I know of them. (1874, 133–34)

One cannot help wonder whether these men's performance was not purely for Rose Kingsley's benefit. She had spent several months in their community, helping her brother to keep books for a railroad company, and also took on "civilizing" projects of her own, for which she may have gained something of a reputation.[7] But Kingsley's "terror" of the Indian men can probably best be understood as a literary expression akin to the captivity narratives so melodramatically paraded before the Victorians (see note 5). This seems especially so in the light of Kingsley's later remark that "their cruelties to [white] women are as bad, or worse, than to men" (1874, 134). Kingsley's passage hints at the sensationalized brutality in the rape or abduction of white women by Native men, which served ultimately to rationalize American imperial expansionism. And whereas captivity narratives often shored up the heroine's prized Victorian virtues of courage, fortitude, and purity in the face of danger, Kingsley instead emphasized

---

7. For instance, Kingsley promoted a reading room, "where the young [white] men may spend their evenings, instead of lounging about the town, or going up to drink in the saloons" (1874, 72).

her feminine need to be rescued by the gallant white male, again not stray-
ing too far afield the proper feminine voice.

Beatrice Medicine (1983) interrogates how cultural bias also distorted
understandings of Native American gender relations. Stereotypes of Native
American women as subordinate in marriage and in work relationships,
as virtual slaves to their fathers and then to their husbands, predominated
popular Anglo discourse. For instance, observers incorrectly assumed
that the hauling of heavy loads meant low status for plainswomen of the
Omaha and Pawnee societies (Wishart 1995). On the contrary, the women
gained status from owning many of the moveable goods, including the
dwelling and most of its contents and, like men, carried what they owned
to new locations (but compare to Lerner 1986).[8] The apparently heavy
manual labor performed by Native women was especially an affront to
the pious, protected, and domestic ideal of femininity that was embedded in British Victorian patriarchal discourse: aristocratic and upwardly
mobile middle-class women proved the success of their men by becoming
economically idle and therefore feminine (see chapter 5). Regardless of
how traveling women themselves were ambiguously associated with this
ideal, Native societies were nevertheless judged in these texts by the degree
to which they approximated western ideals of the civilized treatment of
women. To Rose Kingsley, for instance, gender relations of a Ute family
in Colorado did not approximate western ideals at all. She described Indians riding past her hotel, trailing their tent poles, with "the squaws with
the papooses on their backs, laden, besides, with all the belongings of the
tribe, while the *braves* rode on in front with no load save their guns and
bows" (1874, 134, her italics). On another occasion, Kingsley reported that
a "swarm" of Utes came to town, and her brother Maurice recognized one
of the "young braves [as] the greatest thief unhung in New Mexico: he has
five squaws, and makes them all steal for him" (1874, 104). Kingsley went
on to describe the ugly faces of the squaws, who were dressed like the men
(1874, 104).

8. Lerner (1986) argues against such conceptualizations of women's power and prestige; to her, women's heavy labor was the result of a loss of power and men's redefinition
of labor relations.

15. *Indians.* From Rose Kingsley, *South by West or Winter in the Rocky Mountains and Spring in Mexico* (London: W. Isbister and Co., 1874). Courtesy of The Johns Hopkins University.

In these excerpts, Kingsley posits her own life as an index of women's empowerment (Strobel 1991, 49). She construes Native women's treatment as barbaric and thus avoids confronting her own (relative) powerlessness at home and the fact that her power in America derived from imperial relations (Mills 1994, 41). This is itself a patriarchal expression of white racial superiority; the perceived low status of Native women is seen to stem from Native men, not from unequal political-economic relationships with whites (A. Blunt 1994, 80–85). Although Kingsley seems to sympathize with Native women who are "made to steal" for their husband, she fails to suggest that Native women have their own points of view and ignores how they may have welcomed their own social arrangements.

Thérèse Longworth took exception to the dominant view of Native women's lives as drudgery, when she described the lifestyles of Indians in Yosemite Valley. "It is true," she writes,

> that the women carry the heavy burdens, while the men walk at their
> ease, with their bows and arrows, or rifles. But, if the men were bur-
> dened, they could not pursue their game whenever it might appear.
> (1974, 2: 80)

In this more empathetic representation of Native gender relations, Long-worth acknowledged, but dismissed, dominant understandings of Native women's work as unfeminine or inappropriate, perhaps, again, because she was distanced from the more obviously oppressive centers of white power in towns and railway stations. Calling into question an essential-ist construction of gender and racial difference in these narratives, Long-worth foregrounds herself in sympathy with both Native women and men, a rhetorical position perhaps more available to women who perceived travel as an opportunity to escape the social boundaries of the Victorian aristocracy. In other parts of her narrative, Longworth clearly asserts a more feminist voice, either in pointing out her heroic conquering of the self in dangerous mountain settings (see chapter 3), or by supporting suf-frage in Wyoming. From her viewpoint, Native women's physical labor was not detrimental to their welfare (nor perhaps to other women's), and in fact her passage highlights another ambivalence of reformist policies— (white) women's moral authority sprung from their position in the home, yet many reformers argued for more expansive working roles for women outside of the home.

British women's associations with larger social reform movements finds ready rhetorical outlet in their travel narratives, whether by acknowl-edging the potentialities of the primitive (Pfeiffer, Guest, Bridges); in crit-icizing (Longworth, Pfeiffer, Bridges) or praising (Guest) the actions of the U.S. government and white settlers; by finding fault with Native men (Pender, Kingsley); by disclosing the supposed drudgery of Native women's lives (Kingsley); or by offering a more positive portrayal of non-Western gender relations (Longworth). Widely varying interpretations of racial and gender difference emerge from the encounters, with the same individual often positioning herself in multiple ways. Importantly, though, these rhetorical positions were primarily framed around the racialization of reform rhetoric itself (helping the downtrodden to become civilized). While these women were not American Indian reformers, they did adopt aspects of reform rhetoric in order to position themselves legitimately and purposefully within their own narratives. Furthermore, multiple Native American subjectivities emerge from these documents, racialized and gendered in a number of ways: the chivalrous Indian male (Bird, see note 6); a "not unkindly old woman" (Pfeiffer); a European-looking baby (Bridges); justifiably angered people (Longworth); persistent survivors (Pfeiffer); "beasts" running around on all fours (Kingsley); hardworking squaws (Kingsley, Longworth); and nonviolent hunters and fishers (Longworth and Guest), among others.

Though some of the reformers' discourse challenged Anglo-American capitalist greed and ignorance, their positions left little ideological space for imagining Native peoples on their own terms. A focus on these texts inevitably neglects Native peoples' own self-representations and portrays them only in relation to (advancing) Euro-Americans. Susan Miller (1997, 64) noted that in recent academic scholarship and museum exhibitions, nineteenth-century American Indians are represented as only violent or subordinated, images that wrongly suggest that "our native ancestors had [nothing] else on their minds back then," such as quill-making, deliberating over political issues, or playing ball. Despite the limitations built into reading Native agency or viewpoints from these ruling-class documents, I close out my discussion with an attempt to recover some of those self-representations of Native Americans from the travelers' texts.

Textual Boundaries of Train-Station Encounters

Although British travel narratives are limited in their ability to expose Native people's viewpoints, both travelers and Native Americans were textually produced only as they came in contact with one another, and in that sense the British subject-author emerged only through engagement with specific Native peoples within specific material circumstances. The othering process of Orientalism focuses on European social and cultural values and their ability to influence the travel text, and in effect has the potential to reproduce the very European centered discourses that it seeks to replace. Namely, it assumes the passivity of the colonial subject, and therefore has the potential to recolonize the subject (Mills makes a similar point [1996, 127]). Pratt argues that reading colonial texts simply as "symptoms of imperial ideologies" diffusing from Europe is incomplete in the way that it reproduces metropolitan authority (1992, 5–6, 111–43). She writes that "while the imperial metropolis tends to understand itself as determining the periphery . . . it habitually blinds itself to the ways in which the periphery determines the metropolis" (1992, 6). In her model of the contact zone, colonial cultures met and produced each other.

The postcolonial critic Gayatri Spivak (1988) has led the way in retrieving the voices and histories of subaltern subjects, those objects of colonial processes whose own speaking positions have been silenced. While she is interested in uncovering voices of resistance against oppression, she also argues for subaltern voices that are heterogeneous and not "essentialized fictions" (Spivak 1988). A postcolonial focus on difference (e.g., Ashcroft, Griffiths, and Tiffen 1995; Kaplan and Pease 1993) likewise attempts to eliminate the centrality of the European observer by locating the resistance and agency of subalterns in the contact zone, thus demarcating their influence on hegemonic discourses. Though the material circumstances of many Native peoples in the late nineteenth-century American West was one of war and poverty, in which British travelers could easily be construed as wrongful trespassers, following Susan Miller's (1997) lead it is important to keep in mind that these were probably not "the only things on their minds."

Several scholars have focused on direct quotations of oppressed people in travel texts as a rhetorical maneuver that establishes sympathy and reciprocity, a "subject-to-subject" discursive position associated with feminine discourse (Blake 1990, 353–54; Mills 1991, 3, 97–98; 1994). Direct quotations potentially subvert the authority of the powerful, all-seeing observer, as they work against the aesthetic homogenizing of diverse groups of people, locating both the travel*er* and the travel*ee* in the landscape. And yet, none of the travelers here directly quoted a conversation with an indigenous woman or man—they appear as speakers of only sentence fragments (single words and phrases). For instance, F. D. Bridges commented that "nothing will induce the Indians to come on this lake [Tahoe], 'where one time was one big fire,' they say" (1883, 385–86). Emily Pfeiffer recalled meeting a man in Yosemite who "came up and addressed us in his Indian speech, . . . the word 'tabac,' which he was evidently begging of us, being the only [word] we understood" (1885, 228). Certainly, interpreters or Indian English-speakers could have been located had they been desired, and attempts to place the reader in sympathy with the uncomprehending traveler are unconvincing.

Furthermore, while travelers sometimes claimed that they conversed with Native Americans, the content of those conversations were never disclosed. Theodora Guest, for instance, wrote of "interviewing" some Ute Indians in Salt Lake City, out of which came simply a description of their appearance—they were "horrible-looking, dirty, miserable" (1895, 85). She also reported meeting the Sioux chief Rain in the Face and his party of twenty-one aboard the train near St. Paul, Minnesota. But, here again, she focused on aesthetic appearances: the squaws were "not so bad looking" and the men were taller, smarter and cleaner than "the miserable specimens" in Utah (1895, 172–73). More than anything, these passages recall the objectifying aesthetic gazes discussed previously (with "smarter" itself derived from "taller" and "cleaner"). These passages also highlight, though, Guest's co-presence with poverty-stricken people at a train station in one case, and well-positioned people riding the trains to New York, as Guest herself was, in the other.

The little interpersonal communication and interaction that took place between British travelers and indigenous peoples, both verbal and nonverbal, was usually at train stations, a setting of profoundly unequal power relations, within which only certain kinds of communication could occur. In passages already cited, several British travelers complained about being stared at by Native people at train stations or noted the capacity of Native people to appear at depots in order to be seen by railroad passengers (Pender 1978, 17–18; Pfeiffer 1885, 247–48). At the station in Reno, Nevada, Iza Hardy wrote of finding that "the noble red man and his wives had come out for to see us; and we returned the compliment by all turning out on the platform to see them" (1884, 219). Her mother, Lady Hardy, similarly described a scene at a train station in Colorado, in which "the men stood in groups, solemnly regarding us with their big black eyes, still as statues; the women squatted on the platform or peeped at us from round corners" (1882, 260). In these passages, the traveler appears self-consciously aware of being the object of the gaze of men and women on the platform. This interaction marks Native peoples as both that which is signified in the text and as producers of signification. Although both Hardys surveyed the scene as 'objective' outsiders, the onlookers' gazes simultaneously embodied and located them in the landscape, fully disrupting an interpretation of Native people as passive objects.

Many encounters at train stations involved Indian families begging from travelers, often in the stereotyped stoic silence of the noble Indian (cf. Faithful 1884, 201; I. Hardy 1884, 219), but also in ways that challenged the stereotyped, homogenous subaltern position. Mrs. Vincent (1885), for instance, in her account of her world tour in 1884–1885, quoted a Piute mother begging from her at a train station in Nevada: "one mother brought her 'papoose' (baby), slung on to her back in a long basket . . . [and] begged for 'two bits for the wee papoose'" (1885, vi, 96). Longworth also challenged the stereotype of the silent and passive Indian:

> After entering Wyoming territory, the Indians began to collect around the cars at each station. They besieged the doors and windows, and were wildly importunate for white bread and cakes. They were wretched, famished-looking creatures, clad in tatters of European dress. Their natural food and clothing have been wrung from them by the appropriation of their lands for the rail. They hung about the small stations subsisting on charity, and fully expecting that each passenger should share with them whatever he possessed. (1974, 2: 25)

As well as placing Indians in a proactive begging position, demanding compensation, Longworth here situated their poverty within the larger social context of white-Indian relations: their poverty was not the outcome of intrinsic racial characteristics, but was inflicted from external sources.

Such passages require analysis, too, in the light of the highly publicized concerns of London's educated elite in the 1880s to solve problems of poverty. As bourgeois tensions heightened over social unrest and proximity to the "dirt and disease" of the poor, proscriptions on how to extend charity, as well as how to interact properly with the poor, proliferated (Walkowitz 1992, 26–27; Humphreys 1995; Wood 1991; McClintock 1995). The amended poor laws of the mid–nineteenth century had divided the poor into "deserving" and "undeserving" charitable cases, and the Victorian concepts of thrift, hard work, self-control, and self-help coalesced into the widely held belief that only the most genuinely destitute (e.g., children and the sick) should receive relief, while the able-bodied, whose depraved and deviant situation was considered self-inflicted, should be employed in the workhouses, where a proper morality and concept of work would be stimulated (Wood 1991; Humphreys 1995, 104–10). Charity itself was described by some of the leading national organizations as sinful. They argued that beggars, vagrants, and drunkards were undeserving cases and should be shunned; handouts would only inhibit them from becoming wage earners again (Humphreys 1995, 104). In particular, female charity workers were warned against being duped by undeserving impostors, as their "hearts and sympathies were so easily touched by tales of woe" (as quoted in Humphreys 1995, 111). The idea that the poor primarily needed to help themselves aids us in interpreting many travelers' conflation of poverty with laziness, dirt, and disgust. Rose Pender, for instance, contended that the Indians at the train station in Carson City, Nevada, "do not work, yet to beg they are not ashamed. They are indeed a disgusting people" (1888, 46–47). While otherwise sympathetic to their poverty-stricken conditions, Thérèse Longworth, too, appeared indignant that the Wyoming Indians "fully expect[ed] that each passenger should share with them whatever he possessed."

A heterogeneity of Native voices in reaction to conditions of poverty can be read in the texts, not least in passages that locate resistance to such conditions via nonverbal communication. A traveler paying a nickel or a dime to look at an Indian baby was a common practice at train stations along the western railroad routes; a part, no doubt, of the larger-scale commodification of anything Native. In the following excerpt, Emily Pfeiffer described her encounter with a woman of the "Sioux" (although Utes were more likely to be in Nevada) tribe at a train station in Nevada, whose nonverbal communication with her arguably established some mutuality between the two women. As Pfeiffer offered the mother a nickel for a look at her baby, she remarked that "the young squaw has clearly a turn for business":

> I hold the coin within range of her vision, and an almost imperceptible quiver of an eyelash tells me that she has seen it; but the squaw knows full well that the sight she has to offer is worth more ... and her great eyes continue to look past us or through us, contemplating, as it might seem, the immensities. (1885, 181)

As the woman finally accepted a silver dime, Pfeiffer described the situation as one in which

> the quick eye recognizes the difference in a flash, and tilting the papoose in such a manner that no other shall share the spectacle with the one who has paid for it, she makes a sign to me to bend low, and quickly removes the curtain. A little reddish brown face, with round, rather hanging cheeks, and eyes and mouth just opening in a cry, is exhibited to me for a moment, and the curtain of the peep-show is abruptly closed, when a low laugh tells the Indian woman's enjoyment of the discomfiture of the bystanders. (1885, 181–82)

The mother in this scene displays considerable power to determine the basis for the encounter with Pfeiffer and as such this passage can be read as Native American resistance literature (Kaplan and Pease 1993, 365–495; Ashcroft, Griffiths, and Tiffen 1995, 85–113). The mother's ability to set the terms of the display of the baby, as well as her enjoyment over the "discomfiture of the bystanders," subverts and undermines Pfeiffer's otherwise uncontested privilege to give alms or not. While the Indian mother appears capable of eroding the power of the traveler, Pfeiffer herself must be read as complicit with the mother's strategy of resistance: it is in her text, after all, in which this scene is played out (even if she presented herself as at first unwilling to impart a nickel to someone who may have appeared to her an "undeserving" case).

Conclusion

> I could hardly divest my mind of the idea that we should be attacked by Redskins; for the name of Fort Wallace is associated with such horrors:

but we met with no worse a misfortune than a very bad supper. (Kingsley 1874, 42)

Rose Kingsley's rhetorical disappointment at not encountering stereotyped threatening Indians at the train depot in Kansas reproduces a theme running throughout all of the travelogues I have examined in this chapter: images of American Indians appear in the texts in their capacity to consolidate travelers' positions as discerning, civilized English ladies. The postcolonial critic Homi Bhabha argues that, to succeed, colonial discourse depends upon images of indigenous peoples that are already known and that must be "anxiously repeated" (1983, 18) and must ultimately deny the heterogeneity of colonial subjects. Although I have outlined many ways in which British Victorian racial and gender ideologies might have been transplanted onto American West soil via these travel narratives, my purpose in reading them has been to show how Native American and British women's racialized and gendered social and spatial frameworks intersected in multiple ways and, notwithstanding the refined English lady or stereotyped dangerous Indian, produced a heterogeneity of both British women and Native American subjects. British travelers' gendered and genteel-class identities were played out relationally in several contact zones of the West, which were gendered and racialized in diverse ways. The imperial relations at train stations were particularly important, as these were where most of the contact took place.

This range of discursive subjectivities, of both travelers and Native peoples, unsettle the notion of essentialized gendered responses and an homogenous Native American Other in these texts. British women's identities were read through many social sites, such as bourgeois discourses on dirt and poverty; racialized bourgeois notions of women's moral authority; and gendered colonialist discourses on women's styles of writing and feminine concerns. Thus, although most of the travelers represented Native Americans as aesthetic objects racialized in dress, manner, and hygiene, these complex and intersecting speaking positions produced a diverse range of traveler subject positions, from the sympathetic and more reform-minded concerns of Emily Pfeiffer and Thérèse Longworth, to the more Eurocentric modes of imagining racial purity of Theodora Guest and

Rose Kingsley. And although the unequal social relations of train stations severely limited the types of interactions that could take place between travelers and Native peoples, a range of their subject positions also appears in these texts, including ones that posit active resistance to imperial relations in ways other than either stereotyped stoic silence or unrestrained violence. And, certainly, my attempts to recover Native agency in these narratives poses difficult questions about who can speak for whom here and whether these individuals would want their agency to be recovered in this way. As unresolvable as these questions might seem, they are worthy of consideration.

7

Postcolonialism and Native American Geographies

The Letters of Rosalie La Flesche Farley, 1869–1899

THE LA FLESCHE FAMILY has occupied a prominent position in historical and historical geographical works on the Omaha Indians (Mark 1988; Wilson 1974; Green 1969; Fletcher and La Flesche 1992; Ramsey 1997, 148–53). This is due in large part to the controversial role that their patriarch and last traditional chief, Joseph La Flesche[1] (Iron Eyes), played during the period of Euro-American expansion onto the American Great Plains during the mid- and late nineteenth century. Much of the literature on the Omaha stresses that they responded as archetypal assimilationists to American expansionism (Olund 2002; Milner 1982; Green 1969; Wilson 1974, 70). Reformers, missionaries, politicians, and others considered the Omaha the most "progressive" of Indians, due to their early adoption of the ways of the dominant

---

1. Joseph La Flesche (1822–1889) was the son of a wealthy French trader and an Omaha woman. He was adopted by the previous Omaha chief, Big Elk, and in that way came into his chieftainship rather than being born into it, which stirred controversy among many Omaha. Joseph married Mary Gale (1826–1908), daughter of a U.S. Army surgeon and an Omaha woman, in 1843. Between 1848 and 1872 Joseph had eight children, five with Mary (including Rosalie) and three (including Francis) with his second wife, Tainne. He was a practicing polygamist, with likely a third wife as well.

white culture. Controversy surrounding Joseph was exacerbated by his close association with Presbyterian missionaries who worked with the Omaha from 1840 onward. Because Joseph believed that dominance by the white culture was inevitable, he devoted his energies to education. "It is either civilization or extermination," he claimed (quoted in Wilson 1974, 70).

But it was in their attempts to secure title to their land and avoid deportation to Indian Territory (Oklahoma) that initiated the splitting of their reservation into individual allotments of farm land years before the 1887 Dawes Act mandated it. La Flesche family members were the first of the Omaha to receive allotments, which, in 1881, were supported by perhaps only one-fourth of the people (Boughter 1998, 104). Joseph La Flesche established his own village for his "progressive" followers, which his detractors derided as "the village of make-believe white men" (Milner 1982, 154; Mark 1988, 113). He led his group in building frame houses, starting farms, adopting Christianity, and sending his children to reform schools. The La Flesches were an American-educated, prosperous family amid the collectively declining situation of most Omaha.

Rosalie La Flesche Farley, one of Joseph's (and his first wife Mary's) children, is less well known and much less studied than three of her siblings who rose to relative prominence in U.S. history—Susan, Susette, and Francis.[2] In this chapter I draw attention to letters that Rosalie wrote to

---

2. Susan was the first Native American woman to become a doctor. Sara Kinney, president of the Women's Branch of the Connecticut Indian Association, met Susan through Alice Fletcher, and subsequently provided the means for Susan to attend the Philadelphia Woman's Medical College (Pascoe 1990, 7–10, 123ff). Susan graduated from medical school in 1889 and then returned home to become a physician for the Omaha. She devoted a great deal of her energy to campaigning to state and federal agencies for better health care for Indians.

Susette (Bright Eyes), a writer, speaker, and champion of Indian rights, gained national and international recognition while she was on a speaking tour of the East Coast and Europe publicizing the forced removal of Ponca to Indian Territory. Susette, Thomas Tibbles (a white Indian reformer and newspaperman whom she later married), Standing Bear (a Ponca chief), and her half-brother, Francis, engaged in many speaking engagements over several years, and it was largely from Susette's popularity that East Coast philanthropists and reformers, including Alice Fletcher, became involved in the "Indian cause."

16. *Village of Make-Believe White Men on the Omaha Reservation.* Pen and ink copy by F. W. Miller of a sketch made by an Omaha man for the New Orleans Exposition, 1885. Joseph La Flesche's house is the large one within the marked plot to the center-right of the image. Sketch reproduced courtesy of the Peabody Museum, Harvard University.

her brother Francis (Frank), during the years 1896–1899 when she lived and worked with the Omaha on the reservation and he worked for the Department of Interior's Bureau of Indian Affairs (BIA) in Washington, D.C. With the help of Alice Fletcher,[3] Indian reformer and anthropologist,

---

Francis received a law degree in 1893 at National University, collaborated with Fletcher on many projects, and ultimately became a noted author and ethnologist with the Smithsonian Institution, writing and lecturing on Omaha and Osage customs. He also served as Fletcher's assistant when she began setting up the land allotment program in 1882 (Ramsey 1997).

3. For a complete biography of Fletcher see Mark (1988). Fletcher began work with the Omaha in 1881, with the La Flesche family serving as her hosts on the reservation. She developed a close relationship with them, especially with Francis.

17. Rosalie La Flesche Farley, ca. 1890. From Norma K. Green, *Iron Eye's Family: The Children of Joseph La Flesche* (Lincoln, Neb.: Johnsen Publishing, 1969), 106. Photograph reproduced with permission of the Nebraska State Historical Society.

Francis was appointed clerk in the Indian Office and from that position helped monitor and conduct Omaha business in Washington.

Working from the reservation, Rosalie influenced and often directed Omaha land transactions. The letters I examine in this chapter provide an important testament to the complex, contentious deals taking place over Omaha land, as well as to Rosalie's and the La Flesche family's highly fraught positionings amidst this process. These letters tell part of the story especially of the leasing or selling of what quickly became recognized by a host of factions—including land speculators, policy makers, BIA agents, Omaha leaders, judges, town builders, cattlemen—as prime ranch and farm land, ripe for capitalist development.

Unlike her sisters and (half)-brother, who were educated at schools in New Jersey and Virginia, Rosalie had no formal American education beyond the Presbyterian Mission school on the reservation, although she would likely have had a formal Omaha education. Nonetheless, she rose to a prominent position among the Omaha, primarily as bookkeeper and business manager. Rosalie became "the banker, the go-between, the chief financial officer of the tribe" (Green 1969, 104). She kept separate accounts for individuals and for the Omaha as a whole. She also served as distributor and accountant of funds that were earned from sales or leases of land or that had been donated by eastern philanthropic organizations. With her husband Edward Farley, an Irish immigrant with less formal education than herself, Rosalie managed the communal pasture, the "surplus" reservation land left over after individual allotments were made in the 1880s. Rosalie married Farley in 1880; she was nineteen and he thirty. He apparently came to the reservation as an organ salesman and sold Susette an organ for her classroom. When Rosalie and Ed first married they lived at the Presbyterian Mission, where they both taught school, and later moved to a small house on the reservation near the Agency. In 1884, they built a house on Rosalie's allotment just south of the reservation line near the present town of Bancroft, Nebraska. Rosalie and Ed had ten children, two of whom died at birth.

Since she spoke fluent English and moved in numerous Omaha and Anglo-American social contexts, on and off the reservation, Rosalie's house became a meeting place for many while she served as interpreter. Among her frequent house guests were influential Omaha men, Alice Fletcher, and other eastern Indian reformers such as Sara Kinney of the Connecticut Women's Indian Association.

Rosalie left a small but significant body of written records about colonization of the American Great Plains. Four sets of her unpublished writings are found in the much larger group of La Flesche Family Papers archived at the Nebraska State Historical Society.[4] Her two diaries

---

4. The many Omaha archival materials housed at the Nebraska State Historical Society (NSHS) include the La Flesche Family Papers; Correspondence of Rosalie La Flesche Farley, 1887–1899, Series 9; Diary of Rosalie La Flesche Farley, 1898 (microfilm), Series 11; Diary of Rosalie La Flesche Farley, 1899, Series 2; correspondence of the Farley Sons, 1889–1917, Series 4; correspondence of Francis La Flesche, 1886–1923, Series 1; Correspondence of Alice Cunningham Fletcher, 1886–1921, Series 3; Alice Fletcher and Francis La Flesche, "The Omaha Tribe," *Twenty-seventh Annual Report of the Bureau of American Ethnology, 1905–06* (Washington, D.C.: Government Printing Office, 1911). A number of other letters and unsigned fragments of Rosalie's handwriting survive in the La Flesche Family Papers, but since she transcribed letters for her husband, father, and other Omaha who were less proficient in English, I discuss only those that contain her signature.

document her everyday domestic life, such as her many housekeeping and child-rearing duties, and her letters document the extensive social and spatial relations into which she was tied in her business dealings. As businesswoman, she corresponded frequently with Alice Fletcher, her brother Frank, and other bureaucrats in Washington, D.C. She also wrote letters, documenting both personal and business affairs, to her sisters when they were back East lecturing or at school, and to her sons, as they began leaving home to attend school.

Rosalie's letters, all written from her farm, are terse and packed with details about leases on Omaha land, conflicts over land purchases, payments received, and impending litigation. Rosalie wrote to Frank for both "official" government advice for handling these matters as well as for his personal, unofficial advice. Her documentation of specific conflicts and issues provides insights into a number of land disputes, and their contribution is substantive. These letters speak of her efforts to prevail upon her family, other Omaha, encroaching white squatters, local businessmen, and numerous government officials in the allotting, selling, and leasing of Indian land. Perhaps more than anything else, though, these letters provide a unique opportunity to hear the voice of one influential Indian woman who was caught amid a range of competing cultures, economies, and patriarchies.

In this chapter I attempt to make sense of how Rosalie negotiated the many social spaces and subjectivities through which she maneuvered. I begin by first outlining the spaces of colonial relations into which she was embedded with the federal allotment and leasing programs and the local texture these took on within the Omaha Reservation by the time she came

---

Much of Rosalie's correspondence survives in the NSHS collection. Materials I do not substantially discuss are Rosalie's two diaries, dated January to December 1898, and August to December 1899. While small portions of the diaries inform the content of Rosalie's financial affairs, they consist mostly of routine day-to-day activities such as her sewing and cleaning, family social events, and the weather. Also in her diaries, though, are detailed accounts of purchases she made for the house or farm, and rent and boarder payments she received. Rosalie also wrote to her sons while they were starting out as university students, 1899–1900. These letters focus on family news and student life.

of age. This provides a context for examining extracts of Rosalie's letters that detail several of her involvements. In the last section of the chapter I consider the fruitfulness of a postcolonial approach in analyzing Rosalie's self-representations in her letters, and how one might assess her actions—for which, not incidentally, she absorbed a great deal of criticism. I pay particular attention to the gendered and racialized social and spatial relations to which Rosalie was tied and interpret them as products of American colonialism.

My purpose in all of this is twofold. First, I am implicitly interested in bringing Rosalie's own voice to the forefront in discussions of colonial land dispossession and changing land tenure for the Omaha. There remains a pressing need to continue "writing women in"—especially women who represent minority cultures and ethnicities—to such historical geographies of North America. To do so requires reaching beyond public or published documentary sources to the women's private sphere of letters and diaries, the significant genre of literate women's self-expression in the nineteenth century.

Second, I am more explicitly concerned with demonstrating how a postcolonial approach might enable a fruitful interpretation of these archival materials and, by implication, of other Native American historical geographies. Rosalie's story is ripe for postcolonial analysis; she occupied numerous conflicting, obviously distraught, but ultimately personally advantageous, spaces of "Indianness" in late nineteenth-century America. With Olund (2002), I would caution that assimilationist "successes" such as hers, though, must not be allowed to efface or wash over the larger processes and products of American colonialism.

Allotment, Leasing, and the Farley Pasture

The historical geography of Omaha land dispossession is complex and would be difficult to outline in even a book-length work, let alone in an abridged version here. Several works approach that task (Wishart 1994; Boughter 1998; McDonnell 1991, 399–411). At the macro level, an all-too-familiar sounding series of events, including decimation by white diseases, shrinkage of land base through forced treaties with the U.S. government in 1854 and 1865, liquidation of more land in 1871 to raise capital, the destruction of buffalo herds and wild game, and removal to an approximately 150,000-acre reservation in present-day north-east Nebraska, left the Omaha deeply factionalized and distressed by 1880. To exacerbate matters a bill was then pending in Congress to forcibly remove the Omaha, like their Ponca neighbors, to Indian Territory.

To counteract the threat of removal, the Omaha, with the assistance of Alice Fletcher, brought a petition before the 1881 Congress that specified the amount and location of Omaha lands then under cultivation. In response, the 1882 Congress passed the Omaha Allotment Act, which permitted allocations of the reservation in severalty and patents were issued for individual land holdings. By 1884 formal allotments had been made to 1,194 Omaha, involving 76,810 acres (Wishart 1994, 237). Throughout this process, the Omaha served, as it were, as an early test case "proving" the success of allotment to those who wanted to view it this way, despite the severe economic collapse taking place on the reservation, which the BIA and Congress ignored as they formulated the Dawes Act (Boughter 1998, 115–17).

The Omaha were quickly pressured by land speculators and settlers to lease or rent their land, and they did so long before Congress made it official federal Indian policy. Although the Dawes Act prohibited leasing during a twenty-five-year trust period, governmental rules and restrictions on leasing became increasingly liberal.[5] Though allotment derailed the threat of removal, the whole system led to serious abuses and was fraught with threats, coercion, and cheating. With no clear title or property rights, and prevented from mortgaging allotted land in order to acquire the capital necessary to make improvements, many Omaha were

5. The first (1891) leasing law stipulated that only those physically incapable or too old to work the land could lease it. This was amended in 1894 to include anyone with a nondescript "inability" to work the land (a stipulation later retracted, then again reinstated). McDonnell (1991, 43–59) and Boughter (1998, 134–42) provide helpful discussions of changing leasing laws and their terms (fees, acreages, maximum lengths, etc.). The whole system led to serious abuses, with Indian agents themselves often encouraging deals that personally benefited themselves or their friends, or local "land sharks" leasing lands from Indians for next to nothing and then re-leasing them to settlers at huge profits (Boughter 1982, 139).

simply forced into leasing arrangements and lived off the rent of their lands. The reformer's ideal of the assimilated, self-sufficient Indian farmer did not, for the most part, materialize. By 1892, 90 percent of the Omaha had leased all or part of their allotments and had in fact moved off of them, "getting by" on rent money.

Thousands of acres remained after individual allotments were made on the reservation from 1882 to 1887. One of Alice Fletcher's contributions to this process was in ensuring that this land would be held in common, to be cultivated and leased and rented, while being saved for future generations' allotments (rather than the more typical case of selling this surplus land at $1.25/acre). Fletcher proposed a cooperative grazing program for the common pasture. Before allotments, white ranchers had been allowed to graze cattle on reservation land by paying a fee to the agent (although many white squatters simply staked land for their own use, with no regard for the Indians' claims). Their cattle roamed free, often encroaching on the Indians' cultivated fields. After allotments, fences would be built and Omaha would be allowed to graze their cattle on the communal land at no charge while outsiders would be required to continue paying a fee. This pasture was the primary stage on which Rosalie and Ed Farley's business dealings with and for the Omaha were played out and about which Rosalie wrote her letters.

After 1892 the Indian agent was made officially responsible for granting leases, but a middleman was to be appointed to oversee the upkeep of the pasture, put up fences, manage the cattle, handle business transactions, and collect rents. At the end of the year the manager would deduct expenses, and then split any resulting profits between himself and the Omaha. Ed Farley in 1884 applied for pasture manager and was awarded a twenty-year lease on 18,000 unallotted acres at an annual rate of $0.04/ acre (Green 1969, 77–88). As Omaha were given preference and allowed to lease for longer periods of time, most of Ed and Rosalie's negotiations actually stood in Rosalie's name, with Ed designated as her agent. However, they worked together handling the pasture, eventually developing it into a large business operation that was making profits by 1889 and paying out several hundred dollars to the Omaha annually. Rosalie and Ed continued to renew leases and expand their operations, but the cattle business eventually grew to depend more on a feedlot than grazing on open pasture.

From the beginning the pasture was wrought with difficulties, and it led to a long succession of lease disputes and legal battles for Rosalie and Ed. Apparently, Ed had been profitably managing the pasture—he had 5,000 head of cattle on the range by 1888, was introducing new strains into the Omaha herds, and was among the first in the region to introduce winter feeding (Green 1969, 90–92). Although Rosalie and Ed made a profit and increased their acreage, their successes produced numerous complaints from Omaha as well as from outsiders who wished to take over the common lands. Many believed that Rosalie and Ed took more than their share of Omaha profits (Green 1969, 90–92; Wilson 1974, 355ff). Even Rosalie's sister, Susette, claimed that Ed mismanaged the cattle ranch and cheated her people (Boughter 1998, 107). As one La Flesche family biographer put it:

> The pasture became big business; but, through the years, it was beset by controversy, envy, intrigue and underhanded dealings which almost led to a small scale civil war. It meant success to the Farleys but it was dearly bought as balanced against the labor, the misunderstandings, the slander and suffering it brought to Rosalie and Ed. (Green 1969, 89)

Whatever the truth of the situation, many people wanted to challenge Ed and Rosalie's control and use of the pasture, and did so.

Rosalie's Letters

The twelve extant letters that Rosalie wrote to her brother Frank from 1896 to 1899 speak to the transformation of land tenure on the Omaha reservation and strategies Rosalie and others adopted to survive it.[6] Small portions of the letters describe social events on and off the reservation (usually involving her sons or other family members), but they mostly focus on business, legal, or political transactions. The letters seem intended to keep Frank (and others such as Alice Fletcher) abreast of the proceedings on

---

6. My editorial changes to Rosalie's letters are marked in brackets. References to individual letters are by date within the text.

the reservation, and name the involvements of nearly forty different individuals. Rosalie also detailed to Frank the specific banking transactions she made on behalf of individuals. Some of these transactions apparently involved Frank's own allotment (e.g., 14 July 1897), but she also documented the names of individuals who made payments on loans, or who were behind on their payments (e.g., 7 June 1896).

Rosalie's letters, written in English, often ask advice of Frank or of others occupying higher levels of the federal Indian bureaucracy, and they express gratitude for help rendered. Though it is unclear to which event(s) she was specifically referring in her first letter, dated 5 April 1896, for instance, she wrote that, "We know this much[,] if Miss F [letcher] had not gone to the office in my behalf our answer woul[d] have been "No" at the very star[t]." A few months later Rosalie wrote to Frank again after controversially but successfully obtaining a new set of leases on Omaha land that would be put toward "agricultural purposes." Her letter read:

> Will you please inclose in envelope and direct to [Major Larraber, of the U.S. Bureau of Indian Affairs] or hand to him? Am glad you told me to do this as I have been wanting to [write to him] ever since I received your last message but did not know whether it would be just the thing to do. I would indeed feel guilty if I forgot those to whose earnest efforts I was indebted for the favorable ending of my undertaking. Capt. sent the leases to me Wednesday. (9 July 1896)

In her (prior) letter of 7 June 1896, she had ensured Frank that the "Council signing the lease [referred to above] was in accordance with the act of Congress Oct 1894 authorizing the leasing of tribal lands for farming purposes for five years etc."

Rosalie's letters demonstrate a woman well versed in both Native American and Anglo-American law, the encroaching jurisdiction of one over the other, and her attempts to put both to use for her own purposes. In another letter to Frank, dated 28 October 1897, she declared:

> Always when I come up against anything you hear from me.
>   The Agent—Capt. Mercer has sent me a notice to appear before him the 5th of Nov in a case brought before him . . . to establish heirship or

ownership to the "Oldest grandmothers" land,[7] and I write in haste to ask you if the Interior Department had made any rulings in cases of this kind? [A]nd could you send me a list of authorities that will apply in this case?

In these ways Rosalie's letters make explicit the possibilities open to her for directing affairs with and through her friends in Washington, and the manner in which she was helped by them. Her letters contain many such references: "Am so glad to hear Miss Fletcher will speak to some of the members of the Board of Indian Commissioners, this will help so much . . . [W]e will soon have to push the matter" (22 January 1897), and in a letter dated 14 July 1897: "In regard to the Sloan case . . . You know how it is. I must move carefully in this matter but will do everything I can in a quiet way."[8]

Rosalie's letters make reference to a series of lawsuits in which she became embroiled over the common pasture. In 1890, Rosalie had obtained a lease for 2,632 acres (for five years, renewed each year for $0.25 an acre). In less than a year a lawsuit was brought against her in Federal District Court charging that the lease was fraudulent. William Peebles, a white land speculator, would-be Indian agent, and recurring opponent of Ed and Rosalie for rights to the common pasture, was behind the lawsuit. He charged that the Omaha had not authorized the agent to enter the agreement (there were, in fact, fewer than the required number of Omaha signatories), and that the lease was delaying allotment and therefore hurting

7. This letter refers to a family dispute over eighty acres of land named in a will over which Rosalie was executor.

8. According to Wilson (1974, 301, 369), Tom Sloan was a lawyer who worked for Indian reforms and also was one who had made claims on land leased to Rosalie. In an immediately subsequent letter dated 27 July 1897, Frank wrote to Rosalie saying he thought that the Sloan case had been settled. The matter was not easily solved, however; in a letter dated over two years later, 1 September 1899, Frank informed Rosalie that the agent asked to have some Omaha money set aside to defend the Sloan case. Shortly after that, on 4 December 1899, Frank wrote to Ed saying that Tom Sloan offered to pay the asking price ($2.50/acre) for a parcel of "his and my land," and that Frank was considering letting Sloan have it.

the Indians. Peebles and his group of white speculators from the town of Pender, Nebraska, encouraged squatters and others, who otherwise would not be entitled to allotments, to lay claim to unallotted lands in hopes of buying them later (that is, leases would be withdrawn if the land was allotted). Peebles was determined to nullify Rosalie's lease on the common pasture, and he attempted several strategies to do so, including telling the Omaha that he could arrange for a better deal than Rosalie's.

Peebles's lawsuit was defeated on appeal when it was found that he had forged names of Indians on a document that identified him as their representative. Later, Rosalie brought a countersuit of conspiracy against Peebles, arguing that because he advertised that pasture land was soon to be allotted, no one was interested in renting it and Ed and Rosalie lost business. During the conspiracy trial, each juror was asked whether the fact that Mrs. Farley was an Indian would in any way affect their decision. "They all said they did not [hold and biases], yet in his summation, Peebles's attorney appealed to racial prejudices, reminding the jurors of every atrocity ever committed by Indians" (Boughter 1998, 145).

Rosalie eventually lost the case, though the original jury could not find a verdict against her and asked to be excused. Three years later the Supreme Court of Nebraska reversed the earlier decision, asserting that the conspiracy had in fact been proven and that squatters should be removed (Green 1969, 92ff; Boughter 1998, 141–46).

Disagreements among the Indian agents, Peebles and other land speculators, and Omaha allottees led to years of further litigation and conflict on the reservation. (At one point, a battle ensued over law enforcement jurisdictions—with the county sheriff arresting the Indian police and the police arresting the sheriff [Boughter 1998, 142–57].) Rosalie and Ed's troubles with the pasture did not end with the Peebles's conspiracy trial. In 1896, a petition (the "Fontenelle petition") was circulating, charging that Rosalie and Ed were not paying the Omaha enough for the new leases. The petition attracted sufficient attention that the Indian Affairs office sent a representative to investigate possible discrepancies, but none were found. Detractors claimed, though, that this was due simply to Frank La Flesche's involvement in interpreting the representative's report. In her letters Rosalie was concerned to prove that her leasing practices were fair, that her operation was productive, and that the Omaha were receiving a competitive income from them:

> Big Omaha said he thought it so absurd for those kicking against the lease—Fontenelle & followers—to claim they were not getting enough for the land leased to me when thousands of acres under pasture east of Bancroft . . . they are leasing this spring to parties for farming purposes for .50c an acre for the first two years and .75c for the three years, and taking it in trade at a big price, and this is allotted land.
>
> About 7000 acres now broken and 4000 acres in flax and corn. 180 teams at work plowing and seeding. It will be all broken inside of three weeks. (7 June 1896)

Rosalie's letters suggest a woman who depended on the support of her brother and others in Washington, but who was also determined and enterprising on her own when dealing with Omaha men, local land speculators, or Washington officials. Her letter to Frank of 9 July 1896 describes her negotiations with a group of local men who had made investments in the newly leased land:

> The contract I was to sign was sent up to me Monday . . . Mr McNish read it over three times to me and explain[ed] matters to me. . . . I still hesitated telling them that I wanted you to see the contract, that at the first reading I saw that they had protected their interests enough, and wanted to be sure that mine were protected also in every way, that I expected to sign but did not wish to be hurried.
>
> They were here all afternoon and read it over and over to me and talked each paragraph over . . . They told me I must have confidence in them, that this contract should have been signed by me before a dollar of theirs was invested but they had so much confidence in me so let it go till the lease was approved, and went right ahead and put their money into the undertaking trusting to my honor, now that the rental had to be paid asked me to sign before they advanced any more money. That when you come I could have you read it and if you thought they were taking undue advantage of me in any way they would be willing to modify or fix any of the paragraphs objected to. All there really is about it is that

they are to advance the money this first year to run it. This money will be paid back out of the proceeds out of the land. I am to have one third of the profits, after this year . . . I did not wish to be unreasonable so signed it. I hated to as I thought you and my friend ought to see it first, but our friend Mr. Rice of the Citizens Bank saw the contract and said he could see nothing wrong in it.

Most of Rosalie's letters discuss the legal or political status of lease applications and allotments. One letter mentions Peebles's campaign for position of Omaha Indian agent, to which Rosalie was vehemently opposed. She told Frank that "It is good to know you will look out about Peebles, we may defeat him after all" (22 January 1897). (Peebles was not appointed.) As Peebles had encouraged squatters to lay claim to unallotted Omaha land, in another letter dated 25 February 1897 Rosalie quoted correspondence from the Indian agent Beck, who was aligned with Rosalie and against Peebles and his sympathizers among the Omaha (but who himself was also mired in leasing irregularities) (Boughter 1998, 149),

> I sent a letter to Capt. about the persons on the land covered by the lease and this is what I have received from him. Madame: . . . Your communication of the 16th., inst., received. I have taken steps to eject the persons illegally occupying the land leased by you and communicated the information to your Attorney before receiving your letter.

In addition, much of Rosalie's writing aligns with reformist rhetoric promoting Omaha assimilation into Anglo culture via the model of the self-sufficient Indian farmer. In a letter of 25 September 1899 Rosalie portrayed Ed as a man working against the "idle landlording" mentality that many assumed to be the cause of Omaha social decline:

> Walter came out to tell Ed he was going to lease the old place to som[e] men in Iowa for 5 years for stock raising but Ed advised him not to. [He told him that] he could raise stock himself there [a]nd make it pay. [S]o he has given i[t] up.

Some of Rosalie's last letters (of 1899) also speak of the eventual allotment of the remaining communal lands as per an amendment to the 1882 federal legislation. This amendment allowed for additional allotments to be made, mostly to women and children who had been left out of the original proceedings. But because the available land was now considered finite, children born after 1893 would be excluded. Documentary evidence shows that Frank La Flesche wrote to Rosalie at the time and suggested that since there would not be enough land to go around, that she should "quietly and quickly" file papers for her own children's allotments (as quoted in Boughter 1998, 155).[9] For this he said that the Indian Council at the time wanted him removed because he had helped Rosalie and Ed "swindle the Omahas" (Francis La Flesche to Rosalie Farley, 1898). At the time of the later allotments Rosalie described events then taking place on the reservation:

We went over yesterday [to the Council meeting]. Special Agent read conditions under which allotments were to be made. Wajapa and Noah thought best to let it come, so when it was put to them they agreed to let it come. [O]f course they were many who really did not understand, I told Noah so but he said "It does not matter let them go." He said "It will strike some of our children but it will strike them just as hard, they wanted the land allotted let them have it." Mathewson had Chase do the interpreting, and he blundered through it shamefully . . .

I happened to stand near Chase & helped him out more than once in putting the Indian into English. Mathewson said, "Now we will go out side of building & count those who want the land allotted as they pass out." This was done. [The allotting agent] said he would report at once to Washington[.] After the count was over, there came Nebraska back into the building saying he would have a few words with the Special Agent. Said he had been very favorably impressed with the conditions [r]ead to them, but understood outside that the children they wanted it for were to be left out. He was told he was too late with his question, his face was a funny looking one, when he finally took it in. He has two under six so has Chase, & a good many others who have been clamoring for allotment. Walter looked pretty [blue?], I felt so sorry for him. Susie

9. This refers to Francis La Flesche to Rosalie Farley, 23 January 1898, Correspondence of Francis La Flesche, 1886–1923, Folder 3, Series 1, La Flesche Family Papers, NSHS.

took it easy, said "Let them have the land allotted & be done with it. My children will be left out but it will not hurt them."[10] (10 May 1899)

In other correspondence of Rosalie's, such as a letter to her son Caryl, dated only 1899, she described in detail the ensuing allotment process:

> The Allotting Agent is camped out . . . we heard he was going to allot in Sec. 7 where we want land so we drove over there only to find him out allotting between Winnebago and Omaha Agency. We waited for him to get in all afternoon and just as we were coming away near sun down he got in to camp. He told us when he allotted out where we want land he would let us know.

Two of Rosalie's diary entries also describe her attempts to secure some of the later allotments. On 4 October 1899 she wrote that she "went to Pilcher place and waited all afternoon for [the allotting agent], said he would let us know when he was ready for us." In a letter dated two weeks later, on 18 October, she added:

> [The agent] told me he came to allot the land to the children and took down their names and beneath each name the description of the land. Said we could change the children around if we wished. I showed him the tract Ed had taken for the children and said it was as Ed had given it to him said as far as he knew there was no one claiming the same tract— clear for our taking. [The agent] gave them drawing of the land.[11]

All but one of Rosalie and Ed's eight surviving children were born before 1893, and thus they were secured individual allotments. The children of

10. Hiram Chase was one of the attorneys hired by the Omaha to fight an extension of the twenty-five-year period in which payments for leases could be held in trust by the federal government. Nebraska (Simon Hallowell) was also on the committee fighting the extension. Wajapa was cousin to and supporter of Joseph La Flesche, and as Olund (2002) points out, he was one of the Omaha who testified before the Senate. Noah Leaming was Rosalie's brother-in-law, husband to her sister Lucy.

11. Correspondence of the Farley Sons, 1889–1917, Folder 1, Series 4; Diary of Rosalie La Flesche Farley, 1899, Folder 1, Series 2; La Flesche Family Papers, NSHS.

many other Omaha, including some of Rosalie's immediate family (such as Susan's), though, were not.

Discussion: Postcolonialism and the Case of Rosalie La Flesche Farley

Rosalie's letters raise some provocative questions about American colonial encounters. Hopefully, bringing attention to her letters suggests some value in incorporating women's spaces, biographies, voices, careers, and contributions into historical geographies of North America and elsewhere. There remains a pressing need to provide an antidote to the Great Man tradition that continues to dominate North American historical geography and thus structure thought and inquiry. Questions of epistemological orientations, narrowly defined subjects of study, available evidence, and research methodologies remain at the forefront of producing more critical and polyvocal historical geographies. Meanwhile, though, we need also to think very carefully about *how* we recover women or other silenced voices in historical geography, and for what ends. What are we learning about gendered subjectivity, for instance, and how it informs an understanding of Euro-American expansionism and Native American land dispossession?

Insights provided by postcolonial studies can aid in interpreting Rosalie's life and writings. However, in attempting to situate her and her texts specifically within North American historical geography, one immediately confronts something of a historical closure around the concept of postcolonialism in the United States that has only recently begun to be addressed. Significantly, postcolonial critics and geographers of Native Americans have not found a great deal of common ground (Rundstrom et al. 2000, 85–110). A substantial literature in North American historical geography traces American expansionism and colonial consolidation of a sort (Mitchell and Groves 1990; Meinig 1986–2004, vols. 1–4). Yet such works take little advantage of the insights and concepts that have come to be associated with postcolonial thought.

By contrast, and in line with other British commonwealth countries that share a history of British colonialism, Canadian geographers of First Nation's peoples have often adopted postcolonial theories and language

(Sparke 1998, 463–95; Willems-Braun 1997, 3–31; Blomley 1996, 5–35; Peters 1997, 56–61; Clayton 2000; Peters 2000, 44–55). Some enthusiasm for postcolonialism is evident in U.S. Native American geography. Several studies are taking up postcolonial projects: identity claims mired in issues of Native "authenticity"; reconquest through place naming; pan-Indian ecology claims; and colonial representation and resistance (Hannah 1993, 412–32; Silvern 1995, 262–85; Herman 1999, 76–102). Yet, this represents a small fraction of that subfield.

American studies scholar Amy Kaplan (1993, 3–21), and after her Hulme (1995, 116–23), Richard King (2000), Rowe (2000), Singh and Schmidt (2000), Sharpe (2000, 103–21) and others discuss the "problem" of postcolonialism in the United States. "Orthodox" postcolonial studies focus on the processes and products of European colonialism and impe- rialism, while American colonial and imperial relations, the American empire itself, has remained nearly invisible within this theoretical ori- entation. As Kaplan points out, there remains "a resilient paradigm of American exceptionalism"—an ongoing denial of American colonialism and imperialism within postcolonial studies (1993, 11–17). Castle's (2001) anthology of postcolonial discourses, for instance, promises to regional- ize works coming out of that field, yet no sustained reflections about U.S. colonialism or imperialism within the United States appear in his book. Instead, it focuses on places that are by now familiar case settings for post- colonial critiques—India, Africa, the Caribbean, British settler colonies, and Ireland.

Postcolonialism in an American context is complicated by a num- ber of factors. If continuing colonial or neocolonial relations in the for- mer European colonies strain the meaning of the "post" of postcolonial, this is perhaps even more the case in an American context. In the United States, formal decolonization and nationalist independence movements of the twentieth century—which arguably initiated the identifiable field of postcolonial studies—have little relevance, at least on the surface. But I would emphasize that the problems and limitations of the linear or chronological approach to "post"-colonial relations is not unique to the U.S. context. Furthermore, there are critics who align mid-twentieth-cen- tury resistance movements in the United States (such as civil rights) with other decolonization movements, arguing these were modeled on Third World liberation struggles (Spivak 1988). The "after" of the colonial in the U.S. context for Jenny Sharpe (2000), on the other hand, represents the neocolonial relations that currently intersect with global capitalism and international divisions of labor, especially with decolonized nations. These theorists, then, collectively focus on the postwar international context in their critique of U.S. postcolonialism, as opposed to the "internal colonization" models of racial or ethnic exclusions (discussed below and in the next chapter).

Another factor complicating postcolonialism in an American context is the popular narrative of heroic Americans who fought a war of independence from Britain and who have thus been seen by many as producing an inherently anticolonial state. When an American "empire" (of the European sort) is recognized, it is typically only insofar as U.S. imperialism extending to distant colonizations of places such as the Philippines and Puerto Rico. I am in agreement with Rowe, however, who argues that the U.S. experience might best be considered one in which the rhetoric of an anticolonial revolution against the old world was used to justify its own imperial expansion both against the European powers on the North American continent and in the practice of its own violent internal colonization (2000, 5–7). And in fact, studies on internal colonization of ethnic minorities and Native peoples have a long genealogy in American studies, since the 1950s if not before (Berkhofer 1978; Drinnon 1980; Slotkin 1973; Tompkins 1992). Richard King further argues that the postcolonial paradigm clearly applies to the United States simply because such internal colonization occurred in the United States and its aftermath has everything to do with American identities, institutions, and idioms (2000, 3).

It seems essential to keep in mind that with its historically explicit economic, strategic, and political expansionist policies throughout its history, colonialism in the American context, as compared with its European counterparts, has always been "close to home" (Kaplan 1993, 18). Study of eighteenth and nineteenth century national consolidation and incorporation of different territories, peoples, languages, and currencies into a "nation" has formed one branch of an American postcolonialism that does not rely on a linear or chronological (twentieth century) frame. A number of American studies or ethnic studies scholars consider the United States ripe for such study, especially of the sexist and racist foundations of the American nation. They approach this primarily but not exclusively through the study of literary texts (Singh and Schmidt 2000).

Thus, while Krupat might argue that there simply is no "post" to Native American colonization (2000, 73–94), Singh and Schmidt assert that Native American and other ethnic fiction in the United States reads much like other postcolonial literatures and thus must be included among them (2000, 4; Pease 1994). They refer to the textual moods, styles, and tendencies of this literature, and the fact that they display the familiar tropes of postcolonialism: double-consciousness, mobility, hybridity, diaspora effects, and "third spaces" that are neither assimilationist nor otherness.

Rosalie La Flesche Farley's life and writing exhibit a complex of gendered and racialized subjectivities and social spaces that American colonialism brought into being—those "tropes of postcolonialism." A postcolonial approach here, then, would infer, among other things, the usefulness of unsettling essentialist identity constructs deployed in colonial contexts. My specific intervention suggests that postcolonial approaches to studying relations of difference in the context of Omaha land dispossession challenges self-evident claims to American national identity and notions of progress and stability embedded in them. As a starting place, then, postcolonialism's consistent and self-conscious sensitivity to the complexities involved in making assumptions and claims about "Indian identity" is essential. To approach archival sources such as those left by Rosalie La Flesche Farley requires, as a first step, a substantial opening up of categories such as victims and villains, colonizers and colonized. Two texts that I frequently cite in this chapter provide a comprehensive background to Omaha land dispossession, but both assume rather unproblematized Omaha identities in their works. Wishart prefaces his 1994 *An Unspeakable Sadness* by stating that the Omaha suffered an across-the-board "loss of subsistence, a loss of history, and a loss of identity" in the face of American expansionism. And according to Boughter (1998), two positions were available to the main protagonists involved in leasing and allotting of Omaha land: "victim" or "villain." Obviously, neither of these positions quite captures the experiences and agency demonstrated by Rosalie La Flesche Farley.

Importantly, though, one must also situate Rosalie's writings within the model of American internal colonization outlined above, with the caveat that the colonial spaces she occupied were themselves fragmented, fraught with a range of competing cultures, economies, and patriarchies. The effect was both a limiting and opening up of possibilities for agency and action on her part.

Her letters capture one voice among many whose perspectives have heretofore been left out (and which earlier American studies' scholars such as Berkofer did not, for the most part, consider). Postcolonialism's consistent and self-conscious sensitivity to colonial discourses focuses on the representational and cultural politics involved in the production of knowledges about and by colonial underclasses (Said 1983). Among the goals of such work is the decentering of European thought and discourses, and highlighting the opposition or resistance to "the whole colonial syndrome" as read from colonial texts (Hulme 1995, 12). With these goals also in mind, one might ask how Rosalie strategized her own and her peoples' survival during this peak transitional moment in changing land tenure on the Great Plains.

Rosalie died in 1900, at age thirty-nine, with one child still under the age of three. She had not been well for years, suffering from frequent headaches, colds, and inflammatory rheumatism (Green 1969, 116–17). After her death a town named Rosalie was settled on the reservation (see the afterword). It is the only place named after a member of the La Flesche family. Her obituary was published in the *Omaha Bee,* and ran in part:

> Mrs Farley never severed her relations with the tribe . . . [she] was one of its most influential personages. Old Iron Eye was a keen, strong man and although he left . . . other children, his mantle fell on his daughter Rosalie. She was a woman of rare business qualifications, conducting large enterprises successfully . . . But her influence among the Omaha was not due to sagacity, she was an earnest Christian woman who . . . persistently and unselfishly sought to induce the tribe to accept the benefits of education and Christianity. She was the resource of the poor, the

sick and the improvident, her life was a benediction, truly she was one of the most remarkable women of the state. (Green 1969, 118)

As both her letters and this newspaper obituary attest, Rosalie occupied a shifting set of social and spatial positions on the reservation. This obituary, while praising Rosalie as one of the "most remarkable women of the state," acknowledged her business abilities as well as her embodiment of civilized, selfless, Victorian womanhood. It draws out her complexly layered identity as not only a "progressive" Indian who had adopted Christianity and the moral authority of female white culture, but also as a successful woman entrepreneur.

Rosalie was seen during her lifetime as a progressive Indian, not only willing to adopt land tenure reform and agricultural practices imposed by the federal government, and exploit the American legal and political systems to suit her own ends, but also succeeding at both better than most. Reform rhetoric of the day such as that articulated by Alice Fletcher posited the hope that successful, prosperous Indians such as Rosalie might emerge. Yet it seems that her experiences might be more plausibly viewed, to reverse Audre Lorde's (1984) famous dictum, as a partial dismantling of the master's house using the master's tools. After all, the quintessential Jeffersonian agrarian farmer served by federal policies such as the Homestead Act (upon which the Dawes Act was modeled) needed to be, above all, of pure European descent. Like both her father and her mother, Rosalie was a "mixed-blood" (with a French paternal grandfather and maternal grandfather who was a Caucasian doctor with the U.S. army), and she herself married an Irishman. As Sarah Carter and many others have suggested in other contexts, such intermarriages produced progeny who subverted the social order to the extent that they could not be considered "legitimate heirs to a European inheritance" (Carter 1997; Stoler 1992, 515). Rosalie's potential inclusion in nation was always mediated by her potential transgressiveness as "savage Indian" in such colonial spaces as courtrooms. Witness again William Peebles's attorney attempting to win the conspiracy case Rosalie had brought against him by reminding the courtroom jury of totally unrelated Indian-white conflicts.

Rosalie successfully competed, possibly at the expense of others in her community, in individualized, capitalist production of Omaha land while adopting American-style Victorian codes of respectability and material values. That she personally prospered amid the serious decline of many of those around her requires an examination of the range of possibilities open to her to occupy colonial space. The small set of letters examined here can provide a window into the larger social and spatial dynamics of colonialism, and the racialized and gendered subjectivities that they produced. Rosalie's writings point to numerous sites of accommodation, appropriation, complicity, and resistance to American expansionism.

Although Rosalie traveled to argue her land cases at the state as well as national level and also traveled to a limited degree for pleasure, most of her life was spent on the reservation, doing business and raising her family. Her letters show the extensive reach of colonial space into which she and other Omaha were thrust, providing one eyewitness account of them. The reservation itself was, of course, a product of American colonization in the first instance, bringing the likes of Alice Fletcher to Nebraska and forcing the Omaha to deal with a colonial hierarchy of numerous local, regional, and national scales. Looming large were numerous congressional acts that threatened forced removal, then forced allotment, then de facto forced leasing, and ultimately forced allotment of the common pasture. All of these measures simply sped disintegration of Omaha land. And yet, Rosalie and Ed were among those who managed to staunchly stay put.

At the very least Rosalie's letters demonstrate her close connection to and even manipulation of the federal Indian bureaucracy and its functionaries, including her brother Frank. They show the manner in which she educated herself on legal and political matters through it in order to make the best of a deteriorating situation. Her letters attest to the successes she enjoyed obtaining and maintaining leases on the common pasture and the personal struggles involved in doing so. To Frank she confessed: "I still hesitated telling them I wanted you to see the contract, that at the first reading I saw that they had protected their interests enough, and I wanted to be sure that mine were protected also in every way." Leasing the pasture personally profited Rosalie and Ed, but it also protected the land from the likes of William Peebles and other white speculators. In this sense

Rosalie's letters demonstrate her resistance to further encroachment of Omaha land by white settlement. Rosalie's letters make clear the pressure she endured from speculators to take over this land, and how she managed to strategically adopt her legal status as Indian when it brought her business advantages, but allow for her own Anglicization when it suited her other purposes.

Rosalie presented herself as someone who conducted business fairly and productively, arguing that the Omaha were receiving a competitive income from the leases she obtained (e.g., letter dated 7 June 1896). But her statements must be viewed from within the context of increasing insecurity that the Omaha faced in general. Her description of the final allotment of the common pasture, of both her own preemptive measures and the dreaded discovery by others that they were among the property-less (letter dated 10 May 1899) posits the deepening fractures among the Omaha produced by colonial imperatives. This process further pitted Rosalie against other Omaha in competition for the land. Rosalie's shrewdness here does not appear as "properly" Indian but thoroughly Anglicized in its individualism. Complaints that she acted in her own best interests rather than for those of the group rely on a discourse of proper Indianness, a discourse itself produced by colonialism, which she also transgressed when it suited her or was demanded by the situation. Her (and her family's) actions on many levels caused divisiveness among the Omaha; to many they were antithetical to anything resembling the protection or survival of the group as a group. By all accounts Rosalie wanted to retain the common pasture, but detractors argued that this was simply for her own personal gain, rather than to preserve tribal commonalties, welfare, or identity.

Rosalie's "progressiveness" must also be viewed through a lens that takes into account the gendered racialized differences of the colonial spaces she occupied. She was a member of a well-connected, elite Omaha family whose social hierarchies both preceded and were entrenched by American colonial expansion. Such social positioning gave her access to people, institutions, and rhetorical outlets that most other Omaha women likely did not enjoy. She became transactor of business via her privileged family connections, and the fact that her letters survive at all attests to the rather exceptional position she occupied. It would prove more the exception than the rule that Rosalie as a woman conducted business with and for the Omaha, and in that sense much of her life and writings speak to the strong similarities between the cross-cultural patriarchies that she also negotiated.

The archive offers Rosalie's self-representation as an Anglicized, "civilized" woman. Her letters demonstrate the many accoutrements of the dominant culture's gendered roles and relations that she took on, no doubt influenced by the American education she received from the Presbyterian missionaries installed on the reservation. Theirs and other reform policies centered on turning their downtrodden Native sisters into properly pure, self-sacrificing moral guardians of their households as well as successful domestic engineers (i.e., housewives). Rosalie in many ways embodied the reformer's success story: the Anglicized Native woman.

Rosalie's letters portray a woman who pursued power, livelihood, and personal success; she presented herself as enterprising but always a gentlewoman. The proper gentility and deference she showed her brother and others might in fact have facilitated the businesswoman persona she also displayed. One might interpret the power and success she enjoyed in business negotiations as deriving from her abilities to adopt and maintain acceptable bourgeois womanhood. Her letters demonstrate her attempts to downplay her own self-interest, for example, in arguing instead that her actions were ultimately intended for the general uplift of the Omaha. Consider again her (25 September 1899) letter describing her husband's efforts at persuading his fellow Omaha to work his own land, rather than lease it to outsiders from Iowa.

But Rosalie's gendered racialized identity is not that straightforward, either. If middle-class Anglo culture at the time measured women's status by domesticity that complemented men's productive movement into the public capitalist sphere, Rosalie's life and writing transgressed the boundaries of that femininity. Her self-image teeters on the protofeminist, New Woman of the late nineteenth century, as she spoke and wrote for many Omaha men (e.g., letter dated 10 May 1899) as well as her husband, and in numerous other ways entered the masculinized spheres of business, politics, and law, both Native American and Anglo American.

She could never, on the other hand, fully embody the position of bourgeois "career" woman of nineteenth-century Europe or America either. While the latter might have been considered marginally acceptable in this role if they simultaneously maintained their proper femininity, Rosalie's situation was quite different. She may have adopted some of the same markers of femininity for much the same reasons white women did—to ease the potential transgressiveness of movement into masculine spheres. Yet the risks associated with adopting markers of white bourgeois femininity might have been considerably greater and the stakes higher for her in the colonial space of the reservation: consider again her letter dated 9 July 1896 and the palpable pressure she felt negotiating a complicated leasing contract alone with land-hungry men of the dominant culture: "I did not wish to be unreasonable so signed it."

In any case, adopting a particular gendered identity may not have been a straightforward strategy on Rosalie's part. In some ways her story might not be too unlike those of other Native women forced to choose among alternate patriarchies, in their attempts to make the best of their individual circumstances (if not to simply survive) (Schuurman 1998, 141–58). Carter, for instance, argues that on the Canadian prairies in the 1890s, Native women were portrayed as dangerous, promiscuous threats to white settlers and community builders. In this way they provided a contrast against which white settler women's femininity could be, literally, invented (Carter 1997). Rosalie too, it seems, might always have been negotiating something akin to this underlying "savage menace" threat.

Late nineteenth-century North American colonial encounters tended to produce such oppositional representations of Native women—good ones and bad ones—as well as setting them both in opposition against Anglo women. Rosalie mediated colonial spaces and subjectivities that cast her a long way from either the ineffective, innocent princess image of Native women or the masculinization of the Indian squaw, the two most popular representations of Native American women in the nineteenth century (Pascoe 1990, 123; Albers and James 1987; Albers and Medicine 1983; see chapter 6). She is also quite distanced from the more sympathetic portrayals of Omaha women that point to the relative power and prestige they enjoyed via their more traditional roles in Indian society (Wishart 1995,

509–18). Yet such representations were never far from popular discourse even well into the 1890s and undoubtedly served to frame all of Rosalie's interactions as well. How her adoption of Anglicized femininity might have mediated her relations with other Omaha men and women beyond those described in these letters is difficult to speculate about, although again her family's privileged social standing in the community would be the place to begin in doing so.

I would conclude by observing that Rosalie La Flesche Farley responded to American colonialism in ways that ensured the comfortable survival of herself, her family, and her many descendents. The town named after her still stands today. She was in many ways an exceptional historical figure. I find her purposeful self-education, her business shrewdness, and her unwillingness to be intimidated very appealing. Her appeal, though, is of course complicated by the situation of those she left behind in her business dealings. Like the stories of other Victorian women who used their class positions to advance their own personal status and rights, Rosalie's story grates uncomfortably against present-day antisexist and antiracist sensibilities. A postcolonial approach to the study of her letters, though, allows a measure of understanding about how the gendered and racialized spaces and subjectivities she occupied were products of an American colonialism that to this day is producing few winners on the Omaha reservation.

✳ 8 ✳

Mining Empire

Journalists in the American West, circa 1870

MIRIAM LESLIE AND SARA JANE CLARKE LIPPINCOTT (also known as Grace Greenwood) were two widely read, influential American magazine and newspaper correspondents of the late nineteenth century. Both of these women took transcontinental tours of the United States in the 1870s and subsequently compiled their serialized newspaper accounts into travel books about their experiences (Greenwood 1872; Leslie 1877). This chapter addresses the need for further feminist postcolonial analyses of American women's travel writing about their American "home" in the nineteenth century. My analysis of Leslie and Lippincott concentrates primarily on what they wrote about American national consolidation via the development of large-scale industrial mining in the American West. The women discussed the principal site of mining at that time, the Comstock Lode in Nevada, as well as other mines in Colorado and California. Western mining was then entering a new phase of industrial-scale, technologically advanced operations that relied on both large capital investments and waged laborers.

I examine what Lippincott and Leslie wrote about the wealthy mine owners and emerging industrialists who served as their hosts and patrons during their travels as well as their writings about the workers they observed. I analyze their writings principally in terms of their feminist "reform politics" as well as their imperial politics. Among other issues, I am concerned with how the women deployed reform rhetoric in the cause of exploited mine workers but also how such rhetoric complicates a straightforward reading of their imperial politics. Imperial development of industrial mining depended on the hierarchies produced out of ethnic, class, and gender differences. The internal colonization processes and practices that these texts supported were integral to American continental expansion (see chapter 7).

My ulterior motive here is to situate Lippincott's and Leslie's writings within current debates about the meaning and applicability of a postcolonial critique for the United States. In so doing I make the obvious though still contested assumption that "colonialism happened" in the United States. The travel writings of these women demonstrate potential sites of engagement for feminism, U.S. historical geography, and colonial and postcolonial studies. The texts provide useful sites for exploring the intersections between the women's gendered subjectivity and imperial development in the American West, while also demonstrating potential postcolonial sites of opposition to, or support of, that development.

As I examine the gendered and racialized foundations of the American nation through these texts, I further consider how miners seemed to negotiate their place in the emergent American nation. In that sense I am mindfully working against the potential of reconstituting women journalists as autonomous subjects unilaterally projecting metropolitan understandings of themselves and others onto their reading public. Part of my project thus entails being attuned to the constitutive and dialogical role of western people and places in the production of these colonial discourses. I agree with Pratt (2001, 280) who argues that sensitivity to such interactive processes is essential to avoid falling into the trap of the "self-privileging imaginary that framed the travel and travel books in the first place."

In attempting to raise the possibility of a postcolonial critique of the writings of Leslie and Lippincott, one confronts the difficulties of applying the postcolonial method to the American context (discussed in chapter 7). Although this chapter does not address the removal of Native and Mexican Americans in the areas of western mines nor their reintegration as waged laborers, it must be understood that the mineral resource extraction industry fundamentally depended on their tragic land dispossession, coordinated primarily through the efforts of the U.S. government, land speculators, and settlers. That arm of internal colonization, however, should not be viewed as separate from other, interrelated forms of American and European imperial expansion of the nineteenth century that involved the integration of mining capital, workers, and technology on global, national, and local scales.

Postcolonial critics' consistent and self-conscious sensitivity to colonial discourses draws attention to the representational and cultural politics involved in the production of knowledges about colonial or imperial underclasses produced by them. Among the goals of such work is to decenter metropolitan thought and discourses and to highlight resistance as read from colonial texts. The "colonial underclasses" in the case of western mining includes European (Cornish and Irish) and Chinese immigrants whose experiences and actions were both constrained and broadened by the colonial spaces of the western mines. How they strategized their own survival amid the processes of immigration and diaspora effects, changing mining technologies, and labor relations and practices can be fruitfully read through the texts of these women. My specific intervention suggests that postcolonial approaches to studying relations of difference in colonial and imperial contexts challenges self-evident claims to American national identity and notions of progress and stability embedded within them. The writings of Lippincott and Leslie, then, can serve as a window into some of the larger processes of American internal consolidation of nation—a window, in other words, into the struggles for power to define who rightfully belongs to nation.

American Women Writing America

Depending on how one defines "travel literature," one might usefully expand traditional notions of nineteenth-century American women's travel writing to include narratives that describe minority ethnic women's experiences of forced removal, immigration, and diaspora. Hundreds of recently reprinted primary works, as well as critical secondary works on nineteenth-century women traveling in America, abound. Georgi-Findlay (1996) provides a useful overview of one hundred years of Anglo-American women's narratives of American westward expansion. Women's writing about the American West ranges from immigrant and settler accounts of westward migrations; to the accounts of army wives traveling in an administrative or military capacity with their husbands during the "Indian wars"; to accounts by tourists on holiday at the newly established national parks; to accounts of missionaries, teachers, and other "frontier" reformers; to accounts more properly identified as belles lettres or fiction. Other writers fit more squarely within what might be termed "booster" literature—women who traveled with husbands who were hired by the railroads to publicize, promote, and write guidebooks for the western regions, both for future settlers and tourists as well as for future railroad reconnaissance purposes.

In some ways Lippincott and Leslie might be loosely characterized as western boosters, as they both traveled as guests of the railroad companies and their hosts and patrons were among the wealthy mine owners and emerging industrialists of the region. Both were also, though, well-established journalists reporting on the West to their East Coast audiences, and in this sense they were quite exceptional women. In 1880, only 288 of the 12,308 people in the United States identifying themselves as journalists were women (Beasley 1993, 10). The genres of journalism and travel writing complemented one another during this period, for instance in the ways that women could "legitimately" contribute to both via the epistolary (letter-writing) form.

One might easily frame Sara Lippincott (1823–1904) as an early "Washington correspondent" sympathetic to reform causes. Writing and lecturing under the pseudonym Grace Greenwood, she was a well-known U.S. East Coast journalist, travel correspondent, lecturer, and feminist of her time. Though not an active member of the reform or progressive movement proper, Lippincott spoke and wrote on reform issues of the day, including in support of abolition, women's rights, prison reform, and against capital punishment (Garrett 1997). Lippincott was one of the earliest newspaperwomen in the United States, for, among others, the *Ladies' Home Journal,* the abolitionist *National Era,* the *Saturday Evening Post,* and the *New York Tribune.* She was the first woman employed by the *New York Times* and was also a writer and editor of children's stories and books of poetry. She supported herself, her daughter, and her husband at times, in a profession that offered few opportunities for women.

18. Sara Lippincott (Grace Greenwood), ca. 1875. Photo reproduced
with permission of PictureHistory.

Lippincott often wrote in the epistolary form in her newspaper correspondence and travel narratives. A popular speaker, she took several
lecture tours through the American West and owned a home in Colorado.
New Life in New Lands: Notes of Travel (Greenwood 1872) is a compilation
of an eighteen-month series of articles she wrote about her transcontinental railroad trip from Chicago through Colorado, Utah, Nevada, and
California between July 1871 and November 1872, originally published
in the *New York Times*. In addition to reporting on Western mining,
she described railroad travel, landscape scenery, the situation of Native
Americans, local political and economic growth issues, and explorations
of Yosemite with John Muir. She also devoted two chapters to Colorado
and its future.

Miriam Leslie's personal flair and marriage to Frank Leslie, founder of
a chain of popular magazines and newspapers, catapulted her to national
consciousness as both a newspaperwoman and eventually print-culture
"empress" (Everett 1985). Entrepreneur Frank Leslie is known for revolu-
tionizing the illustrated news weekly. His *Leslie's Illustrated Weekly* and
Frank Leslie's Illustrated Newspaper were among a chain of his magazines

19. Miriam Leslie (n.d.).
Reproduced with permis-
sion of the Collections of The
New York Public Library,
Astor, Lenox and Tilden
Foundations.

and newspapers popular for the technical and artistic quality of the
engraved illustrations.

Leslie's wife Miriam (1836–1914) was a controversial figure by all
accounts, a flamboyant socialite who reportedly spoke five languages and
who most critics seem to agree was a woman most interested in "con-
spicuous consumption and personal publicity" (Reinhardt 1967, 5; also
see Stern 1953, 1972). Her involvement in the Leslie publishing empire
included editing *Frank Leslie's Chimney Corner* and *Frank Leslie's Lady's
Magazine*. After Frank's death in 1881 Miriam "saved" the failing business, meanwhile legally changing her name to Frank Leslie to protect the
publications from claims by Leslie's sons. In later life she turned to lecturing, apparently beginning her lectures with the acclamation: "Ladies
and Gentlemen, I am Frank Leslie." Whatever or whomever else she might
have been, Miriam was a committed feminist and supporter of women's

suffrage. She left her fortune of $2 million at her death in 1914 to the suffrage cause (Everett 1985).

Miriam and Frank, along with an entourage of twelve editors, journalists, and artists, choreographed a widely publicized five-month grand tour of the American West in 1877. Largely financed by the railroad companies in exchange for Leslie's publicity, the trip promoted both the capitalist development of the railroad and Leslie's own publications. The group published the *Illustrated Newspaper* en route, with the aid of a small printing press on board (Stern 1972). Miriam co-wrote a series of articles about this trip with her husband and his assistant, subsequently compiling some of them into her own *California: A Pleasure Trip from Gotham to the Golden Gate (April, May, June, 1877)*. Her text covers Chicago, Cheyenne, Denver, Salt Lake City, San Francisco, other parts of California including Yosemite Valley, and Nevada. Leslie interviewed Mormon leader Brigham Young, described visits with railroad magnates and mining speculators in San Francisco, and devoted several chapters to San Francisco's Chinatown. On her return trip she visited the sweltering mines of Nevada's Comstock Lode and stirred up a "national scandal" with her negative descriptions of the mining town of Virginia City, Nevada.

Both Lippincott and Leslie were self-proclaimed feminists. At the forefront of their texts were a number of white middle-class women's rights issues such as suffrage, equal pay, and clothing reform. Lippincott asserted that, "I preach everywhere the gospel of equal wages for equal labor," demonstrating as much when she criticized the unequal gendered wage structure of a watch factory in Chicago (Greenwood 1872, 23–24). Both women praised Wyoming as the first territory to grant women's suffrage (in 1869). In one of the few recent critical analyses of Lippincott's writing, Georgi-Findlay (1996) interprets her persona as that of an eastern cultured woman traveling alone. According to Georgi-Findlay, Lippincott sought to establish herself within eastern or European literary or journalistic culture, drawing her authority from that speaking position. However, both she and Leslie also deployed the rhetoric of Victorian women's "moral authority" to speak as feminist advocates of a number of social reform causes.

The social reform causes with which Leslie and Lippincott aligned themselves extended to prison reform, temperance, immigrants' and workers' rights, and the rights and conditions of Native women, Chinese prostitutes, and Mormon polygamous wives. Leslie wrote several chapters on San Francisco's Chinatown and condemned Chinese prostitution as the enslavement of 1,500 women (1877, 165–66). Leslie concluded that the reform of prostitution-slavery ought to rest on converting the slave-masters; as white men "owned" the most beautiful women: "Let us devote what is left of our money and energy and Christian zeal to the conversion of these 'gentlemen'" (1877, 167).

While scholars have paid a great deal of attention to nineteenth-century feminist reformers' desire to improve the lives of women they perceived as disenfranchised or exploited (including Pascoe 1990; Morin and Kay Guelke 1998), one might consider how the logic and rhetoric of feminist reform aligns with reportage of the western mining industry. How, if at all, did Leslie and Lippincott extend their reform rhetoric to the miners and their working conditions in the mines?

The Western Mining Empire

American imperialism supported by mineral resource extraction grew at an unprecedented pace in the American West during the period of these women's travels, and their travels were directly supported by it as well. During the California gold rush of the 1840s many miners worked independently and with little capital investment. By the 1860s, a second phase of industrial mining took hold—large-scale, technologically advanced mining operations that depended upon both large capital investments and waged laborers. This second phase of western mining was key to American empire building and America's entry into the world economy (Robbins 1994).

Richard White (1991) outlines two types of American and European investment in the West generally during this period, that of buying stocks in companies and in loaning money, mainly for livestock, farming, lumber, and mining enterprises. Although more European money was invested in livestock than mining overall, the move toward large-scale underground and hydraulic mining was accompanied by increased capital input. Numerous scholars have documented the extent to which western American mining and railroad development depended on capital investments from Europe, mostly Britain, and the cities of the American Northeast. Considerable American, British, and French investments were made in Colorado mining from the 1870s (White 1991), for instance, and hydraulic mining of gold and quartz in California was heavily capitalized by European and American investors. In Nevada's gold and silver mines, investments came from Britain and east coast cities, but returns from the Comstock Lode especially helped concentrate wealth in San Francisco for the first time. San Francisco's capitalists had provided the bulk of the initial financing for western mining ventures, but when these proved inadequate the industry turned to other sources, in the United States and in Europe (Robbins 1994). Thus, the development of industrial capitalism in the American West via mining was tied directly to American foreign relations through the mining industry's dependence on capital from Europe and the American cities of the Northeast. It was also dependent upon the labor provided by Cornish, Irish, Chinese, and other recent immigrants who worked the mines.

Both Leslie and Lippincott reported enthusiastically on the growth and prosperity of the West. The rhetoric of the "Wild West" typified by men of all classes who displayed unrestrained ambition and greed was reserved for just a few mining towns. Most of the region, though, was portrayed as a "New West" of order, economic enterprise, urbanity, and extraordinary engineering feats (Georgi-Findlay 1996). Both Lippincott and Leslie attributed much of this success to the railroad; it brought tourists and immigrants, increased agricultural output and was "an immense help toward the development of the mines and mineral resources" (Greenwood 1872, 115, 388). White (1991) explains that the railroad provided the infrastructure for the economic development of the West generally, both as it demanded timber and coal for its construction, and as it greatly enlarged the West's access to eastern and European markets. The development of the railroad was inseparable from that of industrial-scale mining, as the latter required the transport of large amounts of lower-grade ores, supplies, and technologies. Positive, enthusiastic depictions of railroad travel, food, and society pervade the women's texts. Leslie gushed over the "national triumph" of the railroad (1877, 109), and Lippincott's final chapter was a tribute to the railroad's role in expanding Colorado's mining industry.

Both Lippincott and Leslie were tied into a network of patronage during their travels (Georgi-Findlay 1996). Both described numerous encounters with bankers, politicians, executives, industrialists, and especially railroad or mining officials who welcomed them into their homes and invited them on excursions, including into the mines. These men are portrayed as bold, manly, beneficent, paternalistic, and refined. Leslie, for example, visited the San Francisco estate of William Ralston, founder of the Bank of California, who reaped a fortune from Nevada's Comstock Lode in the early 1870s by integrating mines, mills, smelters, railroads, and timber production into a single company. Although Leslie frames her discussion around Ralston's tragic death (a probable suicide following an economic crash), she nonetheless characterizes him sympathetically as a "self-made man, [who] rose from the smallest beginning," a man who was "princely" and "audacious" (1877, 123–25). Men of the Bank of California also feature in Lippincott's text. She described the bank as one of the "marvellous growths of this marvellous New World," and its bankers as "distinguished for their uniform courtesy and munificent hospitality" (Greenwood 1872, 194–95).

While both Lippincott and Leslie effused over the development of the railroad, tourism, agribusiness, and industry, and the men made rich through them, they also reported sympathetically on the various colonial underclasses produced or displaced by them, such as immigrant ethnic groups from Asia and Europe (although they were much less sympathetic to Native and Mexican Americans already inhabiting the region). In this way their writings about American imperialism and the western mining frontier intersected with tropes of nineteenth-century American feminism. One significant way in which Victorian gender relations and American imperialism intersected in the women's narratives was in expressions of liberation or assimilation of subjugated or oppressed people (see chapter 6). Much of what the travelers wrote about miners drew on this feminist discourse of reform.

The counterpart to the discourse of paternalistic and refined railroad and mining magnates were those of the happy, law-abiding, "heroic" mine workers who were prospering under such industrialists' care. Lippincott especially invoked the discourse of the romanticized, ideal worker who, like his boss, was first and foremost a gentleman. In Cheyenne, Wyoming, Lippincott claimed that her own escorts, who "got their weapons ready" in her defense, were a bigger threat to her safety than the miners she encountered. Rather than fulfilling the stereotyped role of "desperados, violent and foul-mouthed," the miners "stepped courteously aside" and were respectful toward women (Greenwood 1872, 45–48). Near the mining town of Central, Colorado, Lippincott dined with a group of "honest miners":

> Men in rough clothes and heavy boots, with hard hands and with faces well bronzed, but strong, earnest, intelligent. It was to me a communion with the bravest humanity of the age—the vanguard of civilization and honorable enterprise. Mining life here is sober and laborious and law-abiding; we, at least, saw no gambling, no drunkenness, no rudeness, no idleness. (Greenwood 1872, 81)

Not all the news from the western American mining front was positive, however. In a number of ways both Leslie and Lippincott emphasized the damage enacted by industrialized western mining, on the people and on the land. While on one hand these women praised the beneficence of the mine owners who served as their western guides, on the other they harshly admonished mining speculators who were dishonest and greedy and who conducted business in unscrupulous ways. They were "bloated aristocrats" and "elegant idlers" (Greenwood 1872, 231).

Lippincott and Leslie also complicated their images of the gallant and heroic mine workers with those of the severe hardships the laboring men endured in the wretched conditions of the mines. By all accounts the working conditions in some mines of the Comstock Lode were abysmal, with men unable to withstand the heat, ambient air, and labor for more than an hour at a time (Limerick 1987). Leslie visited the Bonanza gold and silver mine in Virginia City, for instance, witnessing the men enter and return from the shafts. Almost suffocated by the hot, oily smell and steam, and the deafening machines, Leslie herself did not descend the mine, although others of her party did. They later produced a wood engraving depicting the thirsty miners for the newspaper. She described the returning miners as ghastly and fatigued: "Such a set of ghosts one

20. *Miners Refreshing Themselves with Ice-Water in the 1,600-foot Level.*
Underground scene in a Comstock mine. From *Frank Leslie's Illustrated Newspaper* 46 (30 March 1878), 61. Reproduced with permission of the Huntington Library.

never saw: pale, exhausted, dripping with water and perspiration, some with their shirts torn off and naked to the waist, all of them haggard and dazed with the long darkness and toil" (1877, 282).

Lippincott, too, described the difficult (though aboveground) working conditions at Clear Creek, Colorado: "Men are kept at work carting gravel, or wheeling it in barrows, for these sluices. In some places they stood knee-deep in water, dipping up the precious mud. A more slavish business could not well be imagined" (Greenwood 1872, 73). Lippincott was little distressed that large-scale, consolidated mining operations were replacing small-scale, independent ones, though, and declared that "only large means can insure large results":

> Boarded-up tunnels and idle windlasses are far oftener indications of the failure of means in the miner than of ore in the mine. The running of railroads into this region, and the consequent reduction in the cost of transportation, labour, and living, will work a great revolution. (Greenwood 1872, 108–9)

One might characterize this mode of writing as one of "reconciliation" (Georgi-Findlay 1996). Lippincott attempts to reconcile both the destruction of nature and oppressive labor conditions with an ultimately positive image of large-scale industrial mining—and its accompanying society—as honest, orderly, efficient, and, above all, economically prosperous. The costs of empire building in industrial mining were worthwhile so long as mining involved lawful, brave miners and paternalistic bosses; the landscape was only ugly when greedy speculators made a profit from it.

For her part, Leslie's mode of writing was ultimately less one of reconciliation than one of friction and hostility toward the people and places associated with western mining. This is not least demonstrated in her admonitions against injustices to Chinese workers and her concluding chapter that extensively draws out the stereotype of the rough, lawless western mining town of Virginia City, Nevada. The "national scandal" that it incited has informed numerous of her biographies (Reinhardt 1967; Stern 1972; Everett 1985).

Leslie wrote disparagingly of the "immoral" atmosphere of Virginia City, emphasizing the existence of only one church but forty-nine gambling saloons; and a mostly male population with "very few women, except of the worst class, and as few children" (1877, 278). (In fact, in the boom years of the Comstock Lode, the population of Virginia City grew from 2,306 men and 30 women in 1860, to a 2:1 ratio by 1870 [Paul 1963, 72].) Leslie claimed the need for a police escort to walk around the town at night, even though in other towns and cities in the West she scoffed at such advice. In sum, Virginia City had little to recommend itself:

> To call a place dreary, desolate, homeless, uncomfortable, and wicked is a good deal, but to call it God-forsaken is a good deal more, and in

a tolerably large experience of this world's wonders, we never found a place better deserving the title than Virginia City. (1877, 277–80)

Leslie's attack on Virginia City rested on deploying her own moral authority to speak on issues of temperance, gambling, and prostitution. As such, she aligned herself with reform women who presented themselves as moral guardians of others. Although Lippincott closed her book with a "hopeful" depiction of western imperial development based on an advancing railroad, prospering resource extraction industry, and heroic workers, Leslie's text ended with an image of an ultimately irredeemable West. Unlike the exploited, enslaved Chinese prostitutes in San Francisco on whose behalf Leslie readily spoke, the prostitutes in Virginia City were simply "bad" women. In addition, it is in this context of Virginia City that Leslie described the miserable working conditions of the miners. Leslie's alignment with feminist reform doctrines of the day is, thus, considerably more uneven than Lippincott's. Her depiction of an irredeemable West ultimately raises the question, I think, of whether she might be read as somehow resistant to American imperial development in the West and, alternatively, Lippincott as more complicit with it.

Mining a Postcolonial West

Western American "resource bonanzas" in the later nineteenth century have been well documented. William Ralston and a small group of men known as the bonanza kings monopolized western mining capital in San Francisco during this period. Brechin argues that Ralston and his cohorts accomplished this through cheating and deception: "If it took insider trading, backstabbing, wholesale political corruption, and looting of the public trough to make San Francisco great, [Ralston] was only following accepted custom" (1999, 41). Perhaps as many as 30 percent of the bonanza kings were foreign born; Paul (1963) characterizes them as superwealthy Irish immigrants who emerged from penniless backgrounds, first coming to California during the gold rush. These are the sort of men whom Lippincott and Leslie endlessly flattered and praised in their travelogues for their honesty, manliness, and paternalism toward workers. The women's texts are thus complicit with American imperial development via a particular type of gendered and classed identification with these men.

Lippincott's textual reconciliation of the mining West should also be considered with respect to the class background and ethnic makeup of the laboring miners she described. At the time of her and Leslie's travels, Cornish, Irish, and Chinese immigrants made up a significant proportion, if not the majority in some locations, of these workers. Bitter resistance to, and exclusions against, Chinese workers infiltrated the most profitable mining areas throughout the middle and later decades of the nineteenth century, in Idaho, Nevada, and California, with the western labor movement itself beginning on the Comstock (Robbins 1994). Fears of Chinese replacements caused Cornish workers to strike in Sutter Creek, California, and Virginia City, Nevada. The Chinese, who immigrated to the United States in large numbers beginning in the 1850s, by the 1870s provided the main labor force in the building of the Central Pacific Railroad and also comprised up to half of the miners in Idaho and a quarter in California (Paul 1963; White 1991). This amounted to 20,000 workers in California alone, men who primarily worked the abandoned "placers" of the first phase of mining (essentially above-ground ores, as opposed to the underground or harder-to-reach deposits mined later).

Leslie described Chinese laborers she encountered in Mariposa, California, admonishing the western mining establishment for its unfair labor practices involving the Chinese more generally: "The cry of cheap labour so furiously raised against the Chinese, principally by the classes to whom any labour is abhorrent, is as unfounded as it is malicious" (1877, 173). She concluded that the Constitution ensured the right of emigrants to "a share of that freedom and self-government we are so justly proud of," and that if the Chinese were treated justly, "Time, the great assimilator" would "soften the differences" among men (1877, 174). Due to exclusions and ethnic prejudices against Chinese workers, however, most of the men that Lippincott and Leslie encountered in the mining camps they visited were recent arrivals from Ireland and Britain.

By 1870, foreign-born workers outnumbered American-born ones in numerous mining centers, including the Comstock Lode and Gilpin County, Colorado. These were principally Cornish and Irish immigrants (Paul 1963). By 1880 in the Comstock Lode, only 770 of 2,770 mine workers were American-born—the rest were Irish, English, and Canadian. Paul

(1963) explains that mining was a traditional occupation for Cornish men, and by 1881, one-third to one-half of them had left their depressed circumstances in England, readily finding work in places like Virginia City. White (1991) characterizes the men's labor organizing as based on ethnic rivalries rather than class consciousness, as evidenced by Cornish men breaking the strike against the Irish- and American-born at the Comstock Lode; the anti-Chinese sentiments in the Comstock Lode; and ethnic tensions between the Cornish and Irish in Butte, Montana.

When one considers the ethnic immigrant composition of much of the West's mining population, which both women's texts explicitly did, Lippincott's rhetorical "reconciliation" of gallant miners, paternalistic bosses, and difficult working conditions becomes clearer. Industrial mining required formerly self-employed miners and recent immigrants to shift and adapt to a system of waged labor. Lippincott's text can be interpreted as one aiding the imperial development of western mining in the ways in which she constructs a gendered immigrant workforce: her miners are complacent, hard-working, sober, and lawful. Images of these refined gentlemen, courteous and chivalrous to women, replaced those of the rowdy, roughneck independent miners who would prove too subversive within the new system. Miners' working conditions in Lippincott's text are considerably better than in Leslie's; her own visit to the Comstock Lode entailed an excursion deep underground, an experience which she described as "very interesting, easy, and instructive . . . [a] pleasan[t] walk" (Greenwood 1872, 178). Thus in many ways Lippincott's text fulfilled several tendencies of the feminist reform rhetoric of the day, promising livelihood and prosperity to working-class immigrant men who labored diligently and adopted temperance and other moral ideals of the middle class. Moreover, continental expansion of the railroad and mining industries was thought to help cultivate these gentlemanly traits.

During their travels, Lippincott and Leslie encountered numerous national, local, and global cultural identities within the borders of the United States, wealthy industrialists as well as working-class men. Rowe (2000) asserts that little has been written connecting American internal colonization with more recognizably colonial ventures in foreign countries. He points out, for instance, that one of the ways that internal colonization moved forward was by aligning certain groups of people with the savagery ascribed to foreigners.

Leslie's workers in Virginia City and their working conditions do in fact appear quite savage. Although her hopes for the assimilation or domestication of Chinese immigrants demonstrate a link between feminist reform politics and American empire building, the Anglo men and women of Virginia City remain largely unintegrated into that progressive model of empire. One might read Leslie's irredeemable West in a number of ways. Perhaps she was deploying an oppositional strategy against American imperialism, condemning or resisting the unrestrained greed of the men (and some women) who advanced the Comstock boom in particular. Alternatively, one might read her as invoking popular racialized discourses about European and Chinese workers. Might the agitating English workers ultimately prove too incorrigible, especially compared to Chinese workers who were stereotyped as docile and apolitical (owing largely to the indentured servitude under which many came to the United States)? Or, finally, one might read Leslie as rather insecure in her own class identity as a properly genteel, upwardly aspiring member of the literati, who required unrefined others against whom to define herself. Bourgeois descriptions of working-class people as unrefined and savage can be understood within a broader class politics. Leslie's attempts to shore up her insecure class identity were even more acute later when she traveled to France and returned, declaring herself a baroness (Everett 1985).

By contrast, rather than reproduce negative stereotypes of lawless, rowdy western men, Lippincott sought to integrate the mineworkers she met into the American nation. Her feminist reform politics work alongside those of empire-building in that Lippincott explicitly domesticated or assimilated the foreign immigrant (Cornish, Irish) into a courageous and contented worker, located within hospitable working conditions. Promised national inclusion, these foreign men thereby serve as witness to the type of progress possible and indeed inevitable within the industrial-imperial complex of the West and the internal colonizations at work there. Their labor was essential to it.

Finally, though, one must consider how the miners these women observed, talked with, and dined with might themselves have envisioned their inclusion in an expanding American Empire as they negotiated their split European and American identities and spaces that both limited and broadened their opportunities to embody an emerging labor force. These recent arrivals to the United States were negotiating both their material and cultural survival in the midst of the changing economic and technological landscape of western mining. Within a limited range of possible ways that they might have occupied such colonial spaces—dealing as they were with forced migrations (both trans-Atlantic and within the United States), insecure labor relations, and wretched working conditions—still it seems that numerous sites of their accommodation, appropriation, and resistance to American expansionism can be read from the travel texts.

A heterogeneous range of miners' voices appears in these texts, from the courteous, hard-working gentleman miners in Wyoming and Colorado; to the exhausted, fatigued workers at the Comstock Lode; to the rude, drunken gamblers in the other social spaces of Virginia City. As they encountered and addressed Lippincott and Leslie, the men asserted their own range of notions about class and gender. The women appeared on the scene in the first instance as guests of the emerging western elite, brought into the spaces of the mines by the owners whose wealth depended on these men's labors. Their attempts to ensure integration into or survival within this uncertain transitional period in western mining might be achieved through various tactics. For example, to engage a bourgeois gentlemanly demeanor—whether as a straightforward strategy or not—is at once to identify with those owners and travel writers and thereby secure inclusion in the spaces they represented.

However, to expose the corrupt values of elite culture might be another strategy to ensure one's place in the emerging nation—by challenging and revising the principles upon which it has been established. Virginia City, as it turns out, rejected Leslie's depictions of it as a hopeless God-forsaken place and "spoke back" to her. The editor of the local Virginia City newspaper expressed his revenge in print. In July 1878 he devoted an entire front page article to criticizing Leslie's character, arguing that she was in no position to judge other women as she herself was (allegedly) illegitimate, engaged in numerous extramarital affairs, and exploited those around her for her own personal gain (Reinhardt 1967; Stern 1972). His article was titled, "Our Female Slanderer, Mrs. Frank Leslie's Book Scandalizing the Families of Virginia City—The History of the Authoress—A Life Drama of Crime and Licentiousness—Startling Developments."

Although it was the editor of the local newspaper who spoke through this account (not miners), his actions in support of the miners and their families articulates with the history of political activism at the Comstock Lode, based as it was, albeit, on ethnic rivalries as well as on class conflict. In addition, the basis of his rhetoric is the double standard historically deployed against successful women who do not adhere to the Victorian domestic ideal. Nonetheless, one might also consider the editor's attempt at exposing and destabilizing Leslie's own claim to nation as opening up a space within which other, alternative paths to it might be imagined. If nothing else, his voice mapped Virginia City as a vortex of competing moralities—and it is clear that the moral high ground that Leslie earlier claimed was not one that she would sustain for long. The editor contributed a measure of instability to Leslie's already punctured public persona. That said, and despite the scandal that his writing provoked and her legal and financial problems after her husband's death in 1880, Leslie's print culture prowess remained ultimately undaunted.

Conclusion

I am in agreement with Richard King (2000, 8) in recognizing, accepting, and interrogating "the conflicted aspects of postcolonial America [that] should energize rather paralyze critical scholarship." I have taken a provisional step here in linking the travel writing by these women about their American "home" to some of the insights of what might now be considered an American postcolonialism. My focus has been on how gender, class, and ethnic politics articulated with discourses of American expansionism and nation building via these travel texts. The integration of mining capital, workers, and technology on a range of scales must be understood as deeply linked with other colonial processes taking place in the nineteenth-century American West. This chapter demonstrates connections among aspects of American literary culture, early feminism, and American empire building. My comments on these American women's writings undoubtedly raise more questions than they answer, and numerous other sites for a postcolonial interpretation of these colonial texts exist. At minimum my point has been to strategically deflect some of postcolonialism's attention onto American soil, where it most certainly belongs.

ꙮ 9 ꙮ

Afterword

Imprints on a New Historical Geography of North America

A Round Trip in North America, by Lady Theodora Guest, with illustrations from the author's sketches . . . [is] a pleasant series of impressions of travel, not very profound in observation and perhaps rather too copious in merely personal details . . .
　　　　—*London Times,* February 21, 1895, 6

One great merit the book [Lady Howard's *Journal of Tour*] certainly possesses, and that is the complete absence of any ill-natured remarks. It is emphatically the production of a gentlewoman.
　　　　—*Athenaeum* 3 (30 April 1898): 563

Miss Faithful was very well received by the high-priests and priestesses of the Salt Lake community, but she nevertheless raises her voice vigorously—we had almost said manfully—against the system whose effects she witnessed.
　　　　—*Spectator* 57 (27 December 1884): 1740

The honour that is done to these Lady-Errants is not unlikely to encourage still further the feminine spirit of unrest, and the uneasy jealousy that is for ever driving the fair sex into proving itself the equal of the other. There is no need for any such proof. Mrs. Bishop [Isabella Bird] . . . has already shown conclusively of what a woman is capable in the way of pluck and endurance. The paper which she read on [Tuesday] was quite the most interesting contribution that was made this year to the Geographical Section of the British Association. But then, Mrs. Bishop brings very

different qualifications from that of being a mere woman . . . Mrs.
Bishop is a very old and experienced traveller, to whom science
owes a considerable debt of gratitude.
—*Spectator* 67 (29 August 1891): 286

Gender, Travel, and Knowledge

IN THEIR SCHOLARSHIP ON WOMEN TRAVELERS in the past several
decades, historians, critical literary theorists, geographers, and others
have been concerned with the question of whether there is a distinct way
that females recreate foreign experience in travel narratives. Such work
oftentimes begins with the writings of eighteenth- and early nineteenth-
century travelers such as Lady Mary Wortley Montagu (1689–1762), Lady
Hester Stanhope (1776–1839), and Harriet Martineau (1802–1876). The
Victorian "lady travelers" such as Isabella Bird (1831–1904), Kate Marsden (1859–1931), and Mary Kingsley (1862–1900) have become popular
subjects of study for their travels to British colonies in Africa, India, and
East Asia during the high colonial period in the nineteenth century. Many
scholars have been interested in simply adding these women's voices to the
canon of women's history and literature (e.g., Morris 1993); others have
used travel narratives to make connections between gender and landscape
interpretation (e.g., M. Allen 1987); and still others have focused on the
ways in which travel writing serves to maintain as well as challenge insti-
tutional and cultural boundaries of societies (e.g., Frawley 1994). Postcolonial critics (e.g., Paravisini-Gebert and Romero-Cesareo 2001) have
analyzed the ways women's writing mediated relationships between European empires and their colonies.

One of my own interests in studying women travelers (and other nineteenth-century women) is in asking how their gendered identities were
produced in place. The women travelers discussed in this volume maneuvered between conflicting social demands to appear the proper English
lady in diverse settings while challenging the Victorian gender hierarchy

in others. The travel narrative provided some women a forum within which to disclose proper ladylike behaviors and thus consolidate their positions as members of the ruling classes. Some of the women travelers, though, such as Bird (1969), Faithful (1884), Longworth (1974), and Pender (1978), foregrounded a revisionist gender identity in their texts. These travelers expressed a newfound sense of self in the American West in the context of rugged outdoor environments (especially in the mountains) or through a comparison of their own gender roles and relations with those of American women. Studying such maneuvering helps us understand "identity politics" generally, but also more fundamentally, where, how, and why gender identity gets produced in the first place.

That these travel writers were classist and racist has become axiomatic, yet women from the dominant classes enjoyed privileges that allowed them to start challenging gender constructs in ways that were open to them, which arguably gave later generations of feminists (and others) a model for challenging other forms of domination and subordination. Moreover and perhaps more significantly, in the preceding pages we see women "on the margins" of Victorian power relations maneuvering through similar social demands for similar ends. Rosalie La Flesche Farley was ensconced in forms of oppression whose "gendered geography" left little social space to inhabit between or outside of the Indian princess/Indian squaw dichotomy, albeit a social space she found and usefully manipulated for her own ends.

I focused these chapters on how gender and imperial ideologies and discourses influenced women's experiences and writings about western places. It was acutely clear to me that an interpolation of many competing ideologies and discourses was relevant to their experiences—first-wave feminism; upper-class feminine manners and mores; romantic discourse on the beautiful and the sublime; upper-class expressions of superiority, authority, paternalism, and intellectualism; and Orientalist discourse on the inferiority of other races of people. My project in large part was to understand how this bundle of ideologies and discourses intersected with a particular kind of experience the American West itself offered in the later nineteenth century: grand-scale railroad tours were available for the first time; huge wilderness areas were being reserved as national parks;

herds of buffalo still roamed the unfenced, wide open spaces of the central interior; Native Americans were just recently removed to reservations; and hundreds of thousands of European immigrants rushed to the farms, factories, and mines.

A focus on women's travel texts also highlights the fact that exploration itself, of the West or anywhere else, may no longer be constituted only as a physical journey over a material place, as a discovery of a place that is already known to its inhabitants, as in much of classical geography. Rather, exploration as a subject of study must be broadened out to concentrate on intercultural conflicts and relationships, feminine and domestic "room-sized" empires à la Pratt (1992, 160), and may include explorations of self over space as well as arm-chair explorations. Geographers are especially well attuned to acknowledge and study the "situatedness" of the explorer or traveler within his or her intellectual and cultural milieu, and thus the knowledge that she or he produces as likewise situated. Feminist historical geographers have long been interested in "worlding" geographical knowledge in this way (Rose 1995; McEwan 1998b).

An examination of women's social roles, relationships, and personal and professional interests also illuminates the processes by which gendered geographical knowledge is produced. Elite women writers legitimated their transgression into the masculine realm of business, travel, and education partly by producing knowledge of other places that reinforced the travelers' own feminine subjectivities. One way they did this was by filling their notebooks with particularly feminine subject matter, about the dress, hygiene, manners, and domestic-scale customs of the people and places they visited, as opposed to taking a more explicit interest in "masculine" topics such as exploitable resources, transportation systems, and governments. Of course, men can and did write about "feminine" subjects and these women masculine ones, but the more significant point is that dominant social ideologies and discourses dynamically and forcefully operated to produce gendered identities and narrative forms; in turn, these could be alternately reproduced and reinforced, or resisted and challenged.

Scholars in recent years have continued to focus attention on historical women's travel writing and such identity issues (e.g., Sidonie Smith

2001; M. Morgan 2001; Paravisini-Gebert and Romero-Cesareo 2001; Speake 2003; Formichella-Elsden 2004), with many recent works addressing how gendered identities are produced in place. These range from studies about travel's connections to national identity (M. Morgan 2001), to the role of particular places as "stages" upon which to perform gendered identity (Formichella-Elsden 2004, in the case of Italy), to the importance of marginalized women's roles in the navigation and cultural mapping of territories (Paravasini-Gebert and Romero-Cesareo 2001, in the case of servants and slaves in the Caribbean sphere).

Sidonie Smith's *Moving Lives: Twentieth-Century Women's Travel Writing* (2001) articulates well with the goals of the present volume in her attempt to map out relationships between identity and what she calls "technologies of motion." *Moving Lives* is structured around travel books of generally privileged white women from Europe, North America, and Australia, which foreground four technologies of motion: travel by foot, air, railroad, and automobile. Smith argues that such technologies have made new kinds of identities possible in the last century, an altered way of seeing and of seeing oneself. Technologies of motion determine types and duration of social encounters; they affect the organization and passage of space and time; they determine itineraries, destinations, rhythms of travel; and they also affect perception and knowledge—how and what the traveler comes to know on the road and thus the "achievements" possible through travel (2001, 23–26).

Another recent and significant shift has occurred in study of gendered geographies of North America, that is, of masculinity and American empire building. Dana Nelson (1998) had examined the ideologies of the white male fraternity—"national manhood"—and its link to civic nationalism and democracy in early American history. More recent titles, such as Basso, McCall, and Garceau (2001) and Greenberg (2005), belong among a wildly burgeoning scholarly literature dealing with cultures of manhood and American empire building in the nineteenth century. Focusing specifically on the American West, the collection by Basso, McCall, and Garceau (2001) analyzes the "politics of risk" on the Comstock Lode from 1860 to 1880, public hangings, constructions of Chinese manhood in the exclusionist debates of 1869–1878, Indian masculinity in film, among

other topics. Greenberg (2005), meanwhile, focuses on the social and economic transformations that were changing the meaning of manhood and
womanhood in the context of the U.S. annexation of northern Mexico in
1848 that led many American men to embrace both an aggressive vision of
expansionism and an equally "martial" vision of manhood.

These and other such works reinforce the notion that gendered geographies reciprocally manifest as inner discoveries and molding of the self
as well as contribute to the development of material culture and society.
Thus, the twofold goal in continuing to mark women as subjects of study
should be to not only examine why women and men produce certain types
of geographies—which has been the focus of my study—but to incorporate
their observations in studies of places and regions. Nineteenth-century
academic geography distinguished itself from the other social sciences
by eschewing a focus on the individual, including the "proper" feminine
focus on domestic life. (Other disciplines, by contrast, including most
notably anthropology, evolved with a whole range of research on women
and gender.) Thus, it is understandable why women travelers' works would
be among those excluded from academic geography in the past. The question remains, though, how to incorporate such work into today's geography, particularly the historical geography of North America. This is the
question to which I turn to next.

Imprints on North American Historical Geography

Study of women's travel writing helps us not only understand how gender difference itself is produced but also the relationship between gendered identity and the itineraries and goals of travel, and the subsequent
knowledge produced *as* travel writing or exploration account. Feminists
scholars have posed valuable questions about women travelers' lives and
works, and this in turn initiated a sweeping "constructionist" overhaul of
the classical geographical tradition, which had of course been comprised
mainly of male protagonists. The recent shift toward more critical analysis of geography's heroic past is undoubtedly one of the most important
advances to have been instigated by feminist research on travel, travel literature, and gender (e.g., Driver 2001). Naylor (2005) provides a useful
overview of recent works that discuss the constructed or produced nature

of geographical knowledge historically and its connections to broader social milieus. These include the sites of scientific knowledge production; the uneven distribution and diffusion of ideas; the process of constituting fields in and through which science was gathered; the rise of scientific subcultures and networks among them; and the institutionalization and policing of the sites of these subcultures.

Even within the limited context of the works collected in this volume, it is apparent that the lives and works of Victorian women travel writers, journalists, naturalists, and others have much to offer historical geography. Constance Gordon Cumming's drawings of Yosemite Valley remain valuable collectors' items in California, and Isabella Bird's books are among the most popular sold today at bookstores in the vicinity of Colorado's Rocky Mountain National Park. When considering how these and other women's works might be considered relevant to the historical geography of North America, two questions present themselves: what "imprints" did the women make on the places they visited and lived, and how can these imprints be incorporated into our studies of nineteenth-century North America?

Most of the women's writings reflect a personal focus on the travel experience, and thus their discoveries were often introspective ones revealing their own personal feelings and attitudes. Of course, feelings and attitudes must themselves be subjected to contextual scrutiny (Scott 1988b). Thus I have closely analyzed in the preceding chapters connections between ideology, discourse, knowledge, and identity. These women were also diligent observers of American West landscapes and people, however, and their observations of—and "imprints" upon—the places they visited and lived intersected at a number of scales, from interior domestic spaces to regional- and global-scale development of technology, resources, and economy.

Though I will not rehearse the much larger debate within geography here, suffice it to say that it is clear that many human geographers have responded to the persuasive call for a reorientation of the scale of historical geographical study (Marston 2004). Though study of the domestic scale has been well integrated into other subdisciplines within Anglophone human geography at least since the 1970s, it is only very recently that we see entire volumes of historical geographical studies focused on the domestic scale. (See, for example, A. Blunt and Dowling's 2006 book, *Home.*) Because the domestic scale is embedded within and intersects with events and processes taking place at other scales, study of the domestic is as important to our understanding of places in past times as is the development of large-scale industry, survey systems, settlements patterns, and other components of "masculine" culture on the ground, those topics that have nonetheless remained central to the most celebrated historical geographies of North America discussed in the Introduction (see Hurt 2006).

Interior domestic spaces and topics were legitimate—and legitimizing—subjects of observation for the women studied in this volume. Isabella Bird, Rose Kingsley, and Rose Pender described the daily upkeep of their cabins or living quarters in great detail (e.g., Bird 1969, 73), meanwhile commenting in similar detail on the household work, activities, and domestic pleasures of their various hosts (e.g., R. Kingsley 1874, 192–94). What value can such observations have to historical geography?

Some of the first scholars writing about women travelers (Middleton 1965; Birkett 1989) would have dismissed such "knowledge" or information as unimportant and in fact detrimental to their project. They were primarily interested in marking women for historical study and celebrating their achievements *as women* and consequently produced eccentric heroines of history in their work. That is, informed by liberal feminism, such works generally rendered the domestic sphere as stifling and not "feminist" enough, and thus in attempts to create feminist heroines out of early women travelers, descriptions of the interiors of homes, styles of dress, food, children's behavior, and so on were minimized in favor of more "masculine" topics such as mountain climbing and the collecting of botanical specimens on jungle expeditions. In this way women travelers could fit comfortably into an already-constituted masculine geographical tradition, since their contributions were cast as similar to men's.

Meanwhile, early poststructuralist literary theorists informed by studies of colonial discourse (e.g., Mills 1991, after Said 1978) focused on elite (white) women travelers' racism, classism, and even sexism during their colonial encounters. Though an essential corrective to what had gone before, this focus had the tendency to obscure the individuality and agency of women travelers, casting them as "author-functions" (after Foucault 1972), and obscuring the extent to which the travelers were testing new gender roles for themselves. In addition, some of this work, by drawing attention to women's participation in colonial administration and missionary activities, for example, rendered domestic subjects as not only trivialized—by the publishing industry, the public, and possibly even the women themselves—but also somehow trivial information. Mills characterizes "lengthy descriptions of the domestic," along with racism, as those portions of the women's texts that feminist readers of the 1990s found impossible to tolerate (1991, 4).

Both theoretical positions downplayed the importance of a "geography of the domestic"—and certainly a further paradox is that in emphasizing the domestic, I am calling attention to the domestic roles and relations from which at least some of the women themselves may have been attempting to distance themselves. In any case, many geographers today are better attuned to appreciating the importance of social reproduction to the survival and sustainability of families and communities, and indeed, of whole economic, political, and cultural orders (e.g., Marston 2000, 2004). Shifting our focus in historical geography to the scale of the domestic—whether it is the social geography of the interior of train compartments described by Hardy (1882) and Longworth (1974); descriptions of subsistence work of immigrants and Native peoples by Cummings (1886) and La Flesche Farley (1892); domestic class relations and work described by Bird (1969), R. Kingsley (1874), and Leslie (1877); in-home education on natural history, botany, and plant illustration experienced by Guest (1895), North (1982), and Cumming (1886); family relationships and home-based leisure time activities described by Bridges (1883) and R. Kingsley (1874); women's clothing standards challenged by Bird (1969); and so on—all provide immeasurably more complete pictures of how domestic- and household-scale activities, practices, and choices fueled and in fact in many aspects enabled political-economic and cultural patterns at other scales. This study has suggested a number of ways by which this happens. It thereby points to, but does not develop, the extent through which American empire building itself was enabled through domestic-scale activities such as home decoration, cooking skills, children's education, gardening, women's domestic economy (and so on), in the manner of Anne McClintock's thesis of "commodity racism" (1995) or Kristin Hoganson's "cosmopolitan domesticity" (2007).

Beyond these sorts of domestic-scale contributions to historical geographies of North America, the women discussed in this volume made "imprints" in other ways as well. Pursuant to the nineteenth-century travelogue genre, their narratives provided recommendations on hotel and train accommodations, quality and costs of food, and advice on how to visit the major tourist attractions. One can speculate that the impact of their assessments was tremendous, given their book sales and sizable subscription base of the major British and American newspapers and magazines in which their writings were serialized and reviewed (e.g., the *London Times,* the *New York Times, Spectator, Leslie's Illustrated Weekly,* etc.), not to mention the large audiences many of the women addressed during their speaking tours and at home.

It should be noted that the women also sometimes wrote very explicitly as "geographers" in the masculinist exploratory tradition, circa 1880, describing such landscape features as the design and layout of Native American houses (Bates 1887), and quantity and quality of raw materials and resources available for extraction (R. Kingsley 1874; Leslie 1877). Recall Rose Kingsley's cordial relationship to the owners of some of the largest haciendas in Mexico, culminating in the final chapter of her book, "Mexico and Its Resources" (1874, 399–411). Journalists Leslie and Lippincott widely circulated news of mineral deposits in Nevada's Comstock Lode, though ambivalence about their removal pervaded both women's texts. Thus, as such well-connected women's "advice" on the future development of the American West quickly worked its way into established centers of calculation and cycles of accumulation (Latour 1987)—whether through their publications or through the likes of railroad developers such as William Palmer—it did so in ways that cracked the canon, if you will, of the masculinist exploratory tradition, since they wrote in both the authoritative mode supporting capitalist development as well as the mode of ethical environmentalist recognizing limits to progress (among others).

All of that said, it is perhaps ironic that the woman who made arguably the biggest "imprint" of the women covered in this volume was Native American, Rosalie La Flesche Farley. Her correspondence reveals a woman well versed in both Native American and Anglo-American law, the encroaching jurisdiction of the latter over the former, and her attempts to put both to use for her own purposes. Such a persona stands in stark contrast to how outsiders represented her (and her family and community) at the time.

Attempts to determine the long-term impacts or influences of La Flesche Farley's efforts to secure land must begin with the fact that a town was named after her, what is now the village of Rosalie, Nebraska—population 178—which sits in the south-central portion of the Omaha Indian Reservation in northeast Nebraska.[1] I do not know how many places in Nebraska or the Great Plains are named after women, but no doubt very few. It is the only place named after a member of the La Flesche family, even though three of Rosalie's siblings as well as her father rose to greater relative prominence in U.S. history than she did. The town of Rosalie was platted on the "surplus" pasture land left over after individual allotments were made on the reservation (discussed in chapter 7). The town's main street is called Farley Avenue, and there is also a Rosalie Avenue and two streets known by their Omaha names, Ne Shu Du and Wa Shu Sha.

The Omaha Reservation sits picturesquely on the western shore of the Missouri River, overlooking the historic scene of the Lewis and Clark expedition. The first time I visited the Omaha Reservation (summer of 2000), I was deeply struck by how prosperous it appeared—crops thriving, wave after wave of tall green, gold, and brown plants of corn, soybeans, oats, alfalfa, and barley fields interrupted only by roads and highways. The place looked alive, but also strangely de-peopled. The large corporate-size farms that had taken over most of the reservation produced a contradictory scene of both growth and emptiness. It was not until I later returned with the intention of taking a closer look at the town of Rosalie that I realized that the pattern set in place 100-plus years ago had persisted. As outlined in chapter 7, after allotment most of the Omaha were forced into leasing arrangements and lived off the rent of their lands. To this day most of the reservation ranch and farmland is not in the hands of Omaha, and

1. Themes in this section are developed more fully in Morin 2003.

most of the Omaha people living on the reservation reside in its three deteriorated towns—Rosalie, Macy (location of tribal headquarters, government offices, schools, and community buildings), and Walthill.

As with many towns on the Plains, Rosalie, or Luezalie in Omaha, emerged as a product of the railroad. The town was platted in 1906, and the Burlington–Great Northern line arrived there in 1907, which brought new businesses, travelers, and mail. Rosalie became a shipping point for cattle, and for much of the twentieth century it was a town of cattlemen and women and farmers. They built square houses out of cottonwood, many of which still stand today. The town was officially incorporated in 1909 with 220 residents. One of the most significant features of Rosalie today is the grain elevator towering over the Chicago, Burlington, and Quincy railroad line that continues to pass alongside the town on its north-south run through the reservation. Today only a gas station and post office remain in town; the dilapidated storefronts are in ghostly ruins, and the main street is deserted. The twenty-four or so blocks constituting the residential part of the town are filled with trailers, shacks, mud, broken fences, and many of the people are elderly.

The story of the village of Rosalie resonates with the much larger obituary of the rural Great Plains often depicted by journalists these days—collapsed homesteads, abandoned ranches, dying towns, brain drains. Sixty percent of the counties in the Great Plains lost population between 1990 and 2000, yet as the "European failure" on the Great Plains accelerates, Native Americans, accounting for significant population gain in the area, are "coming home." Nebraska, for example, witnessed a 20 percent increase in its Native American population over the turn of the twenty-first century. According to the *New York Times* (Egan 2001), "There are [now] more Indians and buffalo on the Plains than any time since the 1870s."

Rosalie La Flesche Farley died at the age of thirty-nine of inflammatory rheumatism, leaving a husband and eight children. Undoubtedly the long succession of lease disputes and legal battles she fought over the communal pasture—within and outside her community—took their toll on her health. To this day, tribal historian Dennis Hastings claims that there is an "offish" feeling amongst the Omaha toward her and the La

Flesches.[2] She and her family did manage to stay put on Omaha land and resist further encroachment by speculators, but not without other tragic losses. Thus, Rosalie's "imprint" is both psychic and material: her correspondence and the dilapidated town serve as important reminders of the struggles and insecurities that accompanied colonialism on the Great Plains, but moreover, that complicity and resistance to it took many forms and served many outcomes, both individual and social.

Such outcomes, though, also cannot be separated from the gender ideologies and constructs that enabled them. In the end, incorporating the many voices of women—British women travelers and naturalists, American journalists, and a Native American businesswoman—into our historical geographies of North America helps us become better attuned to the fundamental importance of gender ideology, discourse, and difference to the shaping of both our past and contemporary worlds.

2. As Hastings declared in an interview with me on 25 January 2001, Rosalie "didn't help the Omaha, was only concerned with herself . . . those La Flesches . . . they didn't help us."

References

Index

References

Adams, William Henry Davenport. 1883. *Celebrated Women Travelers of the Nineteenth Century.* London: W. Swan Sonnenschein.

Albers, Patricia C., and William R. James. 1987. "Illusion and Illumination: Visual Images of American Indian Women in the West." In *The Women's West,* edited by Susan Armitage and Elizabeth Jameson, 35–50. Norman: Univ. of Oklahoma Press.

Albers, Patricia C., and Beatrice Medicine. 1983. *The Hidden Half: Studies of Plains Indian Women.* Lanham, Md.: Univ. Press of America.

Allen, David E. 1976. *The Naturalist in Britain: A Social History.* London: Allen Lane.

Allen, John, ed. 1997. *North American Exploration.* 3 vols. Lincoln: Univ. of Nebraska Press.

Allen, Martha M. 1987. *Traveling West: Nineteenth Century Women on the Overland Routes.* El Paso: Texas Western Press.

Armitage, Susan. 1987. "Through Women's Eyes: A New View of the West." In *The Women's West,* edited by Susan Armitage and Elizabeth Jameson, 9–18. Norman: Univ. of Oklahoma Press.

Armitage, Susan, and Elizabeth Jameson, eds. 1987. *The Women's West.* Norman: Univ. of Oklahoma Press.

Armstrong, Nancy. 1987. "The Rise of the Domestic Woman." In *The Ideology of Conduct: Essays in Literature and the History of Sexuality,* edited by Nancy Armstrong and Leonard Tennenhouse, 96–141. New York: Methuen.

Ashcroft, Bill, Gareth Griffiths, and Helen Tiffen, eds. 1995. *The Post-colonial Studies Reader.* London: Routledge.

Athearn, Robert G. 1962. *Westward the Briton.* Lincoln: Univ. of Nebraska Press. (Orig. pub. 1953. New York: Charles Scribner's Sons.)

Ballantyne, Tony, and Antoinette Burton, eds. 2005. *Bodies in Contact: Rethinking Colonial Encounters in World History*. Durham, N.C.: Duke Univ. Press.

Barber, Lynn. 1980. *The Heyday of Natural History, 1820–1870*. Garden City, N.Y.: Doubleday.

Barnett, Clive. 1998. "Impure and Worldly Geography: The Africanist Discourse of the Royal Geographical Society, 1831–73." *Transactions of the Institute of British Geographers* 23: 239–51.

Barr, Pat. 1970. *A Curious Life for a Lady: The Story of Isabella Bird*. London: Macmillan.

Basso, Matthew, Laura McCall, and Dee Garceau, eds. 2001. *Across the Great Divide: Cultures of Manhood in the American West*. New York: Routledge.

Bates, Emily Catherine. 1887. *A Year in the Great Republic*. 2 vols. London: Ward and Downey.

Bazant, Jan. 1977. *A Concise History of Mexico from Hildalgo to Cardenas, 1805–1940*. Cambridge: Cambridge Univ. Press.

Beasley, Maurine Hoffman. 1993. *Taking Their Place: A Documentary History of Women and Journalism*. Washington, D.C.: American Univ. Press.

Beebe, Lucius, and Charles Clegg. 1958. *Narrow Gauge in the Rockies*. Berkeley, Calif.: Howell-North.

Berkhofer, Robert F., Jr. 1978. *The White Man's Indian: Images of the American Indian from Columbus to the Present*. New York: Vintage.

Berman, Morris. 1975. "'Hegemony' and the Amateur Tradition in British Science." *Journal of Social History* 8: 30–50.

Best, Gerald M. 1968. *Mexican Narrow Gauge*. Berkeley, Calif.: Howell-North.

Bhabha, Homi K. 1983. "The Other Question . . . " *Screen* 24: 18–36.

Bird, Isabella L. 1969. *A Lady's Life in the Rocky Mountains*. Norman: Univ. of Oklahoma Press. (Orig. pub. 1879. London: John Murray.)

Birkett, Dea. 1989. *Spinsters Abroad: Victorian Lady Explorers*. Oxford: Basil Blackwell.

Blake, Susan. 1990. "A Woman's Trek: What Difference Does Gender Make?" *Women Studies International Forum* 13: 347–55.

Blodgett, Peter J. 1990. "Visiting the Realm of Wonder: Yosemite and the Business of Tourism, 1855–1916." *California History* 69: 118–33.

Blomley, Nicholas. 1996. "Shut the Province Down: First Nations Blockades in British Columbia, 1984–1995." *BC Studies* 3: 5–35.

Blunt, Alison. 1994. *Travel, Gender, and Imperialism: Mary Kingsley and West Africa*. New York: Guilford Press.

Blunt, Alison, and Robyn Dowling. 2006. *Home*. London: Routledge.

Blunt, Alison, and Gillian Rose, eds. 1994. *Writing Women and Space: Colonial and Postcolonial Geographies*. New York: Guilford Press.

Blunt, Wilfrid. 1950. *The Art of Botanical Illustration*. London: Collins.

———. 1971. *The Complete Naturalist: A Life of Linnaeus*. London: Collins.

Boorstin, David. 1969. Introduction to *A Lady's Life in the Rocky Mountains*, by Isabella Bird. Norman: Univ. of Oklahoma Press.

Boughter, Judith A. 1998. *Betraying the Omaha Nation, 1790–1916*. Norman: Univ. of Oklahoma Press.

Bourne, Colonel E. G. 1825. *Notes on the State of Sonora and Sinaloa*.

Brechin, Gray A. 1999. *Imperial San Francisco: Urban Power, Earthly Ruin*. Berkeley: Univ. of California Press.

Brenan, J. P. M. 1980. Preface to *A Vision of Eden: The Life and Work of Marianne North*, by Marianne North. New York: Holt, Rinehart and Winston.

Brennan, Timothy. 2000. "The Illusion of Future: Orientalism as Traveling Theory." *Critical Inquiry* 26: 558–83.

Bridges, F. D. 1883. *Journal of a Lady's Travels Round the World*. London: John Murray.

Brockway, Lucile H. 1979. *Science and Colonial Expansion: The Role of the British Royal Botanical Gardens*. New York: Academic Press.

Buchanan, Handasyde. 1979. *Nature into Art: A Treasury of Great Natural History Books*. London: Wiedenfeld and Nicolson.

Burke, Edmund. 1757. *A Philosophical Enquiry into the Origin of Our Ideas of the Sublime and Beautiful*. Reprint, London: Oxford Univ. Press, 1998.

Burton, Antoinette. 1994. *Burdens of History: British Feminists, Indian Women, and Imperial Culture, 1865–1915*. Chapel Hill: Univ. of North Carolina Press.

Calderon de la Barca, Frances Erskine. 1843. *Life in Mexico, During a Residence of Two Years in that Country*. Boston: C. C. Little and Brown.

Callaway, Helen. 1987. *Gender, Culture and Empire: European Women in Colonial Nigeria*. London: Macmillan Press.

Calvert, Peter. 1973. *Mexico*. New York: Praeger.

Carbutt, Mrs. E. H. 1979. *Five Months' Fine Weather in Canada, Western United States, and Mexico*. Ann Arbor: Univ. of Microfilms International. (Orig. pub. 1889. London: Sampson, Low, Marston, Searle, and Rivington.)

Carruthers, Miss. 1879. *Flower Lore: The Teachings of Flowers, Historical, Legendary, Poetical, and Symbolical*. Belfast: McCaw, Stevenson and Orr.

Carter, Sarah. 1993. "Categories and Terrains of Exclusion: Constructing the 'Indian Woman' in the Early Settlement Era in Western Canada." *Great Plains Quarterly* 13: 147–61.

———. 1997. *Capturing Women: The Manipulation of Cultural Imagery in Canada's Prairie West.* Montreal: McGill-Queen's Univ. Press.

Castle, Gregory, ed. 2001. *Postcolonial Discourses: An Anthology.* London: Blackwell.

Chaudhuri, Nupur, and Margaret Strobel, eds. 1992. *Western Women and Imperialism: Complicity and Resistance.* Bloomington: Indiana Univ. Press.

Clayton, Daniel. 2000. *Islands of Truth: The Imperial Fashioning of Vancouver Island.* Vancouver: Univ. of British Columbia Press.

Coats, Alice M. 1969. *Quest for Plants: A History of the Horticultural Explorers.* London: Studio Vista.

Coatsworth, John H. 1974. "Railroads, Landholding, and Agrarian Protest in the Early Porfiriato." *Hispanic American Review* 54: 55–57.

———. 1981. *Growth Against Development: The Economic Impact of Railroads in Profirian Mexico.* DeKalb: Northern Illinois Univ. Press.

Cockcroft, James D. 1968. *Intellectual Precursors of the Mexican Revolution, 1900–1913.* Austin: Univ. of Texas Press.

Comer, Krista. 1999. *Landscapes of the New West: Gender and Geography in Contemporary Women's Writing.* Chapel Hill: Univ. of North Carolina Press.

Cott, Nancy F. 1977. *The Bonds of Womanhood: Women's Sphere in New England, 1780–1835.* New Haven, Conn.: Yale Univ. Press.

Creese, Mary R. S. 1998. *Ladies in the Laboratory? American and British Women in Science, 1800–1900: A Survey of Their Contributions to Research.* Lanham, Md.: Scarecrow Press.

Crofutt's Trans-continental Tourist's Guide. 1872. New York: Geo. A. Crofutt, Publisher.

Cronon, William, ed. 1995. *Uncommon Ground: Toward Reinventing Nature.* New York: W. W. Norton.

Cumming, Constance Gordon. 1886. *Granite Crags of California.* Edinburgh: Blackwood.

———. 1904. *Memories.* Edinburgh: Blackwood.

Davidoff, Leonore. 1983. "Class and Gender in Victorian England." In *Sex and Class in Women's History,* edited by Judith L. Newton, Mary P. Ryan, and Judith R. Walkowitz. London: Routledge.

Davidson, Lillias Campbell. 1889. *Hints to Lady Travellers.* London: Iliffe and Son.

Davin, Anna. 1978. "Imperialism and Motherhood." *History Workshop* 5: 9–65.

Davis, John F. 1975. "Constructing the British View of the Great Plains." In *Images of the Plains: The Role of Human Nature in Settlement,* edited by Brian W. Blouet and Merlin P. Lawson. Lincoln: Univ. of Nebraska Press.

Demars, Stanford E. 1991. *The Tourist in Yosemite, 1855–1985.* Salt Lake City: Univ. of Utah Press.

Dettelbach, Michael. 1996. "Global Physics and Aesthetic Empire: Humboldt's Physical Portrait of the Tropics." In *Visions of Empire: Voyages, Botany and Representations of Nature,* edited by David P. Miller and Peter H. Reill. Cambridge: Cambridge Univ. Press.

Deutsch, Sarah. 1987. *No Separate Refuge: Culture, Class, and Gender on an Anglo-Hispanic Frontier in the American Southwest, 1880–1940.* New York: Oxford Univ. Press.

Domosh, Mona. 1991a. "Towards a Feminist Historiography of Geography." *Transactions of the Institute of British Geographers* 16: 95–104.

———. 1991b. "Beyond the Frontiers of Geographical Knowledge." *Transactions of the Institute of British Geographers* 16: 488–90.

Domosh, Mona, and Karen M. Morin. 2003. "Travels with Feminist Historical Geography." *Gender, Place and Culture* 10: 257–64.

Drinnon, Richard. 1980. *Facing West: The Metaphysics of Indian-Hating and Empire-Building.* New York: New American Library.

Driver, Felix. 2001. *Geography Militant: Cultures of Exploration and Empire.* Oxford: Blackwell.

Egan, Timothy. 2001. "As Others Abandon Plains, Indians and Bison Come Back." *New York Times,* 27 May.

Everett, G. 1985. "Frank Leslie (Henry Carter)." *Dictionary of Literary Biography: American Newspaper Journalists, 1690–1872.* Vol. 2. Detroit: Gale Research.

Faithful, Emily. 1884. *Three Visits to America.* Edinburgh: David Douglas.

Farrar-Hyde, Anne. 1990. *An American Vision: Far Western Landscape and National Culture, 1820–1920.* New York: New York Univ. Press.

Fletcher, Alice, and Francis La Flesche. 1992. *The Omaha Tribe.* Lincoln: Univ. of Nebraska Press. (Orig. pub. 1905–6. Washington, D.C.: Smithsonian Institution.)

Formichella-Elsden, Annamarie. 2004. *Roman Fever: Domesticity and Nationalism in Nineteenth-Century American Women's Writing.* Columbus: Ohio State Univ. Press.

Foster, Shirley. 1990. *Across New Worlds: Nineteenth-Century Women Travellers and Their Writings.* New York: Harvester Wheatsheaf.

Foucault, Michel. 1970. *The Order of Things.* New York: Vintage.

———. 1972. *The Archaeology of Knowledge and the Discourse on Language.* New York: Pantheon.

Franco, Jean. 1989. *Plotting Women: Gender and Representation in Mexico.* New York: Columbia Univ. Press.

Frawley, Maria H. 1994. *A Wider Range: Travel Writing by Women in Victorian England.* London: Associated Univ. Presses.

Frost, Alan. 1996. "The Antipodean Exchange: European Horticulture and Imperial Designs." In *Visions of Empire: Voyages, Botany, and the Representation of Nature,* edited by David P. Miller and Peter H. Reill, 58–79. Cambridge: Cambridge Univ. Press.

Garrett, Paula K. 1997. "Prodigal Daughters and Pilgrims in Petticoats: Grace Greenwood and the Tradition of American Women's Travel Writing." Ph.D. diss., Louisiana State Univ. Agricultural and Mechanical College.

Gates, Barbara T. 1998. *Kindred Nature: Victorian and Edwardian Women Embrace the Living World.* Chicago: Univ. of Chicago Press.

Georgi-Findlay, Brigitte. 1996. *The Frontiers of Women's Writing: Women's Narratives and the Rhetoric of Westward Expansion.* Tucson: Univ. of Arizona Press.

Glenn, Evelyn N. 1994. "From Servitude to Service Work: Historical Continuities in the Racial Division of Paid Reproductive Labor." In *Unequal Sisters: A Multicultural Reader in U.S. Women's History,* edited by Vicki L. Ruiz and Ellen C. DuBois, 405–35. New York: Routledge.

Gottlieb, Robert. 1993. *Forcing the Spring: The Transformation of the American Environmental Movement.* Washington, D.C.: Island Press.

Gould, Stephen Jay. 1997. "The Invisible Woman." In *Natural Eloquence: Women Reinscribe Science,* edited by Barbara T. Gates and Ann B. Shteir, 27–42. Madison: Univ. of Wisconsin Press.

Green, Norma K. 1969. *Iron Eye's Family: The Children of Joseph La Flesche.* Lincoln, Neb.: Johnsen Publishing.

Greenberg, Amy. 2005. *Manifest Manhood and the Antebellum American Empire.* New York: Cambridge Univ. Press.

Gregory, Derek. 1994. *Geographical Imaginations.* Cambridge: Blackwell.

———. 1995. "Between the Book and the Lamp: Imaginative Geographies of Egypt, 1849–50." *Transactions of the Institute of British Geographers* 20: 29–57.

Greenwood, Grace [Sara Jane Clarke Lippincott]. 1872. *New Life in New Lands: Notes of Travel.* New York: J. B. Ford.

Guest, Lady Theodora. 1895. *A Round Trip in North America.* London: Edward Stanford.

Hall, Catherine. 1988. *White, Male and Middle Class: Explorations in Feminism and History.* New York: Routledge.

Hannah, Matthew G. 1993. "Space and Social Control in the Administration of the Oglala Lakota ('Sioux'), 1871–1879." *Journal of Historical Geography* 19: 412–32.

Hardy, Iza Duffus. 1884. *Between Two Oceans: Or, Sketches of American Travel.* London: Hurst and Blackert.

Hardy, Lady [Mary] Duffus. 1882. *Through Cities and Prairie Lands: Sketches of an American Tour.* Chicago: Belford, Clarke and Co.

Harvey-Gibson, Robert J. 1981. *Outlines of the History of Botany.* London: Arno Press. (Orig. pub. 1919. London: Black.)

Herman, R. Douglas K. 1999. "The Aloha State: Place Names and Anti-Conquest of Hawaii." *Annals of the Association of American Geographers* 89: 76–102.

Hobsbawm, Eric J. 1969. *Social Bandits and Primitive Rebels: Studies in Archaic Forms of Social Movement in the Nineteenth and Twentieth Centuries.* Glencoe, Ill.: Free Press.

Hoganson, Kristin. 2007. *Consumer's Imperium: The Global Production of American Domesticity, 1865–1920.* Chapel Hill: Univ. of North Carolina Press.

Howard, Lady Winefred [Fitzalan] of Glossop. 1897. *Journal of a Tour in the United States, Canada and Mexico.* London: Sampson, Low, Marston and Co.

Hulme, Peter. 1986. *Colonial Encounters: Europe and the Native Caribbean 1492–1797.* London: Methuen.

———. 1995. "Including America." *Ariel* 26: 117–23.

Humphreys, Robert. 1995. *Sin, Organized Charity, and the Poor Law in Victorian England.* New York: St. Martin's Press.

Hurt, Douglas. 2006. "Teaching and Research in Historical Geography: A Survey of U.S. Practitioners." *Historical Geography* 34: 71–85.

Jeffrey, Julie Roy. 1988. "There Is Some Splendid Scenery: Women's Responses to the Great Plains Landscape." *Great Plains Quarterly* 8: 70–79.

Jehlen, Myra. 1993. "Why Did the Europeans Cross the Ocean?" In *Cultures of United States Imperialism,* edited by Amy Kaplan and Donald Pease, 41–58. Durham, N.C.: Duke Univ. Press.

Johnston, Henry M. 1992. *Missions to Mexico: A Tale of British Diplomacy in the 1820s.* London: British Academic Press.

Jones, Greta. 1980. *Social Darwinism and English Thought: The Interaction between Biological and Social Theory.* Brighton, U.K.: Harvester Press.

Jones, Kristine L. 1986. "Nineteenth-Century British Travel Accounts of Argentina." *Ethnohistory* 33: 195–211.

Kaplan, Amy. 1993. "Left Alone with America: The Absence of Empire in the Study of American Culture." In *Cultures of United States Imperialism,* edited by Amy Kaplan and Donald Pease, 3–21. Durham, N.C.: Duke Univ. Press.

Kaplan, Amy, and Donald Pease, eds. 1993. *Cultures of United States Imperialism.* Durham, N.C.: Duke Univ. Press.

Kay [Guelke], Jeanne. 1990. "The Future of Historical Geography in the United States." *Annals of the Association of American Geographers* 80: 618–21.

———. 1991. "Landscapes of Women and Men: Rethinking the Regional Historical Geography of the United States and Canada." *Journal of Historical Geography* 17: 435–52.

Kearns, Gerry. 1997. "The Imperial Subject: Geography and Travel in the Work of Mary Kingsley and Halford Mackinder." *Transactions of the Institute of British Geographers* 22: 450–72.

King, Ronald. l985. *Royal Kew.* London: Constable.

King, Richard C., ed. 2000. *Postcolonial America.* Urbana: Univ. of Illinois Press.

Kingsley, Charles. 1874. Preface to *South by West or Winter in Rocky Mountains and Spring in Mexico* by Rose Kingsley, vii–x. London: W. Isbister and Co.

Kingsley, Mary. 1897. *Travels in West Africa: Congo Français, Corisco and Cameroons.* Boston: Beacon Press.

———. 1899. *West African Studies.* London: Frank Cass.

Kingsley, Rose. 1874. *South by West or Winter in the Rocky Mountains and Spring in Mexico.* London: W. Isbister and Co.

Koerner, Lisbet. 1993. "Goethe's Botany: Lessons of a Feminine Science." *Isis* 84: 470–85.

———. 1996. "Purposes of Linnaean Travel: A Preliminary Research Report." In *Visions of Empire: Voyages, Botany, and the Representations of Nature,* edited by David P. Miller and Peter H. Reill, 51–69. Cambridge: Cambridge Univ. Press.

Kolodny, Annette. 1975. *The Lay of the Land: Metaphor as Experience and History in American Life and Letters.* Chapel Hill: Univ. of North Carolina Press.

————. 1984. *The Land Before Her: Fantasy and Experience of the American Frontier, 1630–1860.* Chapel Hill: Univ. of North Carolina Press.

Krupat, Arnold. 2000. "Postcolonialism, Ideology, and Native American Literature." In *Postcolonial Theory and the United States: Race, Ethnicity, and Literature,* edited by Amritjit Singh and Peter Schmidt, 73–94. Jackson: Univ. Press of Mississippi.

La Flesche Farley, Rosalie. 1887–1899. Nebraska State Historical Society, La Flesche Family Papers, Correspondence of Rosalie La Flesche Farley, Series 9.

Langland, Elizabeth. 1995. *Nobody's Angels: Middle-Class Women and Domestic Ideology in Victorian Culture.* Ithaca, N.Y.: Cornell Univ. Press.

Latour, Bruno. 1987. *Science in Action: How to Follow Scientists and Engineers Through Society.* Milton Keynes: Open Univ. Press.

Lawrence, Karen R. 1994. *Penelope's Voyages: Women and Travel in the British Literary Tradition.* Ithaca, N.Y.: Cornell Univ. Press.

Lerner, Gerda. 1986. *The Creation of Patriarchy.* New York: Oxford Univ. Press.

Leslie, Frank [Miriam]. 1877. *California: A Pleasure Trip from Gotham to the Golden Gate (April, May, June, 1877).* New York: G. W. Carleton and Co.

Limb, Melanie, and Claire Dwyer. 2001. *Qualitative Methodologies for Geographers: Issues and Debates.* London: Arnold.

Limerick, Patricia. 1987. *The Legacy of Conquest: The Unbroken Past of the American West.* New York: W. W. Norton.

Livingstone, David N. 1992. *The Geographical Tradition: Episodes in the History of a Contested Discipline.* Oxford: Blackwell.

Longworth, Thérèse (Yelverton), Viscountess Avonmore. 1872. *Zanita: A Tale of the Yo-semite.* New York: Hurd and Houghton.

————. 1974. *Teresina in America.* 2 vols. New York: Arno Press. (Orig. pub. 1875. London: Richard Bentley and Son.)

Lorde, Audre. 1984. *Sister Outsider: Essays and Speeches.* Trumansburg, N.Y.: Crossing Press.

Losano, Antonia. 1997. "A Preference for Vegetables: The Travel Writings and Botanical Art of Marianne North." *Women's Studies* 26: 423–48.

Lowe, Edward J. 1874. *Our Native Ferns; or A History of British Species and Their Varieties.* London: George Bell.

Lyon, George Francis. 1826. *Residence in Mexico, 1826: Diary of a Tour with a Stay in the Republic of Mexico.*

Mabey, Richard. 1988. *The Flowering of Kew: 200 Years of Flower Paintings from the Royal Botanic Gardens.* London: Century.

MacKenzie, John M. 1984. *Propaganda and Empire.* Manchester: Manchester Univ. Press.

Mark, Joan. 1988. *A Stranger in Her Native Land: Alice Fletcher and the American Indians.* Lincoln: Univ. of Nebraska Press.

Marston, Sallie. 2000. "The Social Construction of Scale." *Progress in Human Geography* 24: 219–42.

———. 2004. "A Long Way from Home: Domesticating the Social Production of Scale." In *Scale and Geographic Inquiry: Nature, Society, and Method,* edited by Eric Sheppard and R. B. McMaster, 170–91. London: Blackwell.

Martin, Geoffrey J., and Preston E. James. 1993. *All Possible Worlds: A History of Geographical Ideas.* 3rd ed. New York: John Wiley and Sons.

Martin, Tovah. 1988. *Once Upon a Windowsill: A History of Indoor Plants.* Portland, Ore.: Timber Press.

Marx, Leo. 1964. *Machine in the Garden: Technology and the Pastoral Ideal in America.* New York: Oxford Univ. Press.

McClintock, Anne. 1995. *Imperial Leather: Race, Gender, and Sexuality in the Colonial Contest.* New York: Routledge.

McDonnell, Janet. 1991. *The Dispossession of the American Indian, 1887–1934.* Bloomington: Indiana Univ. Press.

McEwan, Cheryl. 1994. "Encounters with West African Women: Textual Representations of Difference by White Women Abroad." In *Writing Women and Space: Colonial and Postcolonial Geographies,* edited by Alison Blunt and Gillian Rose, 73–100. New York: Guilford Press.

———. 1996. "Paradise or Pandemonium? West African Landscapes in the Travel Accounts of Victorian Women." *Journal of Historical Geography* 22: 68–83.

———. 1998a. "Gender, Science, and Physical Geography in Nineteenth-Century Britain." *Area* 30: 215–23.

———. 1998b. "Cutting the Power Lines Within the Palace? Countering Paternity and Eurocentrism in the Geographical Tradition. *Transactions of the Institute of British Geographers* 23: 371–84.

McFarling, Lloyd, ed. 1955. *Exploring the Northern Plains, 1804–1876.* Caldwell, Idaho: Caxton Printers.

Medicine, Beatrice. 1983. "'Warrior Women,' Sex Role Alternatives for Plains Indian Women." In *The Hidden Half: Studies of Plains Indian Women,* edited by Patricia C. Albers and Beatrice Medicine, 782–85. Lanham, Md.: Univ. Press of America.

Meinig, Donald W. 1986–2004. *The Shaping of America*. 4 vols. New Haven, Conn.: Yale Univ. Press.

Merrill, Lynn L. 1989. *The Romance of Victorian Natural History*. New York: Oxford Univ. Press.

Meyer, Michael C., and William L. Sherman. 1983. *The Course of Mexican History*. New York: Oxford Univ. Press.

Meyers, Greg. 1989. "Science for Women and Children: The Dialogue of Popular Science in the Nineteenth Century." In *Nature Transfigured: Science and Literature, 1700–1900*, edited by John Christie and Sally Shuttleworth, 171–200. Manchester: Manchester Univ. Press.

Middleton, Dorothy. 1965. *Victorian Lady Travellers*. Chicago: Chicago Academy.

Miller, David P. 1996. "Joseph Banks, Empire, and 'Centres of Calculation' in Late Hanoverian London." In *Visions of Empire: Voyages, Botany, and the Representation of Nature*, edited by David P. Miller and Peter H. Reill, 21–37. Cambridge: Cambridge Univ. Press.

Miller, Rory. 1993. *Britain and Latin America in the Nineteenth and Twentieth Centuries*. London: Longman.

Miller, Susan. 1997. "Review Essay: The Emperor on the American Frontier." *Great Plains Quarterly* 17: 63–65.

Mills, Sara. 1990. "Discourses of Difference." *Cultural Studies* 4: 128–32.

———. 1991. *Discourses of Difference: An Analysis of Women's Travel Writing and Colonialism*. London: Routledge.

———. 1994. "Knowledge, Gender, and Empire." In *Writing Women and Space: Colonial and Postcolonial Geographies*, edited by Alison Blunt and Gillian Rose, 29–50. New York: Guilford Press.

———. 1996. "Gender and Colonial Space." *Gender Place and Culture* 3: 125–47.

Milner, Clyde. 1982. *With Good Intentions: Quaker Work Among the Pawnees, Otos, and Omahas in the 1870s*. Lincoln: Univ. of Nebraska Press.

Milner, Clyde, II, Carol A. O'Connor, and Martha A. Sandweiss, eds. 1994. *The Oxford Dictionary of the American West*. New York: Oxford Univ. Press.

Mitchell, Robert D., and Paul A. Groves, eds. 1990. *North America: The Historical Geography of a Changing Continent*. Savage, Md.: Rowman and Littlefield.

Mohanty, Chandra. 1988. "Under Western Eyes: Feminist Scholarship and Colonial Discourses." *Feminist Review* 30: 65–88.

Morgan, Marjorie. 2001. *National Identities and Travel in Victorian Britain*. London: Palgrave.

Morgan, Susan. 1990. "Victorian Women, Wisdom, and Southeast Asia." In *Victorian Sages and Cultural Discourse: Renegotiating Gender and Power,* edited by Thais E. Morgan, 207–24. New Brunswick, N.J.: Rutgers Univ. Press.

———. 1996. *Place Matters: Gendered Geography in Victorian Women's Travel Books about Southeast Asia.* New Brunswick: Rutgers Univ. Press.

Morin, Karen M. 1996. "Gender, Imperialism, and the Western American Landscapes of Victorian Women Travelers, 1874–1897." Ph.D. diss., Univ. of Nebraska–Lincoln.

———. 2001. Review of *Landscapes of the New West: Gender and Geography in Contemporary Women's Writing,* by Krista Comer. *Annals of the Association of American Geographers* 91: 232–34.

———. 2003. "Rosalie." *Historical Geography* 31: 71–80.

Morin, Karen M., and Lawrence D. Berg. 1999. "Emplacing Current Trends in Feminist Historical Geography." *Gender, Place and Culture* 6: 311–30.

Morin, Karen M., and Jeanne Kay Guelke. 1998. "Strategies of Representation, Relationship, and Resistance: British Women Travelers and Mormon Plural Wives, *ca.* 1870–1890." *Annals of the Association of American Geographers* 88: 437–63.

Morris, Mary, ed. 1993. *Maiden Voyages: Writings of Women Travelers.* New York: Vintage.

Mulvey, Christopher. 1983. *Anglo-American Landscapes: A Study of Nineteenth-Century Anglo-American Travel Literature.* Cambridge: Cambridge Univ. Press.

———. 1990. *Transatlantic Manners: Social Patterns in Nineteenth-Century Anglo-American Travel Literature.* Cambridge: Cambridge Univ. Press.

Nash, Roderick. 1967. *Wilderness and the American Mind.* New Haven, Conn.: Yale Univ. Press.

Naylor, Simon. 2005. "Historical Geography: Knowledge, in Place and On the Move." *Progress in Human Geography* 29: 626–34.

Nelson, Dana. 1998. *National Manhood: Capitalist Citizenship and the Imagined Fraternity of White Men.* Durham, N.C.: Duke Univ. Press.

Nicolson, Malcolm. 1990. "Alexander von Humboldt and the Geography of Vegetation." In *Romanticism and the Sciences,* edited by Andrew Cunningham and Nicholas Jardine, 169–89. Cambridge: Cambridge Univ. Press.

North, Marianne. 1892. *Recollections of a Happy Life: Being the Autobiography of Marianne North.* 2 vols. London: Macmillan.

Norwood, Vera. 1993. *Made from This Earth: American Women and Nature.* Chapel Hill: Univ. of North Carolina Press.

Norwood, Vera, and Janice Monk, eds. 1987. *The Desert Is No Lady: Southwestern Landscapes in Women's Writing and Art.* New Haven, Conn.: Yale Univ. Press.

Ogden, K. N. 1990. "Sublime Vistas and Scenic Backdrops: Nineteenth Century Painters and Photographers at Yosemite." *California History* 69: 134–53.

Olund, Eric. 2002. "From Savage Space to Governable Space: The Extension of United States Judicial Sovereignty Over Indian Country in the Nineteenth Century." *Cultural Geographies* 9: 129–57.

Paravisini-Gebert, Lizabeth, and Ivette Romero-Cesareo, eds. 2001. *Women at Sea: Travel Writing and the Margins of Caribbean Discourse.* London: Pelgrave.

Pascoe, Peggy. 1990. *Relations of Rescue: The Search for Female Moral Authority in the American West, 1874–1939.* New York: Oxford Univ. Press.

Paul, Rodman Wilson. 1963. *Mining the Frontiers of the Far West, 1848–1880.* New York: Holt, Rinehart and Winston.

Pease, Donald E. ed. 1994. *National Identities and Post-Americanist Narratives.* Durham, N.C.: Duke Univ. Press.

Pease, Donald, and Robyn Wiegman, eds. 2002. *The Futures of American Studies.* Durham, N.C.: Duke Univ. Press.

Pender, Rose. 1978. *A Lady's Experience in the Wild West in 1883.* Lincoln: Univ. of Nebraska Press. (Orig. pub. 1888. London: G. Tucker.)

Perry, Lewis. 1984. *Intellectual Life in America: A History.* Chicago: Univ. of Chicago Press.

Peters, Evelyn. 1997. "Challenging the Geographers of 'Indianness': The Batchewana Case." *Urban Geography* 18: 56–61.

———. 2000. "Aboriginal People and Canadian Geography: A Review of the Recent Literature." *Canadian Geographer* 44: 44–45.

Pfeiffer, Emily. 1885. *Flying Leaves from East and West.* London: Field and Tuer.

Phillips, Patricia. 1990. *The Scientific Lady: A Social History of Women's Scientific Interests, 1520–1918.* London: Wiedenfeld and Nicolson.

Phillips, Richard. 1997. *Mapping Men and Empire: A Geography of Adventure.* London: Routledge.

Pletcher, David M. 1958. *Rails, Mines, and Progress: Seven American Promoters in Mexico, 1867–1911.* Ithaca, N.Y.: Cornell Univ. Press.

Ponsonby, Laura. 1990. *Marianne North at Kew Gardens*. Exeter: Webb and Bower.

Poole, Annie. 1884. *Mexicans at Home in the Interior*. London.

Pratt, Mary Louise. 1992. *Imperial Eyes: Travel Writing and Transculturation*. London: Routledge.

———. 2001. Review of *Writes of Passage: Reading Travel Writing*, edited by James Duncan and Derek Gregory. *Journal of Historical Geography* 27: 279–81.

Ramsey, Jarold. 1997. "Francis La Flesche." *Dictionary of Literary Biography* 19: 180–96.

Raju, Saraswati, M. Satish Kumar, and Stuart Corbridge. 2006. *Colonial and Post-Colonial Geographies of India*. London: Sage.

Rapson, Richard L. 1971. *Britons View America, Travel Commentary, 1860–1935*. Seattle: Univ. of Washington Press.

Reinhardt, Richard. 1967. *Out West on the Overland Train: Across-the-Continent Excursion with Leslie's Magazine in 1877 and the Overland Trip in 1967*. Palo Alto, Calif.: American West Publishing.

Reynolds, Kimberly, and Nicola Humble. 1993. *Victorian Heroines: Representations of Femininity in Nineteenth-Century Literature and Art*. London: Harvester Wheatsheaf.

Rico, Monica. 1998. "The Cultural Contexts of International Capital Expansion: British Ranchers in Wyoming 1879–1889." *Antipode* 30: 119–34.

Riley, Glenda. 1984. *Women and Indians on the Frontier, 1825–1915*. Albuquerque: Univ. of New Mexico Press.

Ritvo, Harriet. 1987. *The Animal Estate: The English and Other Creatures in the Victorian Age*. Cambridge, Mass.: Harvard Univ. Press.

Robbins, William G. 1994. *Colony and Empire: The Capitalist Transformation of the American West*. Lawrence: Univ. Press of Kansas.

Robinson, Cecil. 1977. *Mexico and the Hispanic Southeast in American Literature*. Tucson: Univ. of Arizona Press.

Robinson, Jane. 1990. *Wayward Women: A Guide to Women Travellers*. New York: Oxford Univ. Press.

Rose, Gillian. 1993. *Feminism and Geography: The Limits to Geographical Knowledge*. Minneapolis: Univ. of Minnesota Press.

———. 1995. "Tradition and Paternity: Same Difference?" *Transactions of the Institute of British Geographers* 20: 414–16.

Rowe, John Carlos. 2000. *Literary Culture and U.S. Imperialism: From the Revolution to World War II*. New York: Oxford Univ. Press.

Rundstrom, Robert, Douglas Deur, Kate Berry, and Dick Winchell. 2000. "Recent Geographical Research on Indians and Inuit in the US and Canada." *American Indian Culture and Research Journal* 24: 85–110.

Rupke, Nicholaas A. 1994. *Richard Owen: Victorian Naturalist*. New Haven, Conn.: Yale Univ. Press.

Russell, Mary. 1986. *The Blessings of a Good Thick Skirt*. London: Collins.

Ruxton, George F. 1846. *Adventures in Mexico*. Oyster Bay, N.Y.: Nelson Doubleday.

Said, Edward. 1978. *Orientalism*. London: Routledge and Kegan Paul.

———. 1983. *The World, the Text, and the Critic*. Cambridge, Mass.: Harvard Univ. Press.

———. 1993. *Culture and Imperialism*. New York: Alfred A. Knopf.

Schaffer, Kay. 1994. "Colonizing Gender in Colonial Australia: The Eliza Frazer Story." In *Writing Women and Space: Colonial and Postcolonial Geographies*, edited by Alison Blunt and Gillian Rose, 101–20. New York: Guilford Press.

Schivelbusch, Wolfgang. 1978. *The Railway Journey: Trains and Travel in the Nineteenth Century*. New York: Urizen Books.

Schuurman, Nadine. 1998. "Contesting Patriarchies: Nlha7pamux and Stl'atl'imx Women and Colonialism in Nineteenth-Century British Columbia." *Gender, Place and Culture* 5: 141–58.

Scott, Joan. 1988a. *Gender and the Politics of History*. New York: Columbia Univ. Press.

———. 1988b. "Experience," In *Feminists Theorize the Political*, edited by Judith Butler and Joan Scott, 22–40. New York: Routledge.

Scourse, Nicolette. 1983. *Victorians and Their Flowers*. Portland, Ore.: Timber Press.

Sharpe, Jenny. 1993. *Allegories of Empire: The Figure of Woman in the Colonial Text*. Minneapolis: Univ. of Minnesota Press.

———. 2000. "Is the United States Postcolonial?" In *Postcolonial America*, edited by Richard King, 103–21. Urbana: Univ. of Illinois Press.

Shteir, Ann B. 1987. "Botany in the Breakfast Room: Women and Early Nineteenth-Century British Plant Study." In *Uneasy Careers and Intimate Lives: Women in Science 1789–1979*, edited by Pnina G. Abir-Am and Dorinda Outram, 31–43. New Brunswick, N.J.: Rutgers Univ. Press.

———. 1996. *Cultivating Women, Cultivating Science: Flora's Daughters and Botany in England, 1760–1860*. Baltimore: Johns Hopkins Univ. Press.

Silvern, Steven. 1995. "Nature, Territory and Identity in the Wisconsin Treaty Rights Controversy." *Ecumene* 2: 276–92.

Singh, Amritjit, and Peter Schmidt. 2000. *Postcolonial Theory and the United States: Race, Ethnicity, and Literature.* Jackson: Univ. of Mississippi Press.

Sinkin, Richard N. 1979. *The Mexican Reform, 1855–1876: A Study in Liberal Nation-Building.* Austin: Univ. of Texas Press.

Skeels, Anna. 1993. "A Passage to Premodernity: Carl Sauer Repositioned in the Field." Master's thesis, Univ. of British Columbia.

Slotkin, Richard. 1973. *Regeneration Through Violence: The Mythology of the American Frontier, 1600–1860.* Middletown, Conn.: Wesleyan Univ. Press.

Smith, Henry Nash. 1950. *Virgin Land: The American West in Symbol and Myth.* Cambridge, Mass.: Harvard Univ. Press.

Smith, Joseph. 1979. *Illusions of Conflict: Anglo-American Diplomacy Toward Latin America, 1865–1896.* Pittsburgh: Univ. of Pittsburgh Press.

Smith, Sidonie. 2001. *Moving Lives: Twentieth-Century Women's Travel Writing.* Minneapolis: Univ. of Minnesota Press.

Smith, Sherry. 1987. "Beyond Princess and Squaw: Army Officer's Perceptions of Indian Women." In *The Women's West,* edited by Susan Armitage and Elizabeth Jameson, 63–76. Norman: Univ. of Oklahoma Press.

Smith-Rosenberg, Carol. 1985. *Disorderly Conduct: Visions of Gender in Victorian America.* New York: Oxford Univ. Press.

Sparke, Matthew. 1998. "A Map that Roared and an Original Atlas: Canada, Cartography, and the Narration of Nation." *Annals of the Association of American Geographers* 88: 463–95.

Sparrow, Walter Shaw. 1905. *Women Painters of the World.* New York: Frederick A. Stokes.

Speake, Jennifer, ed. 2003. *Literature of Travel and Exploration: An Encyclopedia.* 3 vols. London: Routledge.

Spivak, Gayatri C. 1988. "Can the Subaltern Speak?" In *Marxism and the Interpretation of Culture,* edited by C. Nelson and Lawrence Grossberg, 271–313. Basingstoke: Macmillan Education.

Stafleu, Frans A. 1971. *Linnaeus and the Linnaeans: The Spreading of Their Ideas in Systematic Botany, 1735–1789.* Utrecht: A Oosthoek's uitgeversmaatschappij.

Stern, Madeleine. 1953. *Purple Passage: The Life of Mrs. Frank Leslie.* Norman: Univ. of Oklahoma Press.

———. 1972. "Introduction, Mrs. Frank Leslie." *California: A Pleasure Trip from Gotham to the Golden Gate (April, May, June, 1877).* New York: Nieuwkoop, B. De Graaf.

Stoddart, David R. 1986. *On Geography and Its History.* Oxford: Basil Blackwell.

———. 1991. "Do We Need a Feminist Historiography of Geography, and If We Do, What Should It Be? *Transactions of the Institute of British Geographers* 16: 484–87.

Stoler, Ann L. 1992. "Sexual Affronts and Racial Frontiers: European Identities and the Cultural Politics of Exclusion in Colonial Southeast Asia." *Society for Comparative Study of Society and History* 34: 514–51.

———. 1995. *Race and the Education of Desire: Foucault's History of Sexuality and the Colonial Order of Things.* Durham, N.C.: Duke Univ. Press.

Strobel, Margaret. 1991. *European Women and the Second British Empire.* Bloomington: Indiana Univ. Press.

Suleri, Sara. 1992. *The Rhetoric of English India.* Chicago: Univ. of Chicago Press.

Thacker, Robert. 1989. *The Great Prairie Fact and Literary Imagination.* Albuquerque: Univ. of New Mexico Press.

Thurin, Susan Schoenbauer. 1997. "Constance Gordon Cumming." *Dictionary of Literary Biography* 174: 67–88.

Tompkins, Jane. 1992. *West of Everything: The Inner Life of Westerns.* New York: Oxford Univ. Press.

Trigger, Bruce G., and Wilcomb E. Washburn, eds. 1996. *The Cambridge History of the Native Peoples of the Americas.* Vol. 1, *North America.* Cambridge: Cambridge Univ. Press.

Turner, Cordelia Harris. 1893. *The Floral Kingdom: Its History, Sentiment, and Poetry.* Floral Park, N.Y.: John Lewis Childs.

Vicinus, Martha, ed. 1972. *Suffer and Be Still: Women in the Victorian Age.* Bloomington: Indiana Univ. Press.

Vincent, Mrs. Howard. 1885. *Forty Thousand Miles Over Land and Water: The Journal of a Tour Through the British Empire and America.* 2 vols. London: Sampson Low, Marston and Co.

Walkowitz, Judith R. 1992. *City of Dreadful Delight: Narratives of Sexual Danger in Late-Victorian London.* Chicago: Univ. of Chicago Press.

Ward, Sir Henry George. 1828. *Mexico in 1827.* London: Henry Colborn.

Ware, Vron. 1992. *Beyond the Pale: White Women, Racism, and History.* London: Verso.

Weathers, J. N.d. [ca. 1915]. *Commercial Gardening.* Vol. 2. London: Greshem Publishing Co.

Webber, Ronald. 1968. *The Early Horticulturists.* New York: August M. Kelley.

Weber, Max. 1996. *The Protestant Ethic and the Spirit of Capitalism.* London: Routledge.

Welby, Victoria. 1852. *A Young Traveller's Journal of a Tour in North and South America During the Year 1850.* London: T. Bosworth.

White, Richard. 1991. *"It's Your Misfortune and None of My Own": A History of the American West.* London: Univ. of Oklahoma Press.

Willems-Braun, Bruce. 1997. "Buried Epistemologies: The Politics of Nature in (Post)colonial British Columbia." *Annals of the Association of American Geographers* 87: 3–31.

Wilson, Dorothy Clarke. 1974. *Bright Eyes: The Story of Susette La Flesche, an Omaha Indian.* New York: McGraw-Hill.

Wishart, David. 1994. *An Unspeakable Sadness: The Dispossession of the Nebraska Indians.* Lincoln: Univ. of Nebraska Press.

———. 1995. "The Roles and Status of Men and Women in Nineteenth Century Omaha and Pawnee Societies: Postmodernist Uncertainties and Empirical Evidence." *American Indian Quarterly* 19: 509–18.

Women and Geography Study Group of the Royal Geographical Society/Institute of British Geographers. 1997. *Feminist Geographies: Explorations in Diversity and Difference.* Edinburgh: Longman.

Wood, Peter. 1991. *Poverty and the Workhouse in Victorian Britain.* Wolfeboro Falls, N.H.: Alan Sutton Publishing.

Wortley, Lady Emmeline Stuart. 1851. *Travels in the United States, North America, Caribbean, and Peru during 1849 and 1850.* New York: Harper and Brothers.

Worster, Donald. 1985. *Rivers of Empire: Water, Aridity, and the Growth of the American West.* New York: Pantheon Books.

Yonge, Charlotte M. 1887. *The Herb of the Field.* London: Macmillan.

Young, Robert. 1995. *Colonial Desire: Hybridity in Theory, Culture and Race.* London: Routledge.

Index

Italic page number denotes illustration.

geographers/geography: common
ground with postcolonial criticism,
185–86; curiosity-based learning and,
113–14; fathers of, 87, 111–14; "Great
Man" tradition of, 9–10; importance
of extending historiography, 83–84;
overhaul of classical tradition of, 221;
recognition as credible experts, 85;
scholarship on travelers, 217; study of
situatedness of explorers, 219
Geographical Tradition, The (Livingstone), 9
geographic context: development of self-
identity (subjectivities), 2–3; formation of gender/colonial discourses, 3;
production of gender identity and, 2,
52, 217, 218, 219–20. *See also* contact
zones; place/proximity of encounters
Georgi-Findlay, Brigitte, 5, 198, 202
Glacier Point, Yosemite, 56, 59, 74, *75*, *76*
Glen Eyrie, Colorado, 72, 119n. 3, 156
Glenwood Springs, Colorado, 70–71
Goethe, Johann Wolfgang von, 106, 111
Golden Gate Park, 89
gold rush, 203, 209
Gould, Stephen Jay, 94
Granite Crags of California (Cummings),
87, 88–89, 100–102, *101*
Great Plains: commercial/literary
influences on interpretation of, 36;
description of with intimate contact,
41–42, 44; European failure on,
227; Farley's records of colonization of, 172–73; Indian Territory in,
140; influences on women's writing
about, 6; mode of travel's impact on
responses to, 28–29, 32; portrayal of
in women's travelogues, 15–16; residents' observations of, 36–37; return
of Native Americans, 227; romantic

view of, 38–42; views of from trains,
15, 21, 25–26, 27–29, 31–33, 42, 47. *See
also* prairies
Greenberg, Amy, 220, 221
Greenwood, Grace. *See* Lippincott, Sara
Jane Clarke
Gregory, Derek, 43
Guadalajara, Mexico, 119, 121, 124, 126,
127, 130
Guanajuato, Mexico, 124
Guelke, Jeanne Kay, 9, 12
Guest, Lady Theodora: on accommodations, 61; approach of, 16–17,
95; collection of specimens, 34,
103–4; description of men in party,
70; on divided skirt, 59, 60; education of, 224; exploitation of British
natural history hallmarks, 86–87, 94;
femininity of, 114; illustrations of, 96,
97; justification of genocide against
Native Americans, 148, 166–67;
mercantilism and, 108; motivation
for travel, 23; mountaineering adventures of, 55; narration of excursion
up Pike's Peak, 66, 67; and Native
Americans, 146, 152, 160, 162; as
nature artist/writer, 84–86; response
to prairies, 32; significance of work
of, 112–14; support of colonialism,
86, 96; transcontinental railway
journey of, 90n. 7; travel book of, 90,
216; traveling companion of, 23, 55,
90n. 7; trip to eastern U.S., 21n. 1; use
of Latin names of plants, 107; view of
Black Hills situation, 154

hacienda owners, 126, 134–35
Hardy, Iza Duffus: description of
transcontinental trip, 20–21, 23n. 5,

29; disappointment with grasslands, 21; and Native Americans, 149, 162; travel books by, 20; traveling companion of, 23

Hardy, Lady Mary Duffus: description of Native American women, 147–48; description of train travel, 29, 30, 224; motivation for travel, 23; response to prairies, 27, 29; traveling companion of, 23

Hastings, Dennis, 227

Hazelstine, Katherine, *76*

health, 28

health/health care, 169n. 2

Hints to Lady Travellers (Davidson), 58

historians, 11, 217

historical geography: archival approach of, 13–14; common ground with postcolonial criticism, 185–86; domestic scale of, 222–25; dutiful son model, 9–10; erasure of women's writings in, 9; imprint of women writers on, 221–28; incorporation of feminist/gender theorizing approach to, 12–13; lack of analysis of American imperialism, 12; lack of critical/social-theory orientation, 12–13; Leslie's/Lippincott's travel writings and, 197; masculinist language/values of, 11–12; of Native Americans, 138; need for writing women in, 8, 174, 185; of Omaha land dispossession, 174–77; place of women travelers/explorers in, 9, 10; recovering silenced voices, 10, 167, 185; scope of, 87; study of women's travel literature, 221, 222; women's imprints on, 19; works on, 221–22

Hobsbawm, Eric J., 130

Hoganson, Kristin, 225

Home (Blunt/Dowling), 223

Homestead Act, 190

Hooker, Joseph D., 89, 97, 98, 108

Hotel Bernard, 71

Howard, Lady Winefred: activities during male excursions, 70–71, 75–76; description of prairies, 38, 39, 40; on divided skirt, 59, 60; motivation for travel, 23, 24; mountaineering adventures of, 55, 66–67, 74; narration of excursions in Yosemite, 72; and Native Americans, 149, 152–53, 163; on sleeping arrangements on trains, 30–31; tour of Mexico, 118; travel book of, 216; traveling companion of, 23, 24, 55

Hulme, Peter, 6–7, 186

human geographers, 222

Humboldt, Alexander von: belief in unity of nature, 106; erasure of indigenous inhabitants, 109; as father of academic geography, 87; inspiration for, 111; Rose Kingsley's references to, 122; reinvention of landscapes, 43; romantic impulses of, 111–12; time in Mexico, 122n. 5

hunters, 35, 105

Idaho, 210

idealization of motherhood, 4

identity, 14. *See also* gender identity (subjectivity)

immigrants: in agriculture, 219; from China, 198, 204, 208, 210, 211, 219; in Colorado, 70; from Europe, 198, 204, 210–11; mass movement into West, 2, 17, 46; in mining industry, 198, 204, 210–11, 219

on American national consolidation, 18–19; compared to British women journalists, 8; complicity with American imperialism, 209, 211; depiction of patronage network, 205, 209; depiction of railroads, 204; deployment of moral authority, 202; encounters with cultural identities, 211; feminism of, 202; feminist reform rhetoric of, 211, 212; focus of, 8–9; on growth/prosperity of West, 204, 209; on large-scale mining, 207–8; on mineral deposits in Nevada, 225; on miners and working conditions, 205–6, 207, 211, 212, 213; photograph of, *200;* reconciliation of the mining West, 208, 210, 211; report on damage from mining, 206; report on underclasses produced/displaced by industry, 205; support of internal colonization process/practices, 196; transcontinental railway journey, 195, 199, 200; writings of, 198, 199–200, 208

literary heroines, 65–70, 73–74

Livingstone, David N., 9

loggers, 109–11

London Bank, 117

London Times, 58–59, 216

Longmont, Colorado, 79

Long's Peak, Colorado, 3, 73–74

Longworth, Thérèse: on begging by Native Americans, 164; challenge to stereotype of Native American women, 163; description of prairie, 38–39; on dispossession of Native Americans, 153–54, 160, 163, 166; female liberation imagined/lived by, 3; first-wave feminism and, 82; foregrounding of revisionist gender

identity, 218; mountaineering in Yosemite, 55, 82; narration of night in hollow tree, 79–80; on Native American women's roles, 159, 160; portrayal of benefits of suffrage, 81; on privacy on trains, 30, 224; as professional travel writer, 22; resistance to adventure, 70; on riding dress/behavior of companions, 59–60; on sport hunting of buffalo, 35; time spent on prairie, 23; travel books of, 21n. 2, 23n. 4, 79–80, 84n. 1; traveling companion of, 55; travel in winter, 33; on Yosemite, 56, 74, 76, 84n. 1

Lorde, Audre, 190

Loredo, Texas, 121

Losano, Antonia, 95, 108

Lowe, Edward J., 112n. 12

lumbermen, 86, 109–11

Lyon, George Francis, 118

MacKenzie, John M., 7

manhood, 220–21

manifest destiny, 140

Manitou Springs, Colorado, 57, 67, 71, 72

Manzanillo, Mexico, 119, 121, 122, 124, 128, 134

Maripsoa, California, 210

Marsden, Kate, 217

Martineau, Harriet, 217

masculinism, 9–10, 11, 109–10

masculinist exploratory tradition, 6–7, 219, 225. *See also* adventure narratives

Mathewson (government agent to Indians), 183

Mauricio G. (hacienda owner), 135

Maximilian I (emperor of Mexico), 116

McCall, Laura, 220–21

immigrant labor on, 210; contribution to development of West, 204; development of prairies via, 46–47; development of western tourism via, 55–56; environmentalist concerns about, 46; Faithful's view of development of, 45–46; investment opportunities in, 57; in Mexico, 115–16, 120–21, *121,* 136–37; on Omaha reservation, 227. *See also* Mexican National Railway; trains; transcontinental railway journey

Rain in the Face (Indian chief), 162

Ralston, William, 205, 209

Recollections of a Happy Life: Being the Autobiography of Marianne North (North), 89

reconciliation literature, 208, 210, 211

redwoods, 16, 72, 86, 100, 106, 109–10

reformers, 151–52, 168–69

reform rhetoric: civilizing of Native Americans and, 151–60; deployed for mine workers, 19, 196–97, 202; deployed for Native Americans, 6, 176, 182, 190; Farley's alignment with, 182, 193; imperialist politics and, 196–97; influence on women's writings, 6; Leslie's alignment with, 196–97, 208–9; Lippincott's deployment of, 196–97, 211; sympathy concerning Native American dispossession, 18; of Victorians, 6

Reno, Nevada, 149, 162

reservations: allotment process on, 18, 140–41, 169, 171, 174, 175, 188–89, 191, 192; American colonization and, 191; Farleys' protection of land from speculators, 191–92; leasing/sales of lands of, 18, 140–41, 171, 174, 175–76, 177–85, 191, 197–98, 226; loss to

forced treaties, 174; Native American alienation from former lands via, 57; of Omahas, 226–27; removal of Native Americans to, 33, 138, 140, 191, 219

Residence in Mexico, 1826: Diary of a Tour with a Stay in the Republic of Mexico (Lyon), 118

residents' observations of landscapes, 36–37

Rice (Farley's banker), 182

Rocky Mountain National Park, 222

Rocky Mountains: accommodations in, 60–65; American imperialism in, 56–57; Bird in, 1, 61–65; British immigrants/investors in, 57, 70, 120n. 4; descriptions in travel books, 21; engagement with, 27; environmentalists' concern for, 45–46, 48; as focal point for British travelers, 26–27, 42, 57; lack of servants in, 61, 64–65; naturalists in, 16; as tourist attraction, 51, 55–56; women's experiences in, 16, 49–50. *See also* Colorado Rockies; Estes Park, Colorado; Pike's Peak

romanticism: approach of, 37–38; discourse on beautiful/sublime, 6, 25, 38–42, 45–46, 47, 94, 99, 102, 213; female naturalists' association with, 17; influence on women's environmental concerns, 45–46; influence on women's responses to prairies, 25; influence on women's travel writings, 37–38, 44–45, 47, 218; literary conventions of in women's travel books, 15–16, 25, 37–42

Rosalie, Nebraska, 189, 195, 226–27

Rose, Gillian, 9, 53, 83–84

Round Trip in North America, A (Guest), 90, 97